Achieving Inner Balance
in Anxious Times

BARBARA KILLINGER, PhD

McGill-Queen's University Press
Montreal & Kingston • London • Ithaca

ACHIEVING INNER BALANCE
IN ANXIOUS TIMES

© McGill-Queen's University Press 2011

ISBN 978-0-7735-3844-3

Legal deposit first quarter 2011
Bibliothèque nationale du Québec

Printed in Canada on acid-free paper that is 100% ancient forest free
(100% post-consumer recycled), processed chlorine free

Second edition of *The Balancing Act: Rediscovering Your Feelings*,
published by Key Porter, 1995.

McGill-Queen's University Press acknowledges the support of the Canada
Council for the Arts for our publishing program. We also acknowledge the
financial support of the Government of Canada through the Canada Book
Fund for our publishing activities.

Library and Archives Canada Cataloguing in Publication Data

Killinger, Barbara
    Achieving inner balance in anxious times / Barbara Killinger.

Includes bibliographical references and index.
ISBN 978-0-7735-3844-3

1. Peace of mind. 2. Behavior modification. I. Title.

BF637.P3K55 2011   158   C2010-907065-8

Typeset by Jay Tee Graphics Ltd. in 10.5/14 Sabon

Contents

ACHIEVING INNER BALANCE
IN ANXIOUS TIMES

Introduction

Come and find the quiet centre in the crowded life we lead,
find the room for hope to enter, find the frame where we are freed:
clear the chaos and the clutter, clear our eyes, that we can see
all the things that really matter, be at peace, and simply be.
  Shirley Erena Murray, "Come and Find the Quiet Centre"

To find that inner pivotal point of balance, our calm centre of
equilibrium, is no easy feat at the best of times. Today, much
of our emotional and financial security is still being destabil-
ized by anxious uncertainty. We have been witness to media
reports of volatile stocks markets, the threat of major bank
collapses, massive fraud schemes, and widespread corporate
control of our media, government, and institutions of learning. People who suffer from addictions, depression, obsessions, and other psychiatric disorders know anxiety all too
well. It is ever present.

Some of the cultural and societal forces that affect whether
or not our experience of the world is well balanced are relatively recent phenomena, while others, like shifting educa-
tional values, have evolved gradually over time.

Today's "timesickness" is increasingly problematic. In
Marshall McLuhan, Douglas Coupland 's book about the
media guru, the author states his belief that the texture of
daily life in Western media societies changed around 2003
due to the lack of tolerance for waiting of any sort, a need
to have all the facts *now* or suffer a meltdown, and a fear of

becoming irrelevant if one slows down, even once. The new *us* is part of an online phantom world of information where geography is unimportant, and yet, Coupland adds, this complex web of data and people who support us is tenuous and fleeting. "Time speeds up and then it begins to shrink. Years pass by in minutes" (15).

Our shortened attention spans drift easily away as our focus shifts. We become perpetually distracted, and multitasking blurs clarity. As you will learn in these pages, stressful situations result when this inattention is coupled with the negative side of Intuition, with its restless impatience, poor impulse control, and poor judgment. This dynamic prevails as obsessional Thinking comes to dominate our psyche and Feeling, Intuition, and Sensation functions are repressed and turn to their dark side.

When the emphasis in education is placed on practical science and market-driven economic growth rather than the humanities and liberal arts, there are serious consequences for society. Pulitzer Prize winner Chris Hedges warns that the balance of power and control has tipped towards educating students in specialized narrow skills that provide training for a chosen career path, rather than furthering the university's true purpose of educating the mind to ask the broad, universal questions. In his 2009 book, *Empire of Illusion. The End of Literacy and the Triumph of Spectacle,* he blames the bankruptcy of the economic and political systems in the United States on diminishing enrolment and a lack of exposure to the humanities, which have seen a fifty percent decrease in enrolment since the 1960s.

Hedges states that to train students "to debate stoic, existential, theological, and humanistic ways of grappling with reality is to educate them in values and morality" (103). Further, he says, a culture is doomed if it fails to grasp the interplay between morality and power because it mistakes management techniques for wisdom and does not understand that compassion is the true measure of a civilization. Without the clear thinking that is necessary to recognize personal biases and the inadequacies in economic, social, and political structures, no major modifications can take place.

In Canada, funding for the new $200-million Canada Excellence Research Chairs, as an example, overwhelmingly favours the sciences. Yet the humanities, viewed from a broader perspective, benefit our society in vital ways.

The teaching of the humanities plays an important role in preserving democracy, says philosopher Martha Nussbaum, author of *For Profit: Why Democracy Needs the Humanities*. She stresses that the ability to think critically, to argue right and wrong, and to play our role in a democratic society depends on a greater understanding of the world, its different groups of people, their histories, and the way they interact. John Allemang's conversation with Nussbaum, reported in his *Globe and Mail* article "crit.ic.al think.ing," includes an interesting summation of critical thinking. It is described as "the intellectually disciplined process of actively and skillfully conceptualizing, applying, analyzing, synthesizing, and/ or evaluating information gathered from, or generated by, observation, experience, reflection, reasoning, or communication, as a guide to belief and action. In its exemplary form, it is based on universal intellectual values that transcend subject matter divisions: clarity, accuracy, precision, consistency, relevance, sound evidence, good reasons, breadth, and fairness."

Critical thinking, as you will discover, is crucial for the balanced point of view inherent in a technique I developed called *Internalizing*. As you read these pages, you will learn how to analyze your reaction in response to a situation or person in order to be aware of what you *think,* and then to examine how and why you know that. In addition, you will learn to get in touch with how you *feel* about a subject or conversation and to discern exactly what it is in that situation that is causing you to react a certain way. Sometimes it is appropriate to talk about your own *needs* as well. You can then communicate this information, or your *position* as I call it, to those involved. Ideally, you want to be one hundred percent responsible for your own reactions in any given situation.

The pervasive evolution of ever more sophisticated, life-changing technology is another external but present threat to our ability to live a balanced life. It is easy to be seduced by its all-encompassing scope of useful information and far-reaching transformational ways of doing business. The danger lies in the inclination of some individuals to become obsessed with technology and a slave to its use. The lure of getting from idea A to goal B faster and smarter through technological wizardry is highly seductive.

Unfortunately, obsessions eventually take control of the individual, not vice versa. An obsession is narrowly focused thinking that becomes fixated on an idea, goal, object, or person. The individual's relentless, often irrational thoughts and impulsive behaviour together fuel compulsive drives that lack intuition's "big picture" wisdom and limit problem-solving expertise.

At special risk are ambitious, overly-responsible workaholics who already possess perfectionistic tendencies that can lead to a debilitating obsessive fixation on work. Because workaholics are addicted to power and control, and become emotionally crippled during the predictable breakdown spiral that this addiction follows, any major loss of control can immobilize them.

It signals trouble when a hard worker overworks projects by paying obsessive attention to small, picky, often insignificant details until eventually perfectionism silences his or her expertise. The late journalist Barbara Moon, with her virtuoso style and intelligence on almost any subject, delighted yet infuriated producers and magazine editors alike by regularly missing a deadline or meeting it with only seconds to spare. At times, she wrote with an abrasive acerbic wit and took an imperious tone with those who messed with her prose. In his *Maclean's* tribute, "Her Elements of Style," Robert Fulford speculated on the reason for a writer's block that was the "size of Mount Kilimanjaro." Editors wondered whether perfectionism caused her to argue over a comma for half an hour, while Fulford queried whether Moon set her standards so high that even she couldn't meet them. In any case, Moon eventually abandoned writing and became an editor of others' work.

It is ironic that loneliness and alienation are increasing in communities where technology was supposed to eliminate distance and barriers to connection. A sense of isolation can only contribute to increasingly high rates of depression and other mental and physical illnesses. In a 2006 study from the *American Sociological Review*, twenty-five percent of Americans report having no close confidents, a figure more than double that of twenty years earlier. Co-author Lynn Smith-Lovin, professor of sociology at Duke University, sees close relationships as a safety net. "Whether it's picking up a child or finding someone to help you out of the city in a hurricane, these are people we depend on." If something happens to a spouse or partner, that security is gone. When people spend long hours at work, or commute long distances, they have less time and energy to socialize or join groups and are more apt to become isolated, to stay home and watch TV.

Achieving a healthy balance between work and leisure is increasingly problematic. It must be noted that the number of hours of work is but one symptom of workaholism. Nonetheless, "More than 30% of Canadians say they are workaholics," according to a 2007 Statistics Canada study reported on CBC *News*. The study looked at whether quality of life is different for those who see themselves as workaholics and those who do not. Thirty-three percent of Canadians aged nineteen to sixty-four expressed dissatisfaction with their work/life balance: 86 percent felt rushed trying to get through their day; 56 percent said they don't have time for fun anymore. The study concluded that the differences between workaholics and others were primarily in the ways they view and allocate time.

It's not surprising then to learn that a *Forbes'* magazine survey (28 May 2009) rated Canadians the fourth-hardest workers in the developed world. Along with Americans, Canadians reportedly received less paid vacation time than people in almost any other country. Nancy Macdonald reported in *Maclean's* that, even under these conditions, twenty-four percent of Canadians choose not to take all their vacation time.

With so many people laid off or losing their jobs due to the recession, or becoming victims of downsizing and increased workloads, anxiety remains sky high in the workforce. People are working *both* longer and harder just to keep their jobs. As a consequence, financial and emotional security has become all important but frequently evasive. There is an alarming distrust of and fading confidence in our institutions, especially governmental and business regulators. Overall, there is a deepening concern about the lack of integrity and civility in our society, a subject I addressed in my previous book, *Integrity: Doing the Right Thing for the Right Reason*.

None of us can avoid the worrisome impact and slow recovery of this recent recession. The loss of control that such fear-related worry and stress generates has serious ramifications that affect both our emotional and physical health. It has long been acknowledged that there is a strong connection between adrenal arousal and heart disease. In the 1970s, cardiologists Meyer Friedman and Ray Rosenman wrote their *Type-A Behavior and Your Heart*. You will learn more in chapter 4 about psychologist Dr Archibald Hart's findings on how stress and prolonged elevated levels of adrenalin can cause serious damage throughout the body. Excess adrenalin also gives people a dangerously heightened false sense of well-being, even euphoria, because energy increases, the need for sleep is reduced, and there are seductive feelings of excitement. Hart says that it is not surprising that so many people become addicted to this state of arousal. Therefore, he warns, over time both good and bad sources of stress can be equally damaging to our health (21–2).

As a pioneer in the field of workaholism, I have developed techniques that restore the vital inner balance necessary to possess the values and priorities that make it possible to transform a workaholic lifestyle into one that honours the importance of family, co-operative, non-controlling peer relationships, and the values of integrity. Some thirty-plus years working with workaholics and their families has taught me that before change is possible, it is first necessary to understand the complexities and dynamics of this dangerous addiction and how childhood and family experiences – and indeed society itself – have contributed to the loss of inner balance.

Readers of this book will learn how obsession cripples the Feeling function that is so necessary for work-life balance and how the very predictable *Breakdown Syndrome* that this addiction to power and control follows leads to profound personality changes, controlling behaviour, and eventually the tragic loss of integrity. Clients' stories reveal how these formerly idealistic perfectionists lose control of their destiny, and how family members react and suffer the dire consequences of this downward spiral.

The three chapters on the *Internalizing* technique will teach you how to listen to the body's feedback, label each feeling, uncover its source, and re-establish inner control *before* attempting to problem-solve. You will also learn to recognize when it may be necessary to reschedule a discussion to resolve issues to a later time because you are unclear or too emotional to deal with the situation right at that moment.

Wise and intelligent decisions require a holistic and objective overview of information gathered from *both* the Thinking and Feeling functions, each of which has its own language, behaviour, and values. It is important to balance rational and logical thoughts and careful analysis of factual information with input from Feeling's other-directed values of sensitivity, harmony, and personal intimacy. Only then can we have a compassionate understanding of how our decisions will affect the welfare of others involved. Such balance will also help us avoid becoming judgmental and unfairly critical.

Unfortunately, too many of us continue the practice we learned as children, to *externalize* and second-guess what others wished us to do, say, think, or feel. In childhood, that was adaptive as a way of fitting in and being accepted. It was also often done to avoid conflict and keep the peace. As adults, however, projecting and second-guessing others is not only disrespectful but highly manipulative and likely to be wrong.

It is important to add that *Internalizing* is not only effective in counteracting the devastating effects of workaholism, narcissism, and reactive depression, but this process and the other techniques offered here are equally effective with people who have become emotionally crippled by clinical depression, anxiety disorders, and other obsessions. Self-nurturing behaviour and the ability to nurture others each play a major role in choosing a healthy lifestyle. CBC Radio host Andy Barrie was once asked whether he smoked. His answer was, "No. I wouldn't do that to myself." Obviously, his self-nurturing Feeling function was working.

Hopefully, the ideas and techniques offered here will inspire you to begin a life-enhancing journey that will give you the confidence and inner balance necessary to solve life's difficult problems and be fully present to others.

I

Flat Feelings – Tipping the Balance

One Couple's Experience

A lot of folks don't know what's cooking until the pot boils over.

"Morning Smile," *The Globe and Mail*

SPINNING OUT OF CONTROL

A sunbeam slants across my desk, and the morning sun warms the room. Yet an anxious, tense feeling hangs in the air.

Peter, a darkly handsome fifty-year-old entrepreneur, sits rigidly upright and immobile, some distance from his wife, Sally. He casts the occasional furtive glance at her as she tearfully describes the state of their marriage. Peter's face registers little emotion. His brow is deeply furrowed, his cheeks sunken. Ridges stretch up from his tense jaw. His eyes look flat, vacant, and haunted.

In contrast, Sally's eyes, although darkly circled, shine brightly through her obvious pain. She is articulate about her experiences and describes the last few years as an absolute nightmare. Her childhood sweetheart has disappeared into this stranger whom she hardly knows.

"I know I'm depressed and not myself," Sally confides. Then, in a more desperate tone, "I feel numb so much of the time. I don't even know who I am any more!" Sally's voice catches, and tears spill down her cheeks. "It's as though

Peter's rages have absolutely traumatized me. I just can't cope with all this chaos. He's Dr Jekyll one minute, Mr Hyde the next." Sally fights for control, and then almost apologetically completes her thought. "Quite frankly, I'm just as worried about myself as I am about Peter!"

Sally is not alone in feeling traumatized. Peter's anxiety level is sky-high. His prized family business is threatened by bankruptcy. He frets continually that his colleagues and business associates will ask embarrassing questions. He has poured his heart and soul into this firm.

Peter started working for his father part-time at the age of twelve. Even before that he tagged along when his father went into work Saturday and Sunday mornings. "I think now that I was just trying to get this man's attention. My father," Peter explains, "had ice in his veins!" As is so often the case, a workaholic father has produced a workaholic son. When Peter took over the family business, it was the proudest day of his life. It was also, unfortunately, the beginning of a long, slow decline for Peter. Not long after, things started to go awry.

Sally and Peter are typical of the workaholic families I see in my practice. Workaholics like Peter gradually become one-sided and emotionally crippled. Their obsession with work becomes a relentless, compulsive drive to achieve the control and power they feel is necessary to gain others' approval. A successful public persona allows them to enjoy the accolades that hard work brings in our society. Workaholics are perfectionists who need to control all the variables to ensure that things get done their way, the "right" way. Unfortunately, other people must be controlled to achieve this. Work is the arena in which they shine, but soon long hours, over-scheduling, and frantic rushing become the norm. The adrenalin high is their "fix," the drug that frees them from emotional pain. Anger, hurt, guilt, and fear are repressed, and the addiction eventually controls their lives. The workaholic cannot *not* work without getting anxious.

At the end of our first session, I describe to Sally and Peter the therapeutic journey we will take together. Both of them are out of touch with their feelings and emotionally out of control. Our chief task will be to restore their Feeling function so that their psyches will be in balance once again. Both Thinking and Feeling are necessary to make wise decisions. Our journey will take them "from Numb to Joy."

IDENTIFYING THE IMBALANCE

While both Sally and Peter tell me they are numb and confused, Sally alone acknowledges her flat feelings. Peter thinks he is just fine. He's here, he tells me, "only because Sally tells me she's thinking about leaving." He then lets me know that "something's wrong with Sally. She's crying all the time, and for no good reason." Sally is still conscious of her feelings; Peter is not.

A few minutes earlier, I had asked Peter how he was feeling about his wife's unhappiness. His expression turned quizzical. As happens so frequently in my office, Peter turned to Sally, searching for an answer. He needed her to bail him out. It was clear that Peter did not know how he *should* feel. Pointing out this dynamic is one way to help the couple recognize the emotional dependency that occurs when feelings no longer register.

It is scary not to know how you feel, or what you want. Ironically, the strange truth is that negative emotions still work. Anger and envy, for example, surface quite unexpectedly and often are revealed in alarming thoughts. One client hesitantly admitted that he secretly felt superior when he found out a colleague had cancer. "That's not very nice, is it?" he queried, checking out my reaction. Anxiety soars as self-doubt and insecurity make decision-making increasingly difficult.

Sally, under prolonged stress, is suffering depressive symptoms brought on by despair. She tries to suppress her anger as she fights for self-control, but feelings of helplessness and outrage surge. She has worn herself out trying to keep some intimacy alive in this troubled marriage. Sally, a people person, needs harmony in her relationships. Without inner peace, she is prone to extreme psychological and physical distress. She tells me that she has suffered from a series of illnesses that her doctor tells her are all induced by stress.

Disillusioned, and emotionally fatigued, Sally now avoids her friends. "I just don't have anything left to give," she explains.

In fact, both partners have become socially isolated. For the past year, when invitations come, Peter's typical response is, "I'm not going. It's more trouble than it's worth!" In fact, people have become a nuisance. Peter has even stopped attending the business functions the couple never missed before.

Days, nights, and weekends, Peter frantically drives himself. Every avenue must be exhausted to salvage his empire. Failure, for Peter, is unthinkable! So much is at stake – family pride, his reputation, and lost jobs. He knows he can't afford to give in to his panic. He therefore over-controls, and increasingly he pushes others beyond limits so that at least some short-term goals are met. Peter will do almost anything now to block out painful reality, but the adrenalin rush that work used to give him no longer covers his anxiety. Bouts of binge drinking are becoming more frequent. He flies into a fury when Sally confronts him, and denies that he has a problem with alcohol. Peter, flipping in and out of denial, still believes he is firmly in control.

Sally doesn't see all this hyperactivity at Peter's work. In her presence, Peter's rounded shoulders spell defeat. She has noticed that he is increasingly lethargic and oblivious to his surroundings. Simple everyday distractions set off episodes of black moods or extreme irritability. Peter has become like a petulant child, dependent on Sally to run everything. Ironically, Peter was always very protective of his independence.

Riddled with a mixture of guilt, shame, resentment, and insecurity, Peter lashes out at Sally in ugly rages. Sally increasingly can do *nothing* right. Instead of recognizing his own inner chaos, Peter projects his anger outwards. Fear is contagious. Living in such an unpredictable environment, Sally and the children grow increasingly anxious and "hyper" themselves.

Rapid mood swings are common symptoms of extreme anxiety. Sally tells me she is so terrified of risking one of Peter's temper tantrums or rages that she immediately gives in. Anything to keep some semblance of harmony. Peace at any cost is expensive. It means that Sally sacrifices her own needs. Like all martyrs, she feels victimized and bitter. "Nowadays, I cry at the drop of a hat. The slightest provocation, and I'm a bowl of jelly. It's getting that I can't remember what I used to be like!"

Peter has pushed Sally to her limit. Railing against being a powerless puppet, Sally finds her rage erupting into hysteria. Her usual sensitivity and thoughtfulness go out the window. "When I let go, I'm incredibly short and sharp. I lecture and preach, and exaggerate things. All the junk I've been storing up for weeks just comes pouring out." Sally looks chagrined. "I'm really losing it. I've never behaved like this in my entire life."

Peter, on the other hand, appears to have forgotten his angry outbursts completely. He reassures me that he handles all his anger internally. Peter then turns on Sally. "You just admitted you exaggerate." He then explains to me, "Really, I'm sure she makes up a lot of this stuff."

WHO'S AFRAID OF VIRGINIA WOOLF?

We are all probably afraid of anger. Behind negative feelings such as anger, envy, jealousy, and hate lies fear. When Sally says, "I'm really losing it," she no longer feels safe. Not only have Peter's unpredictable outbursts threatened her security, she no longer trusts her own restraints.

When Peter denies his hostility, he avoids taking responsibility for his negative feelings. Instead, he sees Sally as the angry one. A destructive merry-go-round I call the "Terrible Twist" illustrates this projective technique so frequently used by workaholics to control and put down others. A typical exchange goes like this.

In the morning, on the way out the door, Peter tosses over his shoulder, "I'll be home about 6:00 tonight."

By seven o'clock that evening, Sally's feelings have progressed from hurt to frustration. By eight, her rising anger gives way to worry. She has visions of Peter in a car accident, or worse. A disturbing panic rises from her gut.

At 8:45, Peter comes rushing in the front door and is met by Sally, tears streaming down her cheeks. No apology, no explanation are offered. Sally's ensuing confrontation triggers Peter's rage.

"You're acting like a spoiled brat," he screams. A litany of Sally's faults ensues. It ends with the ultimate and all too familiar refrain: "You're always ruining our evenings! No wonder I don't come home any more." Yet again, Sally is made out to be the culprit. Not only is Sally deeply hurt by this twisting of the truth, but she is furious and frightened. Her sense of reality is shaken. Her inner turmoil escalates. Eventually she withdraws into silence and sinks further into depression.

Peter interprets Sally's withdrawal as rejection. In defiance, he stubbornly resolves not to tell Sally any details about his failing business. "Sally asks too many questions," he protests. Peter, too, protects himself with his own armour of silence. Sometimes he sulks for days.

While both feel frightened and abandoned, Peter handles it by running on an even tighter schedule. He avoids thinking about Sally. Sally can't turn herself off so easily.

When hostility in people builds up unchecked, it eventually erupts like a volcano. Overt anger spews forth in the form of ridicule, caustic sarcasm, and smouldering resentment. Bitterness turns into defiance. Temper tantrums give way to acts of destructive rage. Drivers cut off other drivers or go too fast, refusing to follow the rules of the road. People play the devil's advocate and argue just for the sake of arguing. People humiliate others, thus destroying their own and others' security. The ultimate act of rage occurs when someone commits murder or suicide.

When hostility is covert and goes underground, feelings are cut off and denied expression. The person shuns personal responsibility and instead acts out in passive-aggressive ways. Those affected by such behaviour feel victimized, rejected, even abandoned. No healthy resolution is possible without true dialogue.

Peter and Sally had little insight into the magnitude of their anger. The following quiz helped them identify their own passive-aggressive and overt styles of anger.

When others say upsetting things, do you

1. Tune out and block out what is said?
2. Avoid looking at the speaker, and look elsewhere?
3. Remain silent to avoid giving any part of yourself?
4. Get bored easily, yawn, sigh, or grow restless?
5. Rehearse what you are going to say, instead of listening?
6. Distract yourself by doing something else?
7. Send signals indicating you are in a rush?
8. Interrupt others in mid-sentence?
9. Refuse to state your position, or refuse to respond?
10. Often bring the conversation back to your own interests?

Do you avoid responsibility and typically

11. Neglect to follow through on promises?
12. Put off unwanted tasks as long as possible?

13. Tell others what they want to hear, instead of telling the truth?
14. Say yes when you really mean no?
15. Agree to do something in less time than is realistic?
16. Use sarcasm, ridicule, innuendos, or put-downs?
17. Promise things you cannot possibly deliver?
18. Act impulsively, without thinking?

THE EFFECTS OF DEPRESSION AND ANXIETY ON FEELINGS

Both depression and anxiety deaden feelings and cause people to feel numb and flat.

Sally's symptoms indicate that she is suffering a reactive depression, a state brought on by an external situation and relieved when that situation is removed. Her idealistic dreams for her marriage have been frustrated at every turn. Sally is unwittingly carrying Peter's disowned feelings of vulnerability, inadequacy, need, and unresolved guilt as well as her own stored-up anger. Naively oblivious of her best interests, Sally has become a martyr-victim – the good co-dependent in a relationship with an addict. She sacrifices her true Self to maintain a semblance of harmony in the home. The more Peter abdicates his personal responsibilities at home, the more overly responsible Sally becomes. She is left fully in charge of intimacy in their relationship and, unwittingly, she carries the fears and concerns of the whole family. Women like Sally have too often been taught that they should be nice, sweet, cute, silent, self-effacing, and self-sacrificing.

As depression settles in, Sally is zapped of all energy. As Clarissa Pinkola Estes writes in *Women Who Run with the Wolves,* "A woman may try to hide from the devastations of her life, but the bleeding, the loss of life's energy, will continue until she recognizes the predator for what it is and contains it." Desires, goals, and hopes slowly ebb away under such circumstances. Lifeless thoughts, feelings, and desires provide no energy for dreaming or action. Naivety undermines intuition.

Intuition is the soul's spokesperson. It surfaces from the unconscious, is quick, curious, and adventuresome. It willingly takes the necessary risks that make it a powerful ally for justice and fairness. Its role is to measure and weigh information, to sort through extraneous material to discover the essence or core meaning of an idea. It sees the forest, but does not get lost among the trees. It anticipates and forewarns us of people's motivation and intentions. It draws internal maps to tell us the best and wisest direction in which to proceed. It fuels us with enthusiasm and vitality, and gives wings to our imagination.

Sally's fatigue is only one symptom of her depression and the hopelessness she feels. She has also lost weight and her sleeping patterns are disturbed. Sally falls asleep in exhaustion, but sleeps fitfully. At four o'clock, she is wide awake and thrashes about until she falls into a deep sleep, only to be awakened again by disturbing dreams. Her concentration is shot. She gets distracted easily, and after reading a newspaper, she can't retain what she has read. This loss of memory and forgetfulness are common symptoms of depression. It is harder and harder to motivate herself to do even routine chores.

Sally feels mentally, physically, and emotionally drained. Much of the time she feels "like a zombie," as she phrases it. Not only is she avoiding friends, she sees very little of her extended family. Tears come easily, and crying spells are more frequent.

When the couple do have sex, which is rare these days, Sally does not initiate it. Her libido is low, and she has lost confidence in her desirability. She realizes she is distancing herself from problems. Motivating herself to do anything has become difficult, and she finds that often she just doesn't really care what happens. Irrational angry outbursts and cynicism frighten her. "I'm so preoccupied with myself! And so negative about everything. It feels as if I'm permanently wearing dark glasses."

Sally has no trouble recognizing the severity of all of these depressive symptoms. She knows that depression is a dangerous cycle that spirals downwards. The worse Sally feels about herself, the less she is motivated to take any action that might make her feel more effective. Her insecurity and immobilized feelings threaten to seriously undermine her self-worth.

Sally is anxious to get started on her journey back to health. Peter, on the other hand, may falter along the way. His workaholism is an insidious addiction, and recovery will be slow and frustrating for him. Peter's symptoms revolve around anxiety. Panic attacks, rather than depression, are his major concern. He needs to be aware, though, that once his anxiety attacks lessen, denial may close in again. Peter's soul and Self are in jeopardy, but he lacks the insight to know this. Peter's real problem, as we will learn later, concerns his high level of narcissism.

Repeated failures have threatened Peter's perfect persona. Repressed anger breaks through the layers of denial and surfaces in an eruption of rage. Panic attacks rupture the fragile ego temporarily to warn of excessive stress. Anxiety is something Peter can recognize!

Egged on by Sally, Peter reluctantly tells me that, more and more frequently, he finds himself breaking out in sweats. At first it was in the middle of the night. "I'd wake with a start and sit bolt upright. I couldn't breathe, and it felt like a paddle was pressing against my chest."

No, he didn't think he was dreaming. He doesn't think he dreams much. "I felt dizzy and disoriented – almost claustrophobic. My pajamas were soaked!" According to Sally, he would rush from the bedroom and frantically pace up and down the living room until his anxiety subsided. Only then could he begin to breathe normally again. Peter was terrified when these episodes began to occur at work. One day when he was chairing a meeting of the shareholders, he felt his hands go clammy, and beads of sweat appeared on his brow. He could feel his shirt growing damp. "I wonder if they can tell!" Then he worried, "If my panic shows, I'm a goner. They'll lose all confidence in me!" This group had already been witness to one of his angry outbursts two weeks before.

Peter's flights from reality are of grave concern. Not only is his memory terrible, but as Sally explains, "I sometimes worry that he has early Alzheimer's. He not only doesn't remember where I've told him the kids are, he asks me the same question moments after I've answered him the first time." Sally adds, "Peter doesn't seem to remember anything he doesn't want to be responsible for."

There is a danger that Peter's episodic psychotic breaks, where reality and fantasy blur, will become more frequent and severe. The breakdown syndrome of workaholism leads towards a disintegration of the ego. Peter needs to recognize how urgent it is that he gain insight and learn new skills before strong defense mechanisms shut off his chance for a full recovery.

CRISS-CROSSING JOURNEYS

Sally and Peter have one common path – their *mutual need to get back in touch with their feelings* – even though different dynamics drive them. Sally, suffering from a reactive depression, is likely to recover from her depression fairly quickly once the trauma of the current situation is corrected. A more difficult task for Sally will be confronting her co-dependent role in this marriage. She has tried to keep everything and everyone around her in harmony, but in doing so, has sacrificed her own sense of Self. She needs to learn that *giving in* is not true generosity, but a form of dishonesty that leads to a loss of integrity.

Peter faces a more difficult recovery from workaholism and narcissism. His will be a long, arduous journey, full of many setbacks and frustrations. Peter's feelings are deeply repressed because his level of anxiety prevents him from facing the numerous fears, guilt, shame, and insecurity that haunt the workaholic as the predictable breakdown syndrome progresses.

There is much background information to understand before we are ready to learn the techniques and skills necessary to get Feeling and Thinking back into balance. Chapter 2 prepares us with an explanation of how Thinking and Feeling function in the psyche. Chapter 3 goes on to explore the misunderstandings that occur when Feelers and Thinkers communicate. It also examines the Shadow side of these functions, which often wreak havoc in people's lives.

Workaholism, in the past, was little understood. Chapter 4 is devoted to exploring why feelings are lost when a person progresses through the breakdown stages of workaholism and turns from Dr Jekyll into Mr Hyde. Narcissism plays a key role in workaholism, and its self-serving focus profoundly affects all family members. Both workaholism and narcissism are also passed down from parent to child. Chapter 5 explores why narcissism is so prevalent a problem today, and explains its developmental roots and tell-tale characteristics. Chapter 6 demonstrates the dangerous legacies that narcissism brings to the family through a return to Sally and Peter's story.

Chapters 7, 8, and 9 take us through the techniques involved in restoring feelings and becoming a more effective problem-solver. Chapter 10 explores the differences between Feeling and Thinking language and behaviour. Our journey will conclude with a brainstorming technique called *The Logical Circle*, which offers creative solutions when we want to zero in and transform one of the Shadow traits or behaviours that is causing us the most trouble.

2

The Thinking and Feeling Functions

Understanding What Makes You Tick

The true portrait of a man is a fusion of what he thinks he is, what others think he is, what he really is and what he tries to be.

Dore Schary in *Heyday*

PSYCHOLOGICAL TYPE – A BRIEF OVERVIEW

Understanding our personality is of utmost importance if we are to gain insight along our psychological journey towards a balanced life. In the early 1920s, C.G. Jung, the Swiss psychologist, developed his theories of psychological differentiation. In *Psychological Types*, Jung stated that "type differentiation often begins very early, so early that in some cases one must speak of it as innate." He distinguished four basic functions that the conscious psyche requires for adaptation and orientation: Thinking, Feeling, Sensation, and Intuition. One or two functions tend to be dominant, while the others remain inferior or undifferentiated.

According to Jung's theories, ideally all four basic functions should contribute equally: "thinking should facilitate cognition and judgment, feeling should tell us how and to what extent a thing is important or unimportant for us, sensation should convey concrete reality to us through seeing, hearing, tasting, etc., and intuition should enable us to divine the hidden possibilities in the background, since these too belong to the complete picture of a given situation."

YOU CAN'T HAVE ONE WITHOUT THE OTHER

Once we perceive information, it can be used to make decisions, form an opinion, or reach some conclusion. How we make decisions or judgments will differ depending on our dominant type. Therefore, one of the most relevant questions in getting to know yourself is, Is your dominant function normally Thinking or Feeling? Healthy functioning, of course, requires a good balance between both functions. In Jungian theory, if one function works but the other does not, the strong imbalance eventually produces neurotic or pathological behaviour.

Depression, for example, is a sign of imbalance in the psyche. Depressed people become emotional easily, but they are often out of touch with their feelings and unable to make wise decisions. Similarly, when a person is ruled by an obsession, the Thinking function dominates but eventually it becomes fuzzy and confused because it is overused and distorted by anxiety. Judgment is always affected when Thinking or Feeling do not function well. Behavioural changes will become increasingly evident as this imbalance between Thinking and Feeling widens. For instance, Thinking, without the wisdom provided by feelings of compassion and empathy to temper its decisions, allows one to justify and rationalize deceit and to condone unethical behaviour. Uncensored, willful thinking permits one to commit dangerous, even evil acts such as premeditated murder. The defenses of intellectualizing, rationalizing, projecting blame, dissociation, and compartmentalization, as described later in chapter 7, can all be used to justify and excuse insensitive and destructive dysfunctional thinking.

Similarly, Feeling, without the intelligence of Thinking to guide and inform its choices, leads one to remain naive, irresponsible, even ignorant. Hysterical, childish behaviour results when one is hypersensitive, takes everything personally, and overreacts to situations. Insecurity, moodiness, passive-aggressive avoidance, a self-sacrificing martyr-victim mentality, and extreme stubbornness are signs of unhealthy feelings.

Wisdom and maturity develop when both Thinking and Feeling functions inform our decision-making. Marcel, a thirty-year-old client on a leave of absence because of his work-aholism, told me one day that he had started getting flustered the day before. "My mind was racing, and I was cooking up all sorts of ideas about what I was going to say to my boss, when I suddenly realized that my thinking had become obsessive and irrational." He looked pleased with himself as he continued: "I stopped and asked myself what I was feeling at that precise moment. I felt justifiably angry because of what I had just experienced. I decided then to just let myself huff and puff for a while." Then Marcel added, "It really works, you know. All of a sudden I didn't need to be so frustrated any more." By giving both problem-solving functions energy and time, Marcel had kept control over his emotional response.

THINKING AND FEELING

Before you learn my techniques for getting in touch with feelings, it is essential to know whether you are naturally a Thinker or a Feeler.

Thinking and Feeling functions link up with the information acquired through Sensation and Intuition, and use it to make decisions, form judgments, reach conclusions, and develop opinions about both people and things. Each function has its special strength and its own liabilities or negative Shadow side.

Feeling and emotion should not be confused. Emotion is a complex that includes not only Thinking and Feeling functions but also sense impressions, gut reactions, impulses, etc.

Thinking is essentially impersonal. According to Isabel Myers in *Gifts Differing*, "Its goal is objective truth, independent of the personality and wishes of the thinker, or anyone else" (65). Thinking is most useful for impersonal problems, such as drawing up building plans, interpreting a legal document, or analyzing whether information is true or false.

Feeling is best used when handling people and their problems, interpreting human motives, and facilitating a cooperative, mediatory, team model where both the welfare of the people involved and the agenda are considered equally important. People remain motivated if they feel part of the decision-making process.

If a Thinker and a Feeler go to a store to purchase a rug, you will hear the Thinker say, "I think we should get this one. The quality is good, it's a practical colour, and the tight weave will be serviceable."

The Feeler's response might be, "Yuk, I couldn't walk on that rug every day without getting thoroughly upset!"

Both are equally valid responses. The Thinker makes decisions based on logical, rational, practical thinking. The Feeler makes decisions based on what he or she appreciates or values. Unfortunately, in our society and within the individual, thinking often devalues and overruns feeling values.

Thinking

Thinking is reflective and objective. It asks the reasons for doing things. Thinking analyzes and weighs the available evidence. It considers cause and effect, and it stays objective when exploration uncovers unpleasant facts or discovers something is wrong. It wants proof, validity, and reliability.

Therefore, Thinkers give more credence to things that are logical, scientific, and observable. They prefer to wait until results are in before stating their impersonal findings.

Numbers, facts, and figures are highly valued. Thinkers' executive skills include an ability to organize facts and ideas in logical sequence and to be objective when hypothesizing or developing a theoretical approach. Thinkers are best at impersonal jobs. Surgeons operate with an objective distancing. Strong Thinkers are able to fire employees with relatively less trauma and to rationalize their motives for doing so – "It was necessary because it's best for the welfare of the organization." Technicians, scientists, researchers, lawyers, engineers, analysts, and judges tend to be Thinkers.

Thinkers have focused awareness. Consequently, they find it difficult to concentrate on more than one thing at a time. Don't expect a Thinker to read the paper and listen to what you have to say. They heartily dislike interruptions because their inner and outer gathering of data gets distracted. They lose their train of thought.

Thinking processes information by sifting through objective and factual knowledge and then drawing a conclusion. Consequently, the Thinkers' own version of the situation becomes their reality. Unfortunately, logic and reason are no guarantee of being right. Yet Thinkers, convinced of their argument, may be difficult to challenge. Openness is not typically one of their virtues.

Thinkers can react emotionally with some intensity, but more typically their emotions remain less evident because feelings are not communicated. Therefore, people can view Thinkers as cool, aloof, inflexible, arbitrary, and even ruthless, whenever their objective data ignores personal information and values. As Jung puts it, "He may be polite, amiable, and kind, but one is constantly aware of a certain uneasiness betraying an ulterior motive – the disarming of an opponent, who must at all costs be pacified and placated lest he prove himself a nuisance" (241). Thinkers are competitive, and their tendency to take the one-up position is usually met with resistance, distrust, and resentment in the sensitive listener who feels belittled or talked down to. The used-car salesman's pitch typifies this manipulative maneuvering.

Thinkers, because of their competitive nature, tend to be envious and jealous. As well, they can be skeptical, judgmental, critical, pessimistic, and see things as half-empty rather than half-full.

Thinkers can be poor communicators because they package information in their heads prior to speaking. Jungian theory suggests some of the reasons for their miscommunication:

1. Thinkers can clutter up their communication with adjuncts, qualifications, retractions, saving clauses, doubts, etc., but forget to tell you the subject of their discourse.
2. Thinkers tend to be blunt, short, or sharp in their delivery and often neglect to give the listener enough information about how they reached their opinion.
3. Thinkers can take too long and be overly intense about an idea that intrigues them and forget to focus on the relationship with the listener.
4. Thinkers tend to lecture and preach, and thereby bore the listener because there is no exchange of views.
5. Thinkers can fail to personalize and own what they are saying. Instead they talk in generalities, referring to people in general. Or they use theoretical rhetoric to prove their own point.
6. Thinkers enjoy being "historical," bringing up facts and experiences from the past to support their present argument. Such "elephant" memories infuriate the listener, who often has no recollection of the event or totally disagrees with the information when it is presented as evidence of the Thinker's being "right."

Thinkers appear to be listening when they do not interrupt. In reality, they are often lost in thought, rehearsing what they are going to say next. Their focus is arrested on one of the thoughts that interested them personally.

Narrow-minded Thinkers can be domineering, opinionated, and prickly. Outsiders often see them as inconsiderate, insensitive, and arrogant. They can make Feelers feel they have been "run over by a bus!" If teaching, their thoughts are concerned with the material, not the presentation of it or whether the student understands. The first day of my return to school after a fifteen-year absence, I watched in fascination as about a hundred students exited in droves past the professor in the middle of a Psychology 101 lecture. He didn't miss a beat and remained focused on his lecture notes. I was amazed that he didn't seem interested enough to ask the students why they were leaving. Asking for feedback is rare for these Thinkers.

The more Feelings are cut off, the more Thinking will become rigid and unbending, shut off from outside influences and from reality itself. Rigid Thinkers tend to take everything personally and fall back on emotionality and touchiness. If challenged, such Thinkers lash out or withdraw into passive-aggressive anger. Their personal retorts can be vicious and highly irrational. Gradually, their isolation increases as people withdraw because they are afraid or do not trust that the Thinker is capable of being empathic or compassionate.

Tragically, as Jung states, "His originally fertilizing ideas become destructive, poisoned by the sediment of bitterness. His struggle against the influences emanating from the unconscious increases with his external isolation, until finally they begin to cripple him" (244). As a Thinker grows more out of touch with subjective reality, his thinking becomes fanciful and irrelevant to facts as they are. A wall builds up around the person as secrecy and privacy become even more important. Chaos is building up inside, but no one must know!

Fairness is important for Thinkers. It often seems as though they place things on a weigh scale, ensuring that one thing balances another. "If I get this one, then you can have that one" is the exchange. Truth, principles, policies, and laws are valued. Thinkers, however, tend to distrust and ignore decisions made by feeling-based values. Feelings can be deemed flighty, unreliable, and totally illogical or off-the-wall. However, as Isabel Myers concludes in *Gifts Differing*: Thinkers "contribute to the welfare of society by the intellectual criticism of its habits, customs, and beliefs, by the exposure of wrongs, the solution of problems, and the support and research for the enlargement of human knowledge and understanding" (68).

Men slightly outnumber women as Thinkers (60 to 40 per cent), according to Myers-Brigg statistics. In my practice, I find that Thinkers who marry Feeling types often create difficulties because they tend to be "fixers" who problem-solve for a spouse whose thinking they consider inferior. In turn, Feeling types distrust the Thinker's cut-and-dried, matter-of-fact method of discussion. Although both these types just "know" what ideas, which people, and what course of action they value and appreciate, Thinkers want to argue and debate with others to prove that their way of doing things or their thoughts are best. Thinkers contradict each other, each one claiming "the truth," while for Feelers it is enough that something is "valuable" to them. Consequently, it is much easier for Feelers to *agree to disagree*.

Feeling

Feeling, above all, values harmony. Feelers make decisions based on a personal value-based system and on a subjective appreciation of a person or object.

Feelers excel in the social arts because they are sensitive to human interaction. They tend to be well-adjusted and reasonable, and often get what they want easily. They relate well because they are accepting and agreeable, and usually have many friends and acquaintances. Feelers are generally good at sizing up and judging the positive and negative sides of people. Feeling tends to be naturally uncritical, trusting, and optimistic. Feelers like to agree with others, if possible, and give people the benefit of the doubt, at least until evidence to the contrary is acknowledged. Feelers can therefore be naive and subject to others' manipulation. However, feeling itself can become mechanical and calculating if the person neglects to nurture others and be genuinely self-nurturing. Such Feelers may eventually become neurotic.

Sacrifice is easy for Feelers because they have diffuse, open awareness, and their attention is naturally directed outwards towards others. They can do several things at once and still pay attention to the actions and behaviour of family members, friends, and things going on around them. If other-directedness comes at the expense of self-nurturing, however, Feelers may become self-sacrificing victims or martyrs. Such people lose the Self in the service of others and often become bitter, resentful souls who don't feel appreciated for all their efforts. In truth, they are apt to lose their own feelings and become manipulative and controlling people. They give or "give in," but their giving has strings attached. There are unstated expectations about what the other person "should" give back to them. *Giving in*, by the way, has little to do with real generosity!

Because harmony is so important to them, Feelers tend to avoid conflict. Anger can go underground if not expressed. It becomes passive-aggressive in nature and turns into a slow-burning fuse. Eventually this anger turns destructive, both to the Feeler and to those who eventually have to deal with the Mount Vesuvius rages that erupt when the Feeler finally explodes. Withdrawing, sulking, not speaking, or not listening is irresponsible and serves only to delay problem-solving, or inhibits any resolution of problems.

Further, Feelers risk building up enormous resentment and self-pity if they feel unloved or unappreciated. They may give all their energy to others, yet fail to be assertive and stand up for their own needs. Such victims, unfortunately, often fall into despair. Some even contemplate suicide because they feel helpless to change their circumstances. Usually depression becomes a serious problem because repressed anger remains buried beneath consciousness. Feelings of sadness and bitterness are experienced instead. "Smiling depressives" look happy while telling you horrific details of their life, completely out of touch with their own anger. "No, I'm not an angry person," he or she will insist. Anger would mean that they were out of harmony, an unforgivable sin.

Extraverted Feelers like to talk through their thoughts, sort through possibilities, and brainstorm ideas through to a conclusion. Thinkers tend to believe that Feelers ramble, repeat themselves, go into too much detail, or talk too long during this process. When two Feelers are talking, they often interrupt each other, add facilitating or supportive comments, and share experiences. The conversation continues, despite the additions and qualifications, with no apparent problem. Sharing and affirmation are very important.

Feelers, especially Extraverted types, are naturally tenderhearted, diplomatic, tactful, sensitive, and thoughtful. They make friends easily and are able to put themselves in others' shoes. Feelers are enthusiastic, accepting, supportive, and interested in what others do and think. Feelers ask questions and draw out others.

Introverted Feelers, however, resemble Thinkers, as they keep feelings tucked safely inside. They are more shy, timid, secretive, and private. They tend to have one or two close friendships. They may open up after a time when they get to know you. Friends and close relatives complain that they don't say nice things, even "I love you." Their response to this complaint is often utter surprise. Because they do care deeply and often passionately, they find it hard to believe that others don't know this. In fact, the assumption that others are as perceptive and thoughtful as they are leads Feelers to suffer great disappointment. They expect similar behaviour from others, and are often overwhelmed when it is not forthcoming.

Misunderstandings occur frequently between Thinkers and Feelers because of the way caring is shown. Thinkers value doing things for others, such as fixing an appliance or cutting the grass. They think problem-solving for others is "helpful." In contrast, Feelers value affirmation and confirmation from others. They love to hear phrases of endearment and support from loved ones. Typical complaints from a Thinker sound like this: "It's not what you *say,* but what you *do,* that counts. You don't appreciate all the things I do for you. You just want my pay cheque." Or, "You can say you love me a hundred times, but if you turn me away sexually, that's not okay with me. I want a wife who thinks I'm important, who looks after my needs."

The Feeler rejoins, "It's not what you *do,* but what you *say,* that is important to me! I need a sensitive, gentle husband who wants to share and laugh, and who tells me he cares." Or, "How can you expect me to want to be sexual with you when you're so neglectful and thoughtless of my wishes. You never say 'I love you,' even though you know it would make me so happy." Until both Thinking and Feeling are developed within the individual, this dilemma will remain unresolved and irresolvable.

For Feelers, honesty is innate. If they tell a lie, Feelers suffer great dissonance until the truth is out. Small children will tell a fib, but then, after much suffering, they will tell you, "You know what I told you the other day? Well, I really wasn't over at Susan's house!" Ironically, Feelers are sometimes tactful, rather than honest. Hurting other people's feelings is to be avoided because they well understand the pain involved when that happens to them.

Oversensitivity, taking everything personally, is not a healthy response. One must be truly sensitive to *both* oneself and others. Being assertive and firm is therefore important for Feelers. They need to develop the ability to stand up for their own ideas and to understand the valuing process by which they developed them. Otherwise, they will lose confidence when a dominant Thinker steamrolls over their opinions. Harmony-lovers can become demoralized, passive, depressed, and anxiety-prone unless they develop their own objective thinking. Feelers can develop a healthy skepticism by learning to ask themselves these questions:

1. Is this information or opinion really true about me?
2. Is this person attributing something to me that he cannot recognize in himself? In other words, is this a projection?
3. Is this person's blunt, sharp delivery making me defensive? If so, am I really hearing what is being said?
4. Do I actually understand what she is telling me, or are details being left out that might help me figure out what she means?
5. Do I expect him to say thank you graciously, when he really doesn't know how to say it that way?

Isabel Myers, in *Gifts Differing*, points out that Feelers "contribute to the welfare of society by their loyal support of good works and those movements, generally regarded as good by the community, which they feel correctly about and so can serve effectively" (68).

Too frequently, however, those people who are motivated by empathy and compassion can unwittingly sabotage their own well-being. Women Feelers who marry work-obsessed Thinkers, for instance, often take on the disowned feelings of vulnerability, insecurity, and inadequacy of their publicly super-efficient husbands. They feel sad, get depressed, and act out anxiety for both of them. If their ego boundaries are poorly defined, these over-responsible souls overburden themselves by carrying the whole family's problems.

Sadly, to the outside world, this personally irresponsible husband appears together and strong, while his wife gets labelled neurotic! She gets told that, "Everything is her fault," and sadly, she comes to believe that this is true.

This "victim" spouse, parent, and jack-of-all-trades gradually accepts full responsibility for home and children. In the service of others, she loses her true sense of Self and her independence. Depressed, bitter, and resentful, she must seek support outside the family. The status quo is then so entrenched that neither member of this couple can grow because they are trapped in the angst of a dysfunctional family.

WHY THINKERS AND FEELERS HAVE TROUBLE UNDERSTANDING ONE ANOTHER

Now that we have some idea about how Feeling and Thinking function, we will go on to explore how these functions cause problems in our relationships with others. We will look at the different communication patterns of Thinkers and Feelers and examine a controlling tactic that can be highly destructive, especially when used against a Significant Other.

We will also learn how our least-developed or Inferior function can turn against us and undermine our dominant best functions. If your Inferior is negative Thinking, for example, then it will be to your advantage to take the time and energy necessary to develop its positive side. Otherwise, the dangerous Shadow side of your personality will do harm to both yourself and others.

3

Misunderstandings: The $64 Question

What in the World Went Wrong?

Who knows what evil lurks in the hearts of men? The Shadow knows!

CONFUSING, CONFUSED, OR TRAUMATIZED?

Poor communication is the number one reason people give for the breakdown of a relationship. Communicating well is an art that can be learned, but it takes much patience, tolerance, and skill. It also helps to know the different ways people communicate. For example, do they share their thoughts and feelings or is everything kept safely tucked inside?

In this chapter we will discover why Thinkers and Feelers have difficulty communicating with each other and why "The Terrible Twist," a controlling tactic, is so destructive.

We will also learn why the Inferior function is the dark culprit behind many of our upsets and arguments. When this Shadow aspect of ourselves roars to the surface unannounced, atypical personality changes occur that surprise us, and also others. Nobody wins when the Shadow is at play.

CONVERSATIONS BETWEEN THINKERS AND FEELERS

Thinkers and Feelers process information and make decisions in different ways.

Two Thinkers

Andy and Bruce are both born Thinkers.

TWO THINKERS IN CONVERSATION

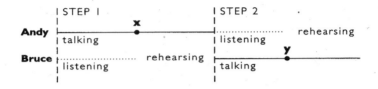

STEP 1:   Andy is talking to Bruce. Bruce listens until Andy says X, an idea that happens to interest Bruce. At this moment, Bruce goes inside his head and processes this information. Bruce begins to formulate his own version of x and starts to rehearse what he is going to say when Andy finishes speaking. Because Bruce is preoccupied with his own thoughts, he hears little else that Andy is saying. Andy finishes talking.

STEP 2:   It is Bruce's turn to speak, and he responds to Andy. Bruce tells Andy what he thinks of Andy's idea, X. Andy, meanwhile, is unaware that Bruce has heard only part of what Andy said. Andy listens to Bruce, until Bruce says Y, an idea that gets Andy's attention. A similar process ensues as Andy becomes preoccupied with his own thoughts about Y. He starts rehearsing what he wants to say to Bruce when Bruce finishes talking.

Andy and Bruce appear to be listening to each other, but it is *selective listening* based on what catches the particular interest of each person. Because Thinkers have *focused awareness*, (which I'll indicate by the symbol ^), they function best when they are able to concentrate on one thing at a time. Some real listening does occur but, since both Andy and Bruce hear only snatches of each other's thoughts, true understanding may be curtailed.

Although Thinkers tend not to interrupt each other, when they become fully engaged in a subject and want to get their point across, they do interrupt and are apt to both speak at once. Overreacting is a dark Shadow side of Feeling, which may be their Inferior function.

Two Feelers

Cindy and Diane are both strong Feelers.

TWO FEELERS IN CONVERSATION

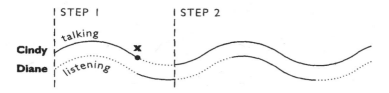

STEP 1:   Cindy is talking through her problems, sorting out what she thinks about a subject. Diane listens, until she hears Cindy mention that she has experienced X, an upsetting situation. Diane recognizes that she too has had a similar situation happen in her own life. Diane then jumps in to briefly share her own experience, and then resumes listening to Cindy's thoughts on the subject.

STEP 2:   Cindy continues talking about her own experience of X. Diane breaks into the conversation several times, and once even speaks at the same time as Cindy. Cindy stops momentarily to let Diane finish her thoughts. Then Cindy continues with her story, while Diane listens.

STEP 3: While Cindy is speaking, she is thinking through her own thoughts. Verbalizing helps her clarify her thinking. Diane in turn acts like a Greek chorus, affirming, sympathizing, supporting, and questioning Cindy's ideas until Cindy finally comes to some resolution of her own problem. Interruptions are no problem for this pair. Both have the Feeler's capacity for diffuse awareness, (indicated by the symbol V). Both are able to concentrate on several conversations at once and still keep track of their own viewpoint. Clarification comes for Cindy as she works through her own ideas. It is helpful to have Diane's support, and she enjoys sharing ideas and opinions along the way with Diane. Cindy herself needs both acceptance and affirmation.

A Thinker and a Feeler

Andy is the Thinker, and Cindy, the Feeler.

THINKER AND FEELER IN CONVERSATION

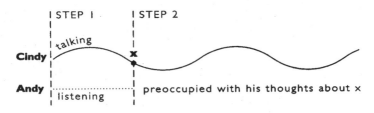

STEP 1: Cindy is talking through a relationship problem with Andy, her husband. She goes to some length to explain her thoughts to Andy. Andy listens until Cindy says X, which is something someone said to her that she found upsetting.

STEP 2: Since Andy thinks this thought, X, is somewhat bizarre, he tries to figure out why Cindy is so upset.

Situation X wouldn't bother him at all! He is absorbed in his own questioning.

STEP 3:   Eventually Cindy realizes there is a blank look on Andy's face. Cindy stops, and verbalizes her anger towards Andy because he isn't listening to her. This is important stuff to her.

STEP 4:   Andy tells her that he thinks her statements about X are ridiculous and totally illogical. "How could you possibly get upset about that?" he asks.

STEP 5:   Cindy explains to Andy that X was only a tangential thought. It really has little to do with the important relationship problem she is trying to solve. "And why are you talking about X anyway? It's got to be the least important thing I said," she adds in frustration.

Cindy gets very upset because, as she says, "He never just accepts my point of view. He always has to add his own two cents!" She feels belittled and offended that Andy didn't even try to simply listen. "It's obvious you haven't the faintest idea what I'm talking about!" Cindy exclaims. "Why don't you ever just listen to me?"

In addition to her initial problem, Cindy now has the extra frustration experienced when she shared her troubled thoughts with Andy. Cindy will soon learn not to "think out loud" to Andy. In doing this, she unwittingly stops sharing and thereby lessens her own generosity, a precious Feeling function. Andy does his own thinking internally first and tends not to share his thoughts until he has reached a conclusion. Certainly, he doesn't talk while he is thinking. Doing two things at once is not Andy's strength.

With communication breaking down, soon neither even tries to understand their differences. Eventually both cease to even care, and little energy goes into talking, let alone listening. Feelings have become too painful and raw, and numbness sets in. Communication, for this couple, occurs only when it is necessary to discuss superficial, impersonal, "safe" topics.

Andy is more interested in ideas, things, and goals. Cindy's interests centre on relationships and people-related issues. No wonder their focus is directed towards different things. Send these two to a movie and listen to the conversation after. Andy will extol the virtues of the film's technology. Cindy will try to figure out all the intricate relationships between the characters. She will worry about what happened to so-and-so, why the heroine didn't see what was coming, and so on.

Solution

STEP 1:   Cindy needs to stop when she sees a blank or far-off look in Andy's eyes, and ask, "Where did I lose you?"

STEP 2:   Andy also needs to take responsibility when he stops listening. At the time he goes inside to start processing x, he needs to warn Cindy, "can you hold on for a minute? I'm trying to figure out why you would be so upset when so-and-so said X. I can't listen and try to figure this out at the same time."

STEP 3:   This gives Cindy a chance to reply that X was only an aside. It isn't important to the way she sees the problem. She herself may be puzzled about why she brought X into the conversation. The reason may be an unconscious one, in which case she won't be able to figure it out immediately. If she does know why she mentioned it, she will be able to explain why she digressed onto that particular tangent.

STEP 4:   Both Cindy and Andy can then resume the conversation, with both of them involved, until Cindy discovers her own solution.

Andy will be able to ask her questions along the way if he finds he is getting lost or distracted again.

STEP 5: When Cindy has reached her own resolution, Andy may clarify his understanding of her intentions by rephrasing what he hears she is going to do to settle this relationship conflict. "So you've decided to phone Mary and explain this to her?" Cindy can then confirm this, or explain further.

The goal for this couple is to develop mutual listening skills and to resolve not to take their different ways of processing information personally. Differing styles of communication need to be understood and appreciated rather than scorned. Otherwise, there will be the familiar arguments about who is right, or challenging questions such as, "Why did you say such a stupid thing?" Such divisive tactics mean no one wins.

THE TERRIBLE TWIST

The Terrible Twist is a controlling, emotionally abusive Shadow tactic that I described in my book *Workaholics: The Respectable Addicts*. Communication becomes highly destructive when it is used, and the recipient of the message is left devastated. Feelers especially need to be aware because Thinkers are naturally competitive and being "one-up" is often important. They are, therefore, more prone to project blame, and see others at fault for something they did. The defense mechanism of projecting blame onto innocent others is a cruel act.

STEP 1: One person does something that the other person feels is thoughtless, such as coming home for dinner hours late without any warning phone call. He or she finally arrives, with no apology or explanation.

STEP 2: The waiting person, at first angry, then hurt, and eventually fearful, is extremely upset and says so: "I was worried sick! Where were you, and why didn't you have the courtesy to call me?"

STEP 3 (The Twist):   The late person becomes highly annoyed at this rebuke. The precipitating behaviour is totally ignored, as if it hadn't happened.

The argument that follows end with a crowning insult: "See, you're spoiling our evening again by getting yourself all upset! It sure doesn't make me want to rush home." And then, to wound even further: "I can't stand your sniveling. Why don't you grow up?"

Such a devastating interchange would traumatize anyone, but since Feeling types are highly sensitive, they are more vulnerable to such abuse. If something goes wrong in a relationship, Feelers tend to take more than their share of responsibility. Some try even harder to make it work. The natural other-directed focus of Feelers too often makes them put other people's happiness before their own. Feelers tend to be *pleasers* who, in order to keep harmony in the family, sacrifice their own inner harmony. The loss of Self is a very real danger for people exposed, over time, to this highly dangerous "projection of blame" defense mechanism.

After my book on workaholism was published, many wives across Canada and the United States phoned to tell me that their eyes had been opened to this terribly abusive tactic. A typical comment: "Thank heavens I finally understand what is actually going on in our house. You know, I really thought I was going crazy!"

One completely demoralized spouse told me, with touching gratitude, that my book actually saved her life. She had planned her own suicide because she had begun to believe her husband's often repeated charge, "It's all your fault!" Her feelings of guilt were too painful, so she became numb and mute. Initially, she had defended herself at every turn, but he used whatever she said and twisted it back against her. She gave up trying to respond because her husband could argue rings around her. She had lost her will and felt totally powerless. The Terrible Twist is a lethal weapon in any power struggle, and should be regarded as emotional abuse.

This woman and any other individuals exposed to this tactic need to develop their own clear objective thinking at such times. You will need to give yourself time to regain the self-control so necessary for objectivity. When you recognize the Terrible Twist, simply state in a firm voice, "I disagree with your view of this situation, and I don't appreciate your comments. I'll talk to you about this later, when I'm not so upset."

Withdraw from the situation and try to write down the exchange in a diary or notebook. This action will help you to gain some objective distance, especially when you see the words in black and white. Then, when you have calmed down enough, ask yourself this crucial question: Was his/her behaviour insensitive or inconsiderate? If you are convinced it was insensitive, choose a time when you are both in a more positive frame of mind. Follow through on your promise to return to discuss the previous situation.

Make sure there is no blaming or judging on your part. Clearly state that you want to establish some mutually agreeable guidelines, so that similar incidents do not occur again. The conversation might go like this: "It's important to me that *we both* be reliable and loyal to one another. I suggest that we make a commitment to call if one of us is going to be later than we promised." Make sure to add, "Would you be willing to meet me halfway on this?"

If the answer is positive, you might add, "I appreciate that. Let's try this for a couple of weeks, and see if this helps our relationship run more smoothly."

If there is no cooperation but instead a continuation of the power struggle, then it is time to realize that you cannot keep a relationship going all by yourself! Remember that the Terrible Twist is emotional abuse and seek help.

Dysfunctional communication is a sign that there are serious problems in the relationship. Often, the Inferior function, working overtime, is one of the culprits.

THE INFERIOR FUNCTION – OUR PHANTOM SHADOW

The Inferior function is largely unconscious and therefore is our least-well-developed function. When we get upset, our negative emotions flood to the surface. We become irritable and sometimes fall into dark moods. Unfortunately, others are often on the receiving end of our unexpected and atypical negative reactions. The Inferior function is autonomous. It has a life of its own! When you overreact to something, "act out" with anger, or "act in" with depression or anxiety, it is a sign that you are in the grip of its power.

The Inferior function, according to Jungian theory, whether it be Thinking, Feeling, Sensation, or Intuition, typically possesses five qualities:

1. It is *primitive*, not well formed, or barely developed.
2. It is *childlike*. We often act in a petulant, childish manner when under its influence.
3. It is *negative* and causes us to withdraw, become grouchy or short-fused, or feel out-of-sorts. Negativity takes different forms, depending on which function is inferior.
4. It is *stubborn*: it digs in its heels and has a habit of hanging around for a long time.
5. It is *rigid* and resolute. Each of us develops patterns of attack, one of which is blaming others, regardless of what happened. The Inferior function, because it is largely unconscious, often runs on automatic pilot, without any help from us.

No one can reason with us when we are caught in the Inferior function's clutches. If it is one of our decision-making functions, Thinking or Feeling, we will find it increasingly hard to make a decision. Our judgment will be distorted by a lack of objectivity and inner control. We may even find ourselves slowly immobilized.

To counteract the Inferior function's negative influence and support our best functions, we need to develop its polar opposite function. Then we will be in better balance psychologically. Thinkers, for example, need to develop their Feeling function so that they become more diplomatic and gracious. Without a well-balanced personality, we become lopsided and risk becoming both bored and boring! As a consequence, our joy and zest for life will fade as repressed energies are consumed by unresolved problems and irresponsible behaviour. It is not fair or responsible to expect our loved ones to carry our disowned craziness or angst!

WHEN YOU ACT OUT WHILE IN YOUR INFERIOR FUNCTION

To illustrate the workings of the Inferior function, we will look at the situation when this function is Thinking (Sally), and when it is Sensation (Peter). My clients Sally and Peter will serve as examples.

Sally – The Feeler

Sally is an Extraverted (E), Intuitive (N), Feeling (F), Judging (J) (ENFJ) personality. Her dominant function is Feeling; her auxiliary or second-best function is Intuition. Her third function is Sensation, and her Inferior function is *Thinking*.

A thumbnail sketch of an ENFJ is offered by Coleen Clark in her booklet on the Myers-Briggs personality types: "Compassionate, caring, idealistic, responsive, charismatic, sociable. Good at organizing & leading people. Need & give affirmation. Need & create harmony."

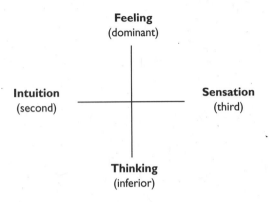

Jung's theory suggests that if Sally is exposed to ongoing stress from the troubled marriage, her Inferior Thinking will become activated. It will start to sabotage her best function, Feeling. Recall how Peter, as he became increasingly frustrated at the loss of control in his own life, projected his anger onto Sally by criticizing and putting her down. This tactic served to make him feel superior, at least temporarily. Eventually, Sally could do nothing right in Peter's eyes because she had begun to challenge his controlling behaviour. She had become the "enemy," someone to defeat.

Sally, in response, grew increasingly afraid and defensive. She became supersensitive and overly emotional, taking things much too personally. Any time she was flooded with emotion, her Inferior Thinking surged up. Instead of withdrawing as she was starting to do, she would lash back at Peter in a fury.

Note that *negative Thinking* is skeptical, critical, judgmental, and pessimistic – "half-empty." It is competitive, and therefore prefers to be right. It excels at one-upmanship. Jealousy and envy motivate the making of comparisons about who is better. Negative thinking gets argumentative, picky, and prickly. It has a short fuse, and its messages are delivered in a clipped, blunt, sharp staccato. Its opinionated statements are not open for discussion.

Negative Thinking leaves out essential information, yet is flustered by the listener's puzzlement. It lectures, preaches, and goes on and on, boring the listener because there is no *exchange of views*. It rarely asks questions of others, and it listens poorly. It gets too intense about its ideas. It turns "historical," bringing up supportive evidence from two weeks, three months, or four years ago. It repeats itself. It fails to personalize and own what it is saying, preferring instead to talk about "people" in general. It uses theoretical rhetoric and quotes from authoritative sources. Quite frankly, it is a roaring pain!

This type of behaviour from the ordinarily nurturing, kind, and gentle Sally has a tremendous impact. It might be expected from a Thinker who is in a bad mood. It is shocking and totally disorienting coming from a Feeler. No wonder Peter becomes even more distrustful and confrontational with Sally.

Sally needs to make a concerted effort to develop her *positive Thinking* function. Effective thinking is rational, logical, sensible, pragmatic, and realistic. It analyses and takes an objective, impersonal look at the facts. It is fair and consistent, and values truth, principles, policy, and laws. Fairness is considered an especially important value.

Peter – The Thinker

Peter is an Introvert (I), Intuitive (N), Thinking (T), Judging (J) (*INTJ*) personality. His dominant function is Intuition; his second-best function is Thinking. His third function is Feeling; and his Inferior function is *Sensation*.

*INTJ*s are described by Coleen Clark as "Independent, reflective, organized, organizing, intellectually astute, skeptical, theoretical, analytical, insightful. Have a private need to control. Good at improving others' ideas but forget to stroke."

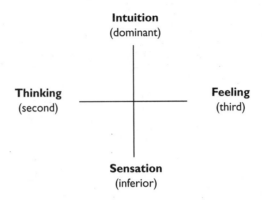

Peter's Inferior Sensation is working overtime because his obsession with work has immobilized his Thinking. Because of the dynamics inherent in workaholism, his positive Feeling and Intuition are repressed and thus not effective. No moderating diplomacy or tact is coming from his Feeling side.

Note that when *negative Sensation* is activated, Thinking becomes dualistic and concrete. Peter sees only two options: black–white, right–wrong, dominant–submissive. He gets lost in obsessive detail. Myopic, he fails to see the big picture any more. He increasingly feels overwhelmed by too much detail or stimuli, and any distractions bring confusion and anger. He is so concrete in his Thinking that the abstract subtleties of Intuition are lost on him. At such times, he seems almost childlike and naive.

When sensation is negative, *selective listening* – hearing only what one wants to hear – becomes problematic. I call it the "3 out of 5" syndrome, meaning the person hears or sees only the details that he or she wishes to hear. To illustrate, a woman once moved in with a man she thought was intelligent, rich, and witty – the three things she wanted to see. This decision was made after knowing him only a few months. The man, it was discovered, was dabbling in some high-flying business ventures. Not only was he totally absorbed in his work, thinking of little else, but he was still emotionally involved with his first wife, despite numerous liaisons since his separation several years before. The important information, the "bookends," as I call them, were forgotten. The woman ignored his workaholism and his constant talk about his ex-wife because this gentleman was extremely charming and persuasive when he wanted something or someone. She had been swept off her feet!

Peter needs to develop his *positive Sensation* by purposely paying attention to its sensory aspects – sight, sound, touch, smell, and taste. These sensations provide much pleasure in life and ground us to the earth and to nature, acting as a constant source of inner nourishment to our souls. Concurrently, he needs to restore his natural intuitive strengths that have been undermined, such as his creativity and imagination, and his ability to see possibilities in the future. He needs to use his objectivity, to stand back and sort out what details are the most important. He might ask Sally to work with him on brainstorming and appreciating the symbolic and metaphoric once again. Peter, as an Intuitive type, used to be good at this.

Peter is experiencing double-trouble. Not only is his Inferior Sensation function causing problems, but he has become emotionally crippled by the dynamics of workaholism. His *positive Feeling* is also barely functioning. He is numb and feels flat and empty. As he says, "I always think something is missing." Peter is battling depression, and his chronic fatigue is the result of his endless pumping of adrenalin. Remember, *negative Feeling* is moody, resentful, and grouchy. It feels hopeless or helpless. It gets overwhelmed, and feels useless and paralyzed. It concentrates on all the things that are wrong or have been done poorly. It generalizes until it sees everything going wrong. It feels sorry for itself.

Negative Feeling is self-focused and self-absorbed and has no ability to be empathetic. It causes people to withdraw and shut themselves off from the world at large. They become

silent and often sigh. They look down and lose eye contact.
They slump forward, feeling exhausted and heavy. Anxious,
they hold their breath and lose concentration. Thoughts get
jumbled, and nothing seems funny or fun any more. An empty,
sick feeling lies in their stomach.

Peter is not available emotionally, either for himself or for
others. He is supersensitive to rejection and avoids situations
where he is vulnerable. He, like Sally, takes everything personally, but he is also quite paranoid. Peter's high anxiety makes
him afraid of life itself.

Peter needs to develop his *positive Feeling*. Positive Feeling
is sensitive, thoughtful, considerate, and warm. It is also generous, tactful, gentle, gracious, diplomatic, and conciliatory. It
values harmony, but can be quietly assertive, if necessary.

It is no wonder that Sally and Peter have grown miles apart.
Sally's negative Thinking responds to Peter's negative Sensation and the dark side of Feeling. Both on a conscious and
an unconscious level, these functions hook onto one another.
A destructive discourse, or passive-aggressive withdrawal,
inevitably follows. No constructive problem-solving is possible at such times.

LOVE YOUR SHADOW!

When the Shadow is at work, it sounds like this: "I don't
know why I just did that!" Or, "My wife told me: 'It's not
what you said, it's the way you said it.'"

The Shadow, a term used by Jung, has three parts. First, the
negative Shadow consists of all the unfavourable aspects of
ourselves that we have repressed or disowned, often for adaptive reasons. Second, the *positive Shadow* contains our admirable but often hidden strengths, which have remained largely
undeveloped. For example, if we are Introverted, a great deal
of our Extraversion lies dormant, waiting to be activated.

Last, but not least, the Shadow contains the wisdom of the
Collective Unconscious. Jung used this term to describe the

innate information and knowledge carried deep within each individual. There are many collectives, both past and present, that influence our behaviour. Our society, for instance, offers laws, rewards, and punishments that filter through to us via informative media and value-related stories. Family values are taught by example and words. Similarly, the collective affiliations we identify with – our schools and our spiritual, financial, and business institutions, for example – all strongly influence our choices. Which partners we choose, what friends we gravitate to, and which work setting we select can be influenced by age, race, status, and historical or political factors.

Carl Jung offers this good advice: Love your Shadow. Nourish it, protect it, and you will stay safe. By welcoming our Shadow into consciousness, we can gain the insight and wisdom necessary to free ourselves from naivety and temptation. Jung, however, warns that considerable effort is needed to recognize the "dark aspects of the personality as present and real. This act is the essential condition for any kind of self-knowledge, and it therefore, as a rule, meets with considerable resistance" (*The Portable Jung*, 145).

It is clear then that a strong will is a pre-requisite for hard-won insights. Only when we begin to recognize when a Shadow trait has been activated, by hearing our tone of voice or a nuanced phrase, or when we become aware of our somewhat bizarre behaviour, will we be able to monitor just *when* and *how* it is being acted out.

Although we may eventually come to tolerate or even "accept" our Shadow side, others will not like it at all! That is because the Shadow is usually projected. As John Sanford, in *The Invisible Partners*, points out, "When something is projected we see it outside of us, as though it belongs to someone else and has nothing to do with us" (10). The good news, ironically, is that only unconscious contents are projected. Projections cease only when identified as such and we choose instead to take full ownership and responsibility for the transformation of our faults and actions.

Jung describes so well the consequences of refusing to see the Shadow in ourselves: "It is often tragic to see how blatantly a man bungles his own life and the lives of others yet remains totally incapable of seeing how much the whole tragedy originates in himself, and how he continually feeds it and keeps it going" (*The Portable Jung*, 147).

Facing up to the wasted years and the sorrow of having damaged others' lives is a daunting task. It takes great courage to honestly say, "I'm sorry." Growth and maturity come when we actually take the necessary steps to make amends, which is the only genuine apology.

The stories told here relate to Thinking or Sensation as the Inferior function. To identify the positive and negative aspects of these functions, as well as those for Sensation and Intuition, refer to the "How to Identify Your Inferior Function" charts in Appendix 3. A more detailed description appears in my book, *Integrity: Doing the Right Thing for the Right Reason*.

UNDERSTANDING THE PROBLEM

Before we begin to discover what we can do to stop doing and saying things that upset others, an understanding of what went wrong is essential. How did we get so out of touch with the positive side of our thoughts and feelings? Have we become emotionally crippled recently, or when was the damage done?

In chapter 4, we will explore workaholism. How do people know if they have become workaholics? What does the loss of balance in the workaholic's life do to his or her personality? Why do workaholics eventually suffer a loss of feelings? What are workaholics afraid of, and why do they become chronically fatigued and burdened with guilt or act badly because of hidden shame?

In chapter 5, we will learn why narcissism plays such an important role in workaholism, and why narcissists lose their feeling values and thereby lack the capacity to be empathic and show compassion. Why is the welfare of others sacrificed to their selfish, self-serving ends? Why is their public persona, the part of their personality that seeks to broadcast their success and accomplishments, so all important?

In chapter 6, we will see how narcissism spills down through generations by exploring the family dynamics in Peter and Sally's family.

We will then be ready to learn some important techniques that will help undo the damage caused when people lose touch with their feelings.

4

The Workaholic Trap

Personality Changes on the Gerbil Wheel

Isn't it amazing how many people there are who long for
immortality – but can't even amuse themselves on a rainy evening.
"Morning Smile," *The Globe and Mail*

THE LOSS OF A BALANCED LIFE

A quote from the author Jack Kerouac says it all: "Who wants
a living – I want a life." Today, family life and work have
become two worlds in conflict. There is no balance in life
when the ideas and goals we pursue come to fruition but we
ride roughshod over our own and other people's feelings and
values. Ironically, although workaholics are overly responsible in public, they become increasingly irresponsible with
their family and themselves.

In my book *Workaholics: The Respectable Addicts*, I illustrate why workaholism is such a dangerous and life-threatening addiction. It changes not only people's personalities but
also the values they live by. It threatens family security and
often leads to family break-up. Surprisingly, it also distorts the
reality of each family member. Along the way, workaholics
eventually suffer the loss of personal and professional integrity.

The focus in this book is on the workaholic's loss of personal
balance. The excessively long hours spent working, the frantic rush of the "Gerbil Wheel" existence, and short-sighted,

"bottom-line" thinking are, after all, only symptoms of a deeper war being waged *within* the individual's psyche.

Workaholics are not addicted to work, as everyone supposes. Ironically, the term itself, as coined by Wayne Oates in 1971 in his *Confessions of a Workaholic,* is misleading. One does not have to have a "real" job to be a workaholic. Many homemakers, and even high school and university students, can become chronic workaholics.

In attempting to understand the workaholic personality, it must be acknowledged that work plays an essential role in defining the Self. Our well-being springs from a sense of accomplishment. We develop our strengths, set goals, and overcome difficult hurdles along the way. Our self-confidence comes through developing skills and mastering tasks that contribute to an entity greater than us. As anyone who has lost a job will attest, without work our personalities suffer profound emotional disorientation and loss of confidence.

A hard worker who maintains a healthy balance between work and play, and is emotionally there for all family members, is not a workaholic.

RECOGNIZING THE WORKAHOLIC PERSONALITY

A workaholic is a person who gradually becomes *emotionally crippled and addicted to control and power in a compulsive drive to gain approval and success.* Actress Bridget Fonda describes her own workaholism to journalist Deirdre Kelly in a *Globe and Mail* article headed "Bridget Fonda: 'Burned Out' at 30."

"Up until now my career has been absorbing a lot of my energies and it still is. But very soon things are going to grind to a halt for a while because I sort of feel burned out. That's the workaholic thing, the thing that makes me work until I feel I've done what it is I need to do before ... I can really rest. But now what's telling me to rest is not that I feel that

I have achieved my life goals but that I feel that I'm on the verge of a breakdown. I suddenly have an image of myself slowing down to a lie-down position and having the grass grow all around me. That's what I feel I want. To be dormant for a while."

A member of a famous screen family, Fonda started her film career at twenty-two. In eight years she had accumulated more than twenty film credits. "Acting is something I care a great deal about. It's something for which I want to do a great job but sometimes I feel that physically I'm exhausted and I can't do as good as I think I can in my head. That's why I've got to stop."

Despite recognizing that perfectionism was unhealthy, Bridget was again working on a new film. Kelly asked whether the race to outdo herself will ever end. "I guess that's what acting is all about … you just can't help it." She explains that horses at the track know what they have to do, and acting is much like that. "The adrenalin kicks in and you do it, you get an urge to stampede, and in the end it feels good even when it feels bad."

Good is rarely enough for perfectionists. Always to be better, or the best, is the ideal. One goal is reached, yet soon after another is set. Goals rarely bring the expected satisfaction, because deep inside the individual is full of self-doubt. He must prove himself once again. Combine the motto "Nothing is ever enough" and Lord Acton's truism that "Power tends to corrupt, and absolute power corrupts absolutely," and you have a recipe for disaster.

As we saw in Peter's story, a public persona that broadcasts success is paramount for workaholics. In fact, workaholism is really about *self-aggrandizement*. Ambitious workaholics become increasingly obsessed with their work performance because of a drive for public and peer approval. The public persona presented to the world is therefore about "looking good." Some workaholics are the Mr Nice Guys who can't say no. Others control and misuse their power to charm and manipulate others for their personal benefit.

Many workaholics do manage to look "great" for long periods and maintain the facade of success, even after repeated failures. In an interview about my book in *USA Today*, Donald Trump was asked by journalist Nancy Hellmich whether he was a workaholic. "I've worked extremely hard over the last year and a half to achieve the success I have attained. There is no such thing as a workaholic if you enjoy what you are doing." This sounds like an alcoholic rationalizing that there is nothing wrong with being an alcoholic as long as you enjoy drinking!

Workaholics feel most vital and alive when their adrenalin is pumping. Getting from goal A to B consumes all their energy. Totally focused and engrossed in their single-minded pursuit of a goal, they compulsively over-schedule, overworking to the point where an extra "fix" is needed just to stay alert and keep up the pace. Rushing becomes the norm. Coffee, alcohol, smoking, drugs are often taken because increased amounts of adrenalin are needed to cover rising anxiety. Over-stimulated, overstressed, and often overwhelmed, workaholics are no longer in control. The addiction is running their lives. Balance is a thing of the past.

Gary's story is but one example. This handsome, bright, and articulate professional engineer came into my office one day looking ashen. "Look, I've got to be frank with you today." He paused. "I'm barely functioning. I'm just not getting it! Ideas are flying past me, and I don't see them!" Obviously in despair, Gary added, "I can't make even the simplest decisions any more! I don't know which way is up!"

When I suggested that he take a minimum of three weeks off to get all the adrenalin out of his system and to take care of himself before he suffered a stroke or heart attack, Gary protested. The company was in yet another crisis, due in part to his poor judgment.

Time out, apparently, was out of the question. When I enquired whether he saw the arrogance implied in this decision, he blushed. We then discussed whether anyone was ever indispensable and irreplaceable in the "big picture."

Workaholism, as I told Gary, can be a lethal addiction. The Japanese named workaholism *Karoshi* in the early 1980s and warned that overwork is life-threatening, even fatal. The National Defense Council for Karoshi Victims published a book called *Karoshi: When the Corporate Warrior Dies*. In the *Toronto Star* article "Overwork kills many, Japanese group says," Hiroshi Kawahito, the group's secretary-general, reported that up to 10,000 Japanese worked themselves to death every year. "We can't name a precise figure ... But when relatively young people die of strokes and heart attacks after working excessively hard, we can't really doubt that it is a case of Karoshi."

Although there was initial reluctance by the Ministry to acknowledge the serious consequence of overwork, Atsuko Kanai, in his chapter "Economic and Employment Conditions, Karoshi (work to death) and the Trend of Studies on Workaholism in Japan," (in *Research Companion to Working Time and Work Addiction*) writes that reported evidence of the harmful influences resulting from excessive fatigue and celebral/cardio diseases caused the Ministry to modify their overly strict standards set out in 1995 and again in 2002 regarding who could be declared a victim and therefore eligible for compensation. However, Kanai reports that the situation was not improving, despite attempts to legislate hours of work and force people to take their allotted vacations.

This changed in 2005, according to a recent article in *The Economist*, "Jobs for Life," when 40 percent of applications for compensation were successful, as compared to 4 percent in 1988. *The Economist* reports that family members may receive approximately $20,000 from the government and sometimes up to $1 million from the company that employs them. For instance, on 30 November 2007, the family of a Toyota employee who had put in 80 hours of unpaid overtime each month for six months before his death in 2002 received compensation for having been a Karoshi victim. This ruling is important because "it may increase the pressure on companies to treat 'free overtime' (work that an employee is obliged to perform but not paid for) as paid work. That would send shockwaves through corporate Japan, where long, long hours are the norm."

A different slant on this problem is found in Hans Griemel's article in the *Globe and* Mail entitled "Government Urges Japanese to Work Less, Have Babies." Griemel reports that, as Japan slogs through its third recession in a decade, young people regard matrimony as "limiting their freedom" and child-rearing as too expensive and a "burden." Both were shunned as sources of fulfillment by about 52 percent of young women and 40 percent of young men. Along with climbing divorce rates and stagnating childbirths, there are also doubts about the ability of future generations to support the swelling ranks of the elderly. "A Lifestyle White Paper" commissioned by the Japanese prime minister's office proposed freeing people from 18-hour work days and mandatory drinks with the boss so they can better balance family life and career. One solution would be to expand child care services, and companies were urged to come up with support systems to enable male employees to help in child rearing.

Unfortunately, despite these hopeful signs, it is obvious that there still is a strong wall of denial in society about the far-ranging problems that workaholism generates.

Our focus here, however, is on the individual.

A PARADIGM FOR THE LOSS OF FEELINGS

What happens inside the psyche when workaholics become obsessive, narrow their focus, and drive themselves obsessively?

Why do they grow numb and feel flat? Why is change so threatening to these "black-and-white" thinkers?

As the obsession with work grows, it consumes ever-increasing amounts of the psychic and physical energy necessary to build ideas, challenge goals, and complete exciting projects and schemes. Everyday family responsibilities are side-lined, and people-related problems at work are regarded as simply a nuisance. Soon, the spouse, child, or co-worker who has been taken for granted, ignored, or in some cases rejected or abandoned act out their hurt and anger by making increased demands for attention. Stretched to the limit already, overburdened workaholics resent these annoying "impositions," and anxiety escalates for all parties.

As overwhelmed workaholics become more obsessively driven, changes take place in the way they gather and process information and in how they make decisions. A brief summary of my paradigm for obsession, based on Jung's theory of psychological types, explains why these shifts that affect the way workaholics function occur , and why there is the tragic loss of feeling during this process.

Thinking

Thinking becomes obsessive as the fascination with work grows. Clarity is lost, and feelings are dulled in order to keep pain and fear from flooding the increasingly fragile ego. Information gained from the Feeling function ceases to moderate the thinking process, and obsessive ruminations take charge. Workaholics plot strategies and devise elaborate schemes, absorbing themselves in endless details. Instead of confronting the problem, they distract themselves by going off on tangents. Anything not to feel anxious!

As obsessive Thinking becomes more confused, circular, and goes nowhere, anything that diverts attention away from the workaholics' current agenda creates anxiety. It's as though

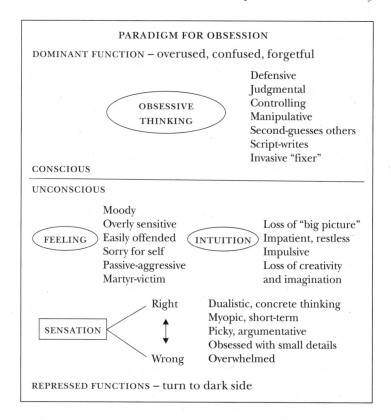

PARADIGM FOR OBSESSION

DOMINANT FUNCTION – overused, confused, forgetful

OBSESSIVE
THINKING

Defensive
Judgmental
Controlling
Manipulative
Second-guesses others
Script-writes
Invasive "fixer"

CONSCIOUS

UNCONSCIOUS

FEELING

Moody
Overly sensitive
Easily offended
Sorry for self
Passive-aggressive
Martyr-victim

INTUITION

Loss of "big picture"
Impatient, restless
Impulsive
Loss of creativity
and imagination

SENSATION

Right

Wrong

Dualistic, concrete thinking
Myopic, short-term
Picky, argumentative
Obsessed with small details
Overwhelmed

REPRESSED FUNCTIONS – turn to dark side

workaholics are wearing side-blinkers or have developed tunnel vision. All their psychic energy is being drained away and life's balance is thrown askew. Soon survival becomes the real issue, rather than competition or being first.

Terry, a young law student, told me that he had had a panic attack sitting in front of the TV the night before. When I enquired whether he had turned the TV off, he looked quite surprised! It had never occurred to him that his overloaded system just couldn't absorb any more stimulation. His self-nurturing Feeling function wasn't working, so he didn't recognize his body's warning signals.

The rational, logical, analytical, realistic side of positive Thinking gives way to its negative, overly skeptical, critical,

judgmental, competitive, and controlling side. The personality of the workaholic is radically changed by this shift.
When I use Gestalt exercises in psychotherapy, directing
clients to sit in different chairs that represent a function
such as positive or negative Thinking or positive or negative
Feeling, a surprising thing happens. Inevitably, it seems that
while sitting in the doing-and-performing *negative Thinking* chair that represents what I call the "fixer" role, the
part that "helps" others in order to exert its power, workaholics make use of invasive projections, blatant or subtle
manipulations, or overprotective rationalizations to bully
the opposite *positive Feeling* chair. It's told basically to pull
up its socks: do this, think that, act as I do. Or a sarcastic
tone of voice is used to denigrate some aspect of the Feeling side of the client's personality. When asked to move to
the Feeling chair and challenge what negative Thinking has
said, workaholics stumble to find a voice or remain speech-
less. Some are totally stunned to realize they have no feeling
vocabulary or behaviour.

Feeling-type clients can also be fascinated but appalled
when they experience the power of their controlling side. I
had forewarned the spouse of a workaholic that I would have
to take an urgent call during our Gestalt session. When the
phone rang, Pat was left stranded in her "Fixer" chair. This
happened to be her Inferior Thinking function, which emerged
whenever she became distraught. I noticed her squirming, and
as soon as I completed the call, she sprang from the chair.
"Thank goodness I'm out of that darned chair! I hate that
controlling side of myself. It reminds me of my bossy aunt.
I call that part of myself "old Ethel." We both laughed, and
many times thereafter I would hear about what old Ethel had
done that week, usually some "fixer" statement that had got
Pat into trouble once again.

Workaholism is, after all, about controlling and gaining
power. Harmony-loving spouses like Pat who can't cope

with ongoing power struggles unwittingly get caught up in counter-control tactics. Such interventions will definitely not be appreciated, as after all, "the workaholic is always right!"

Feeling

When the single-minded focus of obsessive Thinking narrowly focuses on goals and ideas, Thinking goes into overdrive and dominates our attention. At such times, people can be overwhelmed by anxiety as psychic energy drains away. Feeling's capacity for nurturing of self and others has been repressed, and no longer plays a supportive role.

The playful, humorous side of the personality is flattened. No energy is available to counteract and lighten up the intense and overly serious Thinking side. When inner fears, doubts, and guilt dominate the psyche, sensitive, thoughtful, conciliatory feelings are replaced by sullen moods and resentment. Overly sensitive and stubborn, such people take everything personally. Many withdraw into silent submission as a result, but are seething inside. Depression deepens as anger lurks in the shadows. After all, it is easier to adopt the self-pity of the martyr than to take personal responsibility and try to correct what is wrong.

"If I keep running on my Gerbil Wheel, I don't have time to think or confront myself," says Elizabeth, a naive but driven nursery teacher. Instead, this forty-five-year-old woman remains inside her head and intellectualizes. She also develops fantastic schemes to outwit people who, she believes, are jealous or "out to get her." She often dreams about romantic but imaginary encounters. If Elizabeth allowed herself to face her uncertain social skills, she would have to feel her loneliness and fears around aging. "Why should I depress myself?" she protests. She desperately wants to see herself as perfect, so criticism is quickly disregarded. If anger does surface, it is soon squelched to avoid an explosion.

Hard as it is to believe, workaholics like Elizabeth reach a state where *they do not know how they feel.* This phenomena is very difficult for family members to grasp. Their spouse and children know they hurt. They are sad. They feel furious! "Can't my stupid father see what he is doing to his family?" asks Dan, a twenty-year-old arts student. Dan searches for an answer. "Surely he must know what he is doing to my mom!" Dan's disbelief will continue until he learns more about workaholism. Older children and young adults need to be involved in the therapeutic process so that healing can begin to take place. In order to forgive, children need to understand *why* a parent has been unavailable to them emotionally. It is important to break the cycle, so that this generation will not repeat the mistakes of the past.

Intuition

When Feeling stops working, so does Intuition, a sixth feeling that ordinarily sorts out what is important on an unconscious level. Its typical "big picture" view gets sacrificed to immediate gratification. Short-term, concrete goals with high visibility become all important. Today's instant messaging via cell phones, E-mails, and BlackBerrys further encourages impulsive decisions and impatient actions. Intuitive ideas usually pop up unannounced, but sometimes intuition needs overnight reflective time to reveal flaws in a plan. Constant emergencies and general chaos leave no room for Intuition's creativity and its admirable capacity for delaying gratification. "I want it NOW!" is the workaholic's cry.

Imagination, which is able to see endless possibilities, ceases to work as feelings atrophy and the Intuitive function turns to its dark side. Brainstorming stops and metaphors and some abstract thoughts go unrecognized. Instead, workaholics obsess over minute, often insignificant details, and grow picky and argumentative, stuck in their own myopic vision of what is right, or even possible. Stubborn rigidity kills all creative thinking. The person becomes restless and impulsive, easily bored, and never satisfied. Priorities become unclear as objectivity and perspective wane.

Sensation

Negative Sensation eventually dominates the psyche and warps the workaholic's decision-making skills. Dualistic thinking reduces the complex to two simplistic options. If one thing is "right," that makes anything else "wrong." As Heather, a middle-aged bank manager, put it, "Black-and-white thinking is simple – I fail or I succeed!" She laughed nervously. "It's colourful thinking that stymies me! I still can't quite believe all the options we've looked at today." It will be some time before Heather's natural intuitive skills return and work well enough for her to brainstorm effectively. It is difficult for people to comprehend that functions they once relied on have stopped working.

"Don't confuse me with the facts!" is a remark that workaholics might well use. Selective listening is a vital part of negative Sensation. This is another example of "3 out of 5" thinking, in which people focus on the facts that support their own views and often ignore very important information that presents a contrary position.

Workaholics take little time to "smell the roses" and replenish sagging energies with positive emotions. Symphonies and theatres, which used to interest them, become great places to nod off and catch a few winks. Positive Sensation's ability to celebrate all five senses, to be fully present to what is happening in the moment and trust what is observable and concrete, ceases to function well. Instead, future gains are sacrificed for immediate gratification and creature comforts. There is little satisfaction or appreciation because greedy dissatisfaction demands more and drains precious energy away from "what is." To fill up this vacuum and awful emptiness, workaholics turn to adrenaline pumping stimulations such as drugs, excess alcohol or nicotine, and illicit affairs – anything to make them feel alive again.

The obsessed workaholic fails to appreciate the important role that soul-feeding Sensation contributes to a person's sense of well-being. Nor does he or she fully recognize that Sensation gathers *all* the facts and figures necessary to support or reject the accuracy of Intuition's holistic vision. Idealism, in other words, needs to be tempered with realism.

Distortion Generates Fear

The workaholic's reality becomes distorted as obsessive thoughts grow fuzzy and confused, yet overwhelm and devalue information from the Feeling and Intuitive functions. Negative Sensation becomes a powerful force in the personality as suppressed anxiety surfaces as fear-based anger. Such anger is quickly disowned by the workaholic and frequently projected onto others.

Unfortunately, spouses and children are easy targets – family members are less likely to fire you. Thus spouses are criticized, ridiculed, and blamed for everything and anything that goes wrong. Children, workaholics insist, still receive "quality time," but unconditional love and deeply felt affection are scarce. The self-involved, preoccupied workaholic has little time or energy for the small, "petty" things that are important to children. Ball-games are missed. The chair at the head of the table is empty. Although children must still perform and make the workaholic proud, rarely is praise or encouragement forthcoming. Instead, "Why didn't you get 95?" stays with the child forever. The cool, aloof, and demanding parent rarely ventures out from behind his or her wall of reserved or cocky arrogance. Work is to be respected above all else. Family life must revolve around the workaholic's schedule.

"Be like me!" and "Don't challenge anything I do or say" are the not-so-subtle messages conveyed.

UNDERSTANDING THE COMPLEXITY OF WORKAHOLISM

Workaholism is like a perfect tapestry hanging proudly for all to see. Slowly, almost imperceptibly, the threads start to twist and sag until the pattern is barely recognizable. Three distinct threads are woven throughout the workaholic's life, and the dynamics existing between each clearly affects the other two strands. This brief summary will focus on the first and on the conscious aspects of the second in order to show how workaholics become emotionally crippled and out of touch with their feelings. The following outlines the three interacting threads, which are covered in depth in my book on workaholism.

1. *Perfectionism* leads to *Obsession*, which leads to *Narcissism*.
2. *The Breakdown Syndrome* – this involves both conscious and unconscious factors.
3. *Denial, Control*, and *Power* – together they form *The Workaholic Trap*.

1. Perfectionism/Obsession/Narcissism

PERFECTIONISM   Bridget Fonda's insight that her perfectionism was not healthy was correct: the seeds of workaholism do lie in perfectionism. To achieve excellence and mastery, perfectionists try to gain control of *all* the variables that feed into a successful outcome – and that, unfortunately, includes controlling other people!

Perfectionism shapes a person's life-style. If idealistic drives and ambitions are to be fulfilled, a single-minded focus becomes necessary. As concentration narrows, delegating and sharing are discouraged. As demonstrated in *Workaholics*, Thinking eventually dominates and repressed Feeling remains largely unconscious.

Perfectionists believe that they are highly intelligent, even superior, and thus capable of great achievements. Although they are indeed often quite bright, they can also be openly arrogant, ambitious, competitive, and demanding of themselves and others. Although self-sufficient and independent on the surface, they require admiration from others or demand obedience and want their own way. Underneath this self-confident facade lies an insecurity fed by unconscious inner struggles to overcome unresolved childhood fears of helplessness, dependency, and loss of approval and affection.

MR NICE GUY OR MS NICE GAL

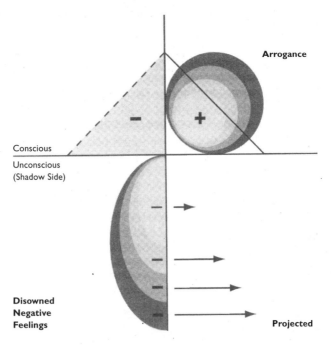

Proud workaholics, torn between arrogance and insecurity, solve the dilemma by consciously identifying with only the positive attributes of their personality. Unflattering feedback is filtered out through *selective listening*. Thus workaholics hear only what they want to hear. In turn, they manipulate others by telling them what they think the other person wants to hear. Workaholics can be extremely charming when they want something!

The control necessary to maintain this Nice Guy or Gal image breaks apart as the workaholic progresses through the breakdown stages of workaholism. "I'm losing it!" is their cry for help. Like Narcissus of the Greek myth who was mesmerized by his perfect reflection, when troubled waters stir up the pool, the workaholic is left with a well-crafted persona but with little sense of an authentic Self.

Joel, a thirty-five-year-old lawyer, told me that he felt paralyzed by bizarre fears. "You may find this hard to believe," Joel projected. "I'm embarrassed even saying this. But I feel like a fraud sometimes, especially when I'm in court. It's almost as though there's a detached part of me that looks on, as if in utter disbelief. It taunts me: 'Who do you think you are!' 'You're such a phony!' 'You're going to blow this one!'"

Joel was plagued with self-doubt even though he had graduated cum laude in his last year at law school. "Am I going crazy, or what?" he asks. The mighty often have a great distance to fall from the pedestal on which parents, classmates, or spouses have placed them. Remember, workaholics had to *do* something to get recognition in the dysfunctional families in which they were loved conditionally and rewarded primarily for their "doing and performing" talents.

OBSESSION   The chief sign of perfectionism is obsession. Obsession occurs when one part of the personality receives a disproportionate amount of psychic energy. Ambitious workaholics, focused on distant goals, fail to attend to warning signs from the body. It isn't until the out-of-touch workaholic experiences dire panic attacks or depression that this extreme distress becomes conscious.

Obsessive thinking works overtime while workaholics dream up schemes and strategies that will move them from goal A to B faster and more effectively than others. The greater the pressure to complete these often grandiose plans, the more frantic the individual becomes. Inflated egos and heady arrogance leave these people totally unrealistic about what is possible. Workaholics promise the earth, by Tuesday!

Work habits thus necessitate rushing, frantic activity, and over-scheduling. After an interview with me for *Pathways* magazine, contributing editor Kim Pittaway wrote: "Speaking with Killinger helped me to recognize one of my own triggers. As a freelancer, I set my own work schedule. In the past, I routinely viewed weekends as potential catch-up time. I'd procrastinate during the week with the rationalization that I could always make it up on Saturday and Sunday." Following our meeting, Kim put a "fence" around her weekends and set them aside as a "work free – play only" zone. This meant that she had to stop procrastinating during the week. It took awhile until guilt about *not* working on weekends vanished.

Without set boundaries, work can spill into everything one does. Soon, you are caught up on a Gerbil Wheel existence and can't get off. There is no time to think, and certainly no energy left to ponder how you actually feel at that moment. Fear of failing is ever present, and thus anxiety fuels this relentless drive.

Severe obsessions stretch your nerves to the limit, as if you are on the proverbial rack. You can't stand the intensity and pain, but you can't get off either. You're hooked! You soldier on, a martyr to your cause, but soon you start to resent everything and everybody. You even begin to hate yourself. Such bad feelings, often too painful to bear, are subsequently repressed. It may look like an exciting life to others who envy the workaholic. But nothing seems to fill the emptiness that is experienced deep in the pit of your stomach.

It is almost impossible to lower a person's sights once he has fallen under the curse of perfectionism. I once bargained with an extremely obsessive final-year high school student about aiming for a 90 percent average, instead of the 98.6 percent he had managed to attain. No talk about the Rhodes Scholar's criteria that the individual must be well-rounded and do well in a number of areas could sway this young man. Many other clients tell similar stories about high expectations but tortured lives. It's like living with your own sergeant-major cracking the whip. Going AWOL is out of the question. Perfectionists would lose their badge of honour if they quit!

Compulsive acts or rituals grow more chaotic as the work-aholic loses control. Counting, checking, cleaning, ordering, straightening, making lists, rewriting, all done to an extreme, are efforts to counteract inner confusion as the workaholic strives to restore order out of growing chaos. When a child or spouse unexpectedly interferes with a compulsive ritual, it is often enough to set off an explosive temper tantrum-like fit of rage.

People around the workaholic walk on eggshells much of the time, uncertain what will trigger the next barrage. When the workaholic is an emotionally drained homemaker, it's like living in the middle of a minefield for the rest of the family. Compulsive activities can become so frantic that the person collapses, unable to function effectively any longer. "I couldn't get out of bed to start my day" is a common complaint signa-ling a breakdown.

An obsessional triangle of guilt, fear, and negativity locks the workaholic in a strange prison where perfection-ism is replaced by an agitated compulsive need to dominate and control even the smallest detail. No wonder the psyche bounces between fear and anger as the workaholic is driven towards despair.

Bouts of rage are common at this point. The stressed psyche, worn out by the constant exercising of dominance, is
totally drained. While "one-up" is acceptable, "one-down" is
not! Submission of any kind, whether brought on by criticism
or a challenge, sets off panic reactions. Obsessive workaholics
often swing between dominance and a submissive rebellion.
By tipping the balance in one direction or the other they can
maintain a comforting, but false, sense of control.

Some workaholics act out their rage in a passive-aggressive manner. They suffer severe mood swings or anxiety
attacks, and "turn off," sulk, or withdraw emotionally and
physically into depression. Others let pent-up feelings build
to dangerous levels. Unfortunately, family members are easy
targets for abuse. Such explosive behaviour would not be
tolerated for long in the working world, unless you happened
to be the boss.

NARCISSISM Perfectionism and obsession lead to high
levels of self-absorption. As fears produce increased levels
of obsessive behaviours, insecure workaholics try to control
everything and everybody around them. Any threats or challenges to their power and ability to control must be countered
to protect the fragile ego.

Narcissism is the real evil of workaholism. The historical
and philosophical background of how and why narcissism
has become a major problem in our society today is outlined
in depth in my book *Integrity: Doing the Right Thing for the
Right Reason*. The excesses of greed and the power trips of
the eighties and thereafter have left us with the legacy of the
"me" generation. The two following chapters are devoted to
understanding narcissism, in the individual and in the family.

2. The Breakdown Syndrome

Many older workaholics can trace the onset of workaholism to a troublesome or traumatic situation in their lives or

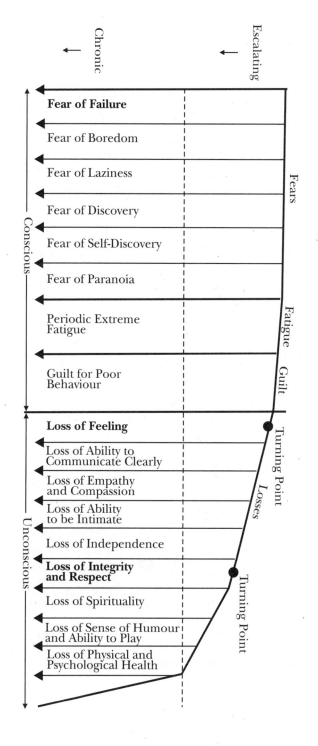

THE BREAKDOWN SYNDROME

Chronic ←

Escalating ←

Fears

Fatigue

Guilt

Turning Point

Losses

Turning Point

Conscious

Fear of Failure

Fear of Boredom

Fear of Laziness

Fear of Discovery

Fear of Self-Discovery

Fear of Paranoia

Periodic Extreme
Fatigue

Guilt for Poor
Behaviour

Unconscious

Loss of Feeling

Loss of Ability to
Communicate Clearly

Loss of Empathy
and Compassion

Loss of Ability
to be Intimate

Loss of Independence

**Loss of Integrity
and Respect**

Loss of Spirituality

Loss of Sense of Humour
and Ability to Play

Loss of Physical and
Psychological Health

that of their families that occurred perhaps several decades before. From that moment on, they decided they were going to be in control of their lives. In earlier days, when wives usually stayed home, they were not in direct competition, as it were. By fully supporting the workaholic's career, the spouse unknowingly furthered the addictive habits of her ambitious bread-winner. Financial security brought the husband the recognition and power he craved, and the life-style he desired for his family. Many wives sold their souls and identity for the sake of harmony and accepted the sacrifice of a close emotional connection to their husbands. Fighting depression, many became obsessive "shopaholics" who sought compensation by overvaluing material goods and status in the community. Others sought solace in alcoholism.

Nowadays, the breakdown is occurring over a five- or six-year period. Our society encourages people to overwork, and greed often underlies the endless search for a more profitable bottom line. Many companies and institutions are workaholic entities that suffer many of the same breakdown symptoms as the individual.

EARLIEST SIGNS OF THE BREAKDOWN   Fortunately, the earliest signs of the breakdown process are recognized by the workaholic. At our busiest times, all of us experience some of the following fears, the chronic fatigue, and guilt. It is when we get hooked by the obsessive need to overwork and a relentless rush of adrenalin floods through our system that we become increasingly overwhelmed and immobilized.

CHRONIC FEARS   Fear gnaws away at insecure people who depend on others to affirm their worth. Feelings ordinarily force us to experience our vulnerability, but workaholics manage to avoid dealing with anything that threatens their self-esteem by intellectualizing in response.

Fear, however, can reach obsessive levels when perfectionists, who have a strong need to control, are faced with the possibility of finding themselves in a one-down position on the workplace hierarchical ladder. Therefore annual employee evaluations, censorship of ideas or projects, threatened demotions, forced transfers, or the ultimate fear of dismissal can generate great stress and a stubborn rigidity that makes it difficult to adjust to any change. The modern trend for industry to reduce middle management is especially threatening. Dismissal is the ultimate outrage. Even low productivity or disorganization of any kind can induce mounting anxiety and often panic attacks in workers, students, and homemakers alike.

In these traumatic recessionary times, job losses, imminent threats of bankruptcy, and possibly corruption charges are driving many workaholics over the edge.

Fear of Failure. G. K. Chesterton wrote: "The reason angels can fly is that they have learned to take themselves lightly." Not so perfectionists. Failing for them is the end of the world. Early years for these ambitious children are relatively free of failure because a strong need for approval drives them to excel. The work ethic is usually a powerful force in their family of origin. Narcissistic parents, who see their children as extensions of themselves, *expect* high levels of achievement. Sometimes, these projected expectations compensate for the parent's own blocked ambitions.

University years often set patterns for future habits. Faced with the brightest and the best, perhaps for the first time in their lives, perfectionistic students might need to struggle. Rather than face lower grades, which for them would signal failure, they burn the midnight oil in a frantic effort to "catch up." Many workaholics who achieved fame or notoriety at college by excelling at sports or scholastics spend a lifetime trying to recapture the past glory of those years.

Promotions that reward hard workers sometimes move workaholics up the corporate ladder, beyond their level of competency. More senior jobs can overtax limited social skills. Often notoriously poor listeners, these arrogant but emotionally crippled people can lack the sensitivity, diplomacy, tact, and grace necessary to work co-operatively to mediate effectively with fellow workers or be able to respond to needs different from theirs.

Even while idealistic expectations prevail, internally the workaholic may be facing ever-increasing self-doubt. Promotions, expansion into new markets, takeovers, and research discoveries bring increased responsibility. Paddling faster while struggling against internal chaos only escalates feelings of impending doom as fatalistic workaholics do battle with the harsh reality of diminishing effectiveness. As power and omnipotence fade, workaholics work even harder. Immersed in the moment, they lose touch with objective long-term goals. When life throws a curve, most of us pick ourselves up, dust ourselves off, and ask probing questions about why and how things went wrong. Workaholics, in contrast, are too afraid to confront their own reality.

Fear of Boredom.   Workaholics abhor the possible vacuum that boredom might create if circumstances forced them to jump off their Gerbil Wheel existence. With a strong need to be right and get their own way, they feel best when nothing distracts them from any goal-directed action that provides them with a sense of purpose or entitlement. Reluctant to turn down work, they cram their days full by over-scheduling. Soon, rushing and being late become the norm. No time is left to contemplate where they are headed or to evaluate the purpose of their life. Narrowly focused, single-minded workaholics become what they fear – boring, shallow people. As J. B. Priestley wrote: "Any fool can be fussy and rid himself of energy all over the place, but a man has to have something in him before he can settle down to do *nothing.*" Long periods of relaxation are threatening, partly because adrenalin withdrawal causes severe distress. Vacations are either avoided on the excuse of one crisis or another, or replaced by brief weekend jaunts. If one or two week vacations are taken, days are crammed full of activities. Workaholics rarely stay away when they are sick, or if they do stay home, they call in to the office regularly to check up on things. When it takes twelve hours to do what used to be done in eight, time off becomes out of the question.

Fear of Laziness. This fear of laziness, which workaholics seem willing to admit to, may be the unconscious compensating for an overly developed sense of responsibility. Life must be serious and goal-directed if workaholics are to succeed at all costs. Their persona must not be seen to be frivolous – no "vegging" allowed, so commuters diligently read their newspapers rather than chat to the person beside them. Others excel at doing two things at once. Drivers use car phones at will, and even those who jog listen to their Walkmans lest they "waste time." Talk to a workaholic on the phone, and you will hear papers shuffling. Silences are filled in with clicking sounds as they think things through. Some may start a language course "for fun," but cancel classes for more urgent business.

Laziness is not to be confused with chronic fatigue due to physical and emotional exhaustion. Those "couch potatoes" who are barely functioning plunk themselves in front of the TV and stare unseeing, or escape to dens or bedrooms where no "performance" is necessary. Laziness, on the other hand, is revealed when hard-core workaholics avoid personal responsibility at home or elsewhere because "they have more important things to do." Psychologically, workaholics are lazy. They seem to have little curiosity about what makes them tick. They rarely read self-improvement books, unless they are motivational ones directed towards improving performance. Denial allows them to hang on to the illusion of the perfect Self.

Fear of Discovery. As fears lead to confusion and turmoil, efficiency and productivity are strongly affected. Workaholics worry about the *visibility* of their mistakes or lowered productivity if they suspect they're not measuring up. Rather than be found out, workaholics cover themselves by lying or withholding essential information from their staff. One client told me that when a colleague was finally let go, management found a pile of unfinished files stashed neatly underneath the couch in his office.

Secrecy and privacy become all-important aids to protect workaholics from scrutiny. They ride on their reputations as long as possible. Carl, a well-respected business executive, was let go in a company power-play. He had built up an elaborate support system by depending on his juniors to do the things he didn't like doing. Now he despaired that he would ever be able to replicate his present success and high sales figures in another company. "I'm not sure I can learn all the things I might need to know for my next job before I leave," he worried.

Initially, delegating work to others who might take away the workaholic's earning power is discouraged. Instead, workaholics regularly stay at the office until seven or eight o'clock to get it all done. Then, as anxiety blocks concentration, the extra hours become a necessity. Later in the breakdown, when exhausted workaholics are stretched to the limit, they must somehow get others in the office to do their work. Some procrastinate until exasperated secretaries or juniors take charge although it's important that colleagues at the peer level not find this out. Yet these same people continue to take on new projects in order to feel powerful and to prop up sagging egos. Mr. Nice Guys rarely say no, at least at work.

Because bodily warning signals go unheeded when feelings are numbed, workaholics do not anticipate the breakdown or "crash" that is lurking ahead. Workaholics will not admit that something is wrong until panic attacks, claustrophobic episodes, an irregular heartbeat, or other health troubles force them to acknowledge that a serious health problem exists. Without insight, workaholics continue to avoid dealing with what is actually happening to them.

Fear of Self-Discovery. Workaholics depend on an external frame of reference to formulate their version of Self. They judge their success by guessing what others perceive them to be. Brenda, a competent office manager, tried to convey an image of self-assurance, but instead she was labeled "conceited" by her staff. In one of our sessions, Brenda revealed her own self-doubt. "I put terrible pressure on myself to always stay up and cheerful. I got to believe my own myth despite repeated feedback from my staff. They told me that I was short, blunt, and sharp. Apparently, people felt I was overly critical and judgmental. I just didn't see it, until it was too late." Her eyes brimmed with the tears she hadn't allowed herself before. "I just wish I had another chance with those people now that I'm getting better. I think that I could do a good job there."

People like Brenda who are out of touch with their own feelings cannot possibly be sensitive to others' vulnerability. Instead, they unconsciously tap into the weaknesses of others, yet remain oblivious to these same foibles in themselves. A strong fear of disapproval keeps denial, dishonesty, and secrecy alive. Hard-core workaholics avoid introspection at all costs. Projection of blame is a popular defense for people who cannot accept the Shadow aspects of themselves. "Promise me that I won't hate myself at the end of this process" is a remark that reveals the self-loathing of a Dr Jekyll turned Mr Hyde. "When I was high on myself," Cynthia admitted, "I could do no wrong! But at three a.m., it was quite a different tale." Cynthia asked herself, "How could I be so blind? Why didn't I remember those screaming episodes my husband keeps talking about? The poor guy still seems so traumatized by all of this."

The journey from perfectionistic idealism to self-knowledge and wholeness is a real victory. Unfortunately, fears and laziness work against the workaholic who might otherwise gain the insight necessary to challenge and develop a strong sense of Self. It's easier to keep feeding the ego, a job narcissists devote their life to, at least until their persona cracks. One spouse told of her husband's disdainful response to a request she had made. "Why would I want to read Dr Killinger's book? She doesn't even know me!" The implication here is that this man is special and different. No book is going to tell him otherwise.

Fear of Persecution.   The ultimate fear is paranoia. As Dr R. Campbell writes in the *Psychiatric Dictionary*, in a paranoid personality, the affected person is "hypersensitive, rigid and unwarrantedly suspicious, jealous, and envious. He often has an exaggerated sense of self-importance, must always be right and/or prove others to be in the wrong, and has a tendency to blame others and to ascribe evil to them" (444).

Sadly, what the paranoid individual fears most may actually come to pass. Workaholics who lack genuine "people skills" find themselves passed by on their climb up the corporate ladder. Their mask of self-deceit is so strong that they can't acknowledge that social niceties are important. Their *Pandora's box* contains self-loathing and countless insecurities, so rather than confront their Shadow traits, paranoid workaholics avoid dealing with anyone who challenges them. Any form of rejection is a force to be feared, so workaholics dismiss others from their consciousness by using dissociation, a defense tactic in which people and things cease to exist for the individual. Loved ones who try to help are seen as persecutors, not the true friends they are trying to be. It takes enormous resolve for recovering workaholics to confront the pain of facing up to what they have done to others.

When turbulent feelings do surface, the workaholic can experience periodic psychotic breaks in which rage spills out unchecked. Pam was a witness to her husband's despair. "While Chuck was shouting abuse at me, his face turned purple. I looked into his eyes and it was like *nothing* was there. I think the poor guy has lost his soul!" Paranoia is a hellish state, and many fear-filled workaholics suffer frequent bouts of rage simply because they are poised on the edge of a nervous breakdown. The miracle is how these loners still manage to do their job at all. Their support systems may gradually desert them, but they march on to their own drum.

CHRONIC FATIGUE Over time, cumulative fears and concerns about performance produce bouts of emotional and physical exhaustion. At first, workaholics find themselves nodding off in a movie or fighting to keep awake at the supper table because all energy is depleted after a day of rushing, missing deadlines, or frantically over-scheduling. Gradually, more frequent bouts of fatigue become debilitating and more public. Chronically exhausted workaholics even become the butt of family jokes as they get used to father falling asleep without warning, anywhere and at any time. The children just nod to each other or raise their eyes and move around him. It doesn't seem to matter how many people are present, or how noisy the gathering. Father sleeps soundly in his chair until he wakes with a jolt, a surprised look on his face.

Exhaustion also can take the form of hyperactivity. Some workaholics become obsessed with exercise and train for some company-sponsored sporting event or even a marathon, rather than give in and rest. They run their life as though on an endless treadmill. "Hyper" types jump from one activity to the next and often have trouble winding down at night. They are scarcely aware of how tired, cramped, and tense they are.

Dr A. Hart, in *The Hidden Link Between Adrenalin and Stress*, explains that the stress response alerts the body to prepare itself for action. Adrenalin and the related hormones act to signal the conversion of stored sugar to glucose so the body can prepare itself for muscle activity. Adrenalin contracts the muscular layer in the walls of the arteries and, together with a speeded-up heart rate, raises the blood pressure and stimulates increased respiration so that extra oxygen is available to the body. In this state, the body fights off disease and discomfort.

As the demand for oxygen and excess energy drops, the body tries to return its systems to normal functioning. Hart writes: "It is then that headaches, diarrhea, fatigue, illness, rapid heartbeats, skipped beats, depression, and generalized anxiety are felt" (72). Adrenal fatigue sets in when high levels of adrenalin are maintained for extended periods. The adrenal cortex becomes enlarged, key lymph nodes shrink, and the stomach and intestines become irritated until the system crashes in severe fatigue. Hart concludes that "the victim's sudden inability to tolerate any stress or raise any energy" is a sign of adrenalin fatigue brought on by too much stress (73).

"Couch potato"–type workaholics, mentioned earlier, are very selective about what they will or will not do on the home front. All their energy must be reserved for the office to protect their public persona. I suspect that the chronic fatigue of workaholism and the phenomenon known as "Yuppie Flu" are closely linked.

GUILT   Guilt is conscious, an uncomfortable feeling that warns us that some irresponsible or unhealthy behaviour is morally or ethically unjust. Workaholics who are still in touch with their feelings suffer pangs of guilt when their hostile actions affect innocent others. Quentin Hyder, in *The Christian Handbook of Psychiatry*, notes that guilt is an awareness of wrongdoing as well as a fear of punishment, both of which can lead to shame, regret, remorse, and low self-esteem. If alienated from their ideal persona, workaholics can experience isolation and loneliness, anxiety and depression.

Guilt is really *self-anger*. Unfortunately, it can be projected outwards, or be repressed but transformed into ugly moods. After one distraught wife caught her husband picking up their young son and throwing him across the room for calling his father a name, she screamed at him to stop and placed herself between them. "You're just getting hysterical, Elaine. Get a hold of yourself, for heaven's sake" was the projection William hurled at her. By doing so, he absolved himself of guilt. Unwilling to face rejection or feelings of inadequacy, emotionally crippled workaholics reject or dismiss others so they can feel superior once again. Without compassion and empathy, they are unable to forgive others or themselves. Many grow increasingly more vindictive and punish others mercilessly when something goes wrong.

Unconscious shame replaces guilt. Directed outwards, shame manifests itself in dark moods, put-downs, sarcasm, and outrage. Directed inwards, shame fosters self-neglect and punishment. Workaholics unwittingly neglect to eat properly or get enough sleep. They are too busy to see their doctor when warning signals of bodily distress should no longer be ignored. Without the feeling and compassion necessary to experience guilt and subsequently change behaviour, workaholics act out their shame. Few recognize just how angry they are and will forcefully deny it.

THE EVILS OF WORKAHOLISM The combination of escalating fears, chronic fatigue, and guilt are emotionally draining. Accordingly, workaholics are easily overwhelmed by excess stimulation or demands on their time. Agitated frustration sets in whenever anyone threatens their ability to control everything and everyone. Their stubbornly rigid need to be "right" and have their own way rarely changes.

There are two key turning points in the downward spiral of the breakdown syndrome, the *loss of feeling*, and the *loss of integrity*. Once feeling ceases to inform judgments, profound personality changes begin. A series of losses occur that are largely unconscious and therefore are not recognized by the individual:

- The *ability to communicate clearly* is lost because workaholics are uncertain about how they feel. Consequently, they watch others to see how they should act and what they should say in certain situations.
- The *ability to be intimate* is threatened. When feelings don't function well, workaholics lose their ability to be thoughtful, empathetic, or compassionate. Warmth is missing and letting go of control to be fully present, even momentarily, is stressful. Workaholics can "perform" in the technical sense, but the partner can feel "like an object" because the workaholic is not there emotionally. Sexual intimacy often ceases, or becomes part of a power struggle that leaves both partners unsatisfied and frustrated.
- *Independence is challenged.* When workaholics depend on others to tell them how they should feel, they cease to be the strong and independent people they once believed themselves to be. Tongue-tied and unable to express their own feelings, others must do it for them. Yet they resent this "interference" and punish the spouse, child, or fellow worker they rely on the most.
- *Loss of integrity and respect* is a sad fate for these formerly idealistic people. As the Shadow side of the

personality exerts its powerful influence and each function
turns to its dark side, workaholics start to do the opposite
of what they would have done before. As one unfaithful
husband who had an affair phrased it: "I know now
why I first came to see you. My Shadow was pulling me
down so hard that I could no longer resist temptation!"
Respectability and trust earned through hard work
and devotion can be lost overnight. In fact, the loss of
integrity in today's world has escalated to alarming levels
in our society as more and more people are committing
fraudulent and unscrupulous acts. Lying, cheating, and
stealing are commonplace. My *Integrity* book documents
why perfectionism, obsession, and narcissism are
contributing to this tragic situation.

- *Loss of spirituality* occurs because one has to love oneself
  before a truly generous spirit is possible. Denial and
  dishonesty lead to a loss of Self – the pathway to the soul
  and one's inner connection with God. Arrogance and
  selfishness discourage an open acceptance of a greater
  Power.

- *Loss of a sense of humour and the ability to play* occurs
  gradually and almost imperceptibly. Workaholics *work*
  at their play, always improving their skills in order to
  reach a better outcome or score. If they can't do well, they
  often avoid the activity. A genuine, hearty laugh becomes
  a thing of the past. In its place is the narcissist's chilling
  laugh or sneer, and dark sarcastic, put-down humour.

- *Loss of physical and psychological health* occurs as the
  breakdown spirals downwards. Excess adrenalin and
  a lack of nurturing and healthy habits take their toll.
  Physiological responses to workaholism include excess
  stomach sensitivity, abnormal blood pressure, heart
  trouble, nervousness, lack of vitality, and total inability
  to relax. Anxiety reactions may include disturbed
  breathing, increased heart activity, vasomotor changes,

and musculoskeletal disturbances such as trembling, paralysis, or increased sweating. Workaholics often report a feeling of pressure in the chest, constricted breathing, dizziness, and light-headedness. Prolonged stress leads to more frequent and severe anxiety and psychosomatic complaints: partial withdrawal where a person dissociates and pretends something didn't happen; panic attacks when a fragile ego ruptures temporarily; a full retreat into a psychotic state in which reality and fantasy blur; or a complete disintegration of the ego or suicide. As noted earlier, death from strokes and heart attacks due to workaholism, or Karoshi, are reported in some Japanese studies.

DENIAL, CONTROL, AND POWER – THE WORKAHOLIC TRAP

This seductive combination is the chief reason that workaholics cannot escape this addiction to save themselves from the grievous losses that have been described.

Denial

Denial and the art of impression management are powerful forces that allow workaholism to grow unchecked. It becomes harder to maintain the illusory "perfect" persona that depends on external affirmation when workaholics become entangled in a web of deceit and lies. Broken promises, saying what others want to hear, and refusing to say no when this would be wise – all add up to the loss of integrity and self-respect. The protective shield of denial crumbles as others dare to challenge their control and power tactics.

Secrecy and privacy become comfortable allies in avoiding dealing with the damage done to others through manipulation and deceit. Denial makes free use of defense mechanisms such as projection of blame, dissociation, and compartmentalization. As long as denial remains strong, families and concerned friends are helpless to intervene as any criticism or challenge whatsoever is denied or met with a counterattack. The person delivering the negative feedback becomes the "enemy" whom the vindictive workaholic must punish or reject lest they themselves be rejected.

Control

Workaholics feel safest when work and life are predictably consistent. The more uncertain life becomes, the more it becomes necessary to micromanage down to the minutest detail and to keep everyone else in line.

To retain their superior, one-up position, many workaholics use a highly manipulative type of control to maintain dominance. The Terrible Twist, a distortion of the truth so that the other person gets blamed for the workaholic's insensitive or thoughtless action, is but one example. Outwardly solicitous workaholics avoid personal responsibility by agreeing to do something and then doing nothing, or just doing their own thing. At the same time, they manage to leave the impression that they are cool, reserved, and removed from the chaos they create. It is others who are seen as angry and hysterical whenever they complain. Workaholics accept high profile work that is "visible" to all, such as committees or boards, yet neglect the mundane but necessary work that keeps the wheels in motion from day to day. Self-aggrandizement is the name of this game.

Blatant overt control is not hard to miss. If you are always right, then it is important to "help", the word they use, by telling others what they should do, say, think, or feel. Difficulties arise because workaholics lack the insight to criticize their own actions and fail to see how their unwelcome "advice" affects others adversely. If people do complain, their resentment is met with irritability, sarcasm, or even tantrum-like rages. Such severe outbursts become more frequent as inner control is lost.

Support ebbs away at an alarming rate as people become genuinely afraid of such retaliatory actions and suspect, quite rightly, that these self-serving individuals have little regard or respect for others' ideas or even their welfare.

Power

Power is the seductive mistress that lures the workaholic's attention away from the family and a balanced lifestyle. Power is driven by greed – an aggressive, instinctual need for more control, more success, more rewards, more recognition. Power can be used for good or evil, but an excess of power combined with a growing arrogance and anxious deep-seated insecurity is a recipe for disaster. Greed is fed by ambition, competition, perfectionism, anger, and guilt. It starts with an internal need to be in control, and spreads to control of other people, objects, organizations, and even whole industries. Strategies, one-upmanship, manipulation, exploitation, and domination are the tactics of power.

Recovery comes only when the power of love becomes stronger than the power of greed. Love encourages empathy, compassion, generosity, good will, and compromise. Its language is appreciation, support, enthusiasm, and sharing. Compassion and competition are like oil and water; they do not mix. Compassion does not deal in winners and losers. It doesn't isolate, separate, or estrange.

Competition can be constructive and creative, but it becomes unhealthy if one constantly needs to measure oneself against others and come out ahead. It is most destructive when motivated by a need to punish others and vindicate oneself. Only through gaining wisdom and exercising compassion will the workaholic ensure that personal control and power are used for good, not evil.

NARCISSISM

Having examined how perfectionism leads to obsession, in chapter 5 we will look at how obsession fosters narcissistic behaviour in the workaholic. High levels of narcissism make recovery from workaholism increasingly difficult, if not impossible.

While workaholism does foster narcissism in formerly functioning individuals, a different type of narcissism called the narcissistic personality occurs in psychologically damaged people who fail to develop emotionally past the adolescent level because of some childhood trauma, neglect, or idealization. Both types can share similar characteristics. Ways to identify signs of our own and others' narcissism will be presented as well.

5

Narcissism

Mirror, Mirror, on the Wall, Who Is the Fairest of Them All?

People who get carried away with themselves often have to walk back alone.

"Morning Smile," *The Globe and Mail*

Normal levels of narcissism are fundamental to the development of self-respect, self-love, and pride. We nurture ourselves each day by meeting our physical and psychological needs. In excess, however, narcissism becomes a destructive dynamic that warps our life energy and blocks psychological growth.

The chief sign of a neurotic narcissism is the loss of feeling, the loss of the *real Self*, the whole personality with its potential for growth and development. The person instead identifies with an idealized view of what she or he feels they should be and thus denies and rejects their actual being. In the extreme, narcissism becomes a personality disturbance in which the person is overly invested in his or her own image or persona, in how she or he wants to be perceived by the world. Narcissists manipulate situations and people to serve their own self-interest. Acting without Feeling's other-directed focus, they strive for power to enhance their image, often at any cost. Ironically, in spite of this exaggerated self-interest, narcissists lack a true sense of an *authentic Self*.

THE DEVELOPMENT OF SELF

The roots of narcissism lie within our earliest childhood experiences. A weakened or damaged Self results when there is faulty interaction between the child and those he or she is mirroring or merging with in the process of self-identification.

The Healthy Self

According to Drs Heinz Kohut and Ernest Wolf, writing in the *International Journal of Psychoanalysis*, there are two types of "self-objects" in healthy ego development. Through *mirroring*, the first type, the child develops the Self by identifying with an accepting and confirming parent who affirms his or her "innate sense of vigour, greatness, and perfection." The child learns to see him or herself through the mirror of the parents' eyes. If positively reinforced, the child will affirm those aspects that are rewarded. Parents who strongly value performance will reward high academic grades, winning at sports, or excelling in the arts. Such high achievement will be further recognized and rewarded by society. Conversely, a child who receives negative looks or sharp criticism will devalue that personality trait or activity and associate it with reflected negative feelings. A healthy Self develops when the child receives positive regard and respect for the *whole* person. In this case both strengths and weaknesses are acknowledged, and the child's "being and feeling" side is supported, along with the "doing and thinking" side. He or she thus becomes a unique Self, an individual who is separate and different from his or her parents.

The second type of "self-object" is the *idealized parent imago*, the parent who serves as a role model of inner strength and calmness, of infallibility and omnipotence. If parents have calm voices, relaxed and yielding bodies, and offer warmth and affection through physical closeness and verbal expressions of love, the child tends to absorb and adopt these affirmative characteristics. If the parents are at peace with their own strivings and values, the child is also more likely to develop unconditional self-acceptance. When conflicts and new challenges test the child's confidence and inner security, the healthy family is there to offer the encouragement and support necessary to learn from life's lessons and transform newfound insights into growth. The Self thus develops in a healthy environment relatively free from the high levels of anxiety created when parents are in conflict and families become dysfunctional.

Unconditional acceptance does not imply permissiveness. Children need parameters within which to develop self-acceptance and self-control. Indulgent parents who overprotect and problem-solve for their children rob them of their chance to develop independence and self-esteem. Shielded from harsh reality, these children remain naïve and vulnerable. When they reach puberty, however, they are expected to assume adult responsibility, with no real preparation for handling life's difficult experiences.

As John Sanford points out in *Evil: The Shadow Side of Reality*, the growing child needs to identify the behaviours that societal standards deem acceptable and establish self-control from within. "In a permissive atmosphere a child's capacity to develop his or her own behaviour monitoring system is blunted. The ego development will then be too weak to enable the child as an adult to cope with the Shadow" (56). As a consequence, this dark, unwanted side of the personality will be repressed or disowned in order to protect the ego's ideal persona. It is important to note that ego ideals may be influenced, on both conscious and the unconscious levels, not only by family but by peer groups, school, and religious teachings.

Performance, what the child does, needs to be recognized as quite separate from the whole Self. When parents comment and give feedback on behaviour based on their evaluation of what is appropriate or unacceptable, their focus needs to be on the child's efforts and determination, not on his or her character. The child who is not labelled a good or bad person as a consequence of faulty behaviour can recover confidence quickly and learn through experience that challenges and failures are a normal part of life's struggles. The child should feel supported at such times, not criticized or judged.

A strong Self can tolerate wide swings in self-esteem in response to victory or defeat, success or failure. Success and joy are incorporated into one's self-image, as are hopelessness and despair. The healthy individual operates within a wide band of fluctuations of feelings. If life gets chaotic, for whatever reason, it is normal to sometimes feel like one is on a roller coaster.

The Damaged Self

In sharp contrast, children in dysfunctional families often receive ambiguous and unpredictable messages from a parent. Their "self-object" role models are confused and confusing. A parent may be emotionally unavailable because of his own narcissism, alcoholism, work addiction, drug addiction, or perfectionism. An unstable environment in which role models are too busy, materially oriented, and self-focused or obsessive, dishonest, unpredictable, and unreliable breeds insecurity in the child and a confused self-image.

Today, the alarming growth of video game-playing addictions is another cause for concern. To escape the anxiety of stress-filled lives, some new generation technically savvy parents are spending excessive hours lost in a virtual world where they can feel in control. Hooked and energized by the rush that an adrenalin high offers, they cocoon themselves away from the family, unaware and emotionally out-of-touch with the needs of their children and spouse.

Without adequate nurturing and stability, children fail to creatively deal with life's inevitable setbacks. There is growing evidence, according to Gabor Mate in his *Globe and Mail* article, "Why Can't Johnny adapt?," that the lack of resilience in our youth poses a major threat to our future as a society. Their fears, frustration, and vulnerability get acted out in the burgeoning drug scene and through bullying and aggressive violent actions. Mate warns that too often primary relationship are with other children, who cannot offer the unconditional love and acceptance that fosters resilience. The less resilient we are, he adds, "the more prone we become to addictions and aggressive behaviours, including self-harm. We also become more attached to objects."

In the narcissistic personality, the damaged ego is too fragile to tolerate wide mood swings. Instead, negative aspects of the personality or undesirable feedback are quickly repressed or dismissed in order to conceal underlying fears, guilt, or depression. To protect and compensate for perceived threats, the ego inflates even more until eventually it puffs up to a state of arrogance. A superiority complex fosters high self-expectations that may produce hyperactivity first in the child and later in the adult. This happens because anxious self-doubt and even self-loathing bubble up dangerously close to the surface of consciousness in response to stress.

Discovering how and when the Self has been damaged is an important part of life's journey. After all, we must first recognize what is wrong and then explore the source of our wounds before it is possible to know how to heal. Self-knowledge and wisdom develop through the work of transformation until the damaged parts of our psyche no longer have the power to cause us ongoing pain, sadness, guilt, or anger.

Unwittingly, perfectionistic parents often discourage or refuse to acknowledge the negative but natural feelings their children express. Repeated episodes of censoring, innocent though each may seem at the time, can foster long-term denial and dishonesty in a child. The seeds of narcissism are thus planted in the next generation.

Alexandra, exploring the roots of her damaged Self in one of our sessions, recalled how negative feelings in her home were definitely unacceptable, even taboo. Many times, she was told by her controlling mother, "If you can't be pleasant, then you'll just have to go to your room until you can put a smile on your face!"

"I was never allowed to think for myself," Alexandra now realizes. "In fact, I sometimes wondered if I really did exist. I felt like a nuisance, someone they didn't want to deal with." Her mother wanted the children to be obedient, and show her respect. Disobedience meant that mother would refuse to speak to her children for hours. Sometimes, if she was really upset, these silences lasted for days at a stretch.

Alexandra remembers desperately wanting to be a part of her family. "So if things went wrong," she explained, "I'd go to my mother and say, 'Mommy, I'm really sorry for whatever I did.'"

Surprisingly, at least to Alexandra, her mother would answer, "Sorry isn't good enough! If you don't know what you did, you'd better go away and think about it some more." Alexandra assured me that she honestly had no idea what she was supposed to have done.

The crucial question for Alexandra became, "What do I have to do in this family to get my needs met and survive?" Her answer was, "I had to deny who I really was." She could talk only about positive things; anger was never to be expressed. In fact, Alexandra felt "bad" whenever she was angry. Her mother apparently kept her own anger tightly controlled, although her pursed lips and frown instilled fear in her child.

Denial became an adaptive habit. Alexandra learned to tell others what they wanted to hear. After a while, little white lies became progressively easier to tell. "It never crossed my mind that I was being dishonest!" was how she phrased it.

Another problematic pattern emerged. Because Alexandra was not allowed to be angry, she learned to project blame onto others. She recalled with chagrin the many times she had set up her brother so that he looked like the guilty party. "I was quiet about it, but I was a real brat!"

Telling people what they want to hear, rather than the truth, fosters the self-serving aspects of narcissism. You learn not only to manipulate others but to kid yourself about all sorts of things. Life consequently gets very complicated and convoluted. The real Self gets lost in the confusion and chaos that the individual creates around him or herself. All the psyche's energy is invested in the ego, the persona that the individual wants the world to see. The centre of the Self, the soul, lacks nourishment and substance, and the person is left with a deep emptiness. Nothing is ever enough to fill this longing for self-acceptance, and so the person must get his needs met through others. The loss of Self is a personal tragedy.

THE LOSS OF FEELINGS IN NARCISSISM

Why is it so difficult to restore the narcissist's ability to feel once again? A healthy person's self-image correlates with and confirms the body's own direct experience. Even though Sally is depressed, she is connected with her body. She says, "I'm crying because I'm so damned mad!" Peter, on the other hand, often honestly does not know how he feels. In the narcissistic personality, the ego is dissociated from the body or Self. Consciousness is thus severed from its life force, the body. Ordinarily, the body's involuntary circulatory, digestive, and respiratory functions send signals to inform the brain about our emotional state. Depending on the information from this feedback, we experience excitement, happiness, depression, or sadness, and so on.

Normal Development

When development is healthy, one of the key functions of the ego is to seek gratification of our needs in the outer world. In order to do this, it must be able to distinguish reality from fantasy. The ego perceives information, co-ordinates action, adapts to reality, delays gratification, and ensures safety and preservation by avoiding injury and punishment. It selects what features of the environment to respond to, and how best to get its own needs met safely. The ego has a high degree of continuity and self-identity. It is capable of observing and criticizing itself, so that we may learn and persevere. The ego is conscious, or at least available to consciousness. It is the "doing-performing-thinking" action centre of our being.

The ego serves to perceive the Self but is not the Self. Nor is it completely separate. At birth, the biological Self comes into being. The psychological concept of Self, in Jungian terms, describes the psychic totality of the personality, including both conscious and unconscious aspects. The Self is experienced through the feeling functions of the body. It can express itself only after there is an awareness and acknowledgment of feelings. Without this expression, the Self remains largely unconscious and undeveloped. What we feel depends on what happens in the body, what information we receive from its involuntary feedback functions.

The ego controls the body's action through its will. Will controls the mind, and therefore is capable of manipulating how we feel. It also interprets or misinterprets how others feel. However, it is important to note that the will or ego is incapable of "creating" a feeling. In *Narcissism: Denial of the True Self*, Alexander Lowen suggests, "One can't truly will a sexual response, an appetite, a feeling of love, or even anger – however much one may 'think' one can ... For body happenings to lead to the perception of feeling, the events must reach the surface of the body and the surface of the mind, where consciousness is located" (30). For example, the impulses triggered by Peter's anger fail to reach the surface of his consciousness, which normally would initiate reactions such as crying or lashing out. Anger is kept safely hidden inside until his defenses prove inadequate to hold back the surging rage bubbling just beneath the surface of his consciousness. Only when this rage breaks through does Peter fully experience his anger.

Dysfunctional Development

In the narcissist, reality becomes increasingly distorted. Not only is there a lack of congruence between the desired self-image, the persona, and the true bodily Self but ego boundaries are blurred to the point that it becomes difficult to distinguish between images of the Self and objects outside the Self. Unfortunately, these objects are often people! Peter rationalizes that if he wants to go skiing, of course the whole family wants to go. It is assumed and therefore becomes his reality. No inquiries need be made. The narcissist's strong will or mind can refuse to see or hear things that there is no wish to acknowledge – especially if the evidence is contrary to what the narcissist wants to believe.

Denial, of course, implies initial recognition. A decision is made to deal with a situation or to deny its existence. In time, however, *the narcissist's denial itself becomes unconscious.* Narcissists carry on as if everything is all right, even if their reality is quite different from what others perceive.

The bodies of many narcissists appear rigid and stiff. Such rigidity may be absent in agile narcissistic athletes, dancers, and actors who move with a grace that suggests that emotion is present. However, in their personal lives, these narcissists act without feeling. Lowen explains the phenomenon: he believes that tension at the base of the skull in the muscles that hold the head to the neck blocks the flow of excitement from the body into the head. The narcissist, cut off from bodily feeling, lives from the neck up, in the mind. It's as though a scarf were tied too tightly around the neck. Not surprisingly, many narcissists complain about neck pain or pain felt in the back which is actually referred from pinched nerves in the neck. Spouses will often describe them as "a pain in the neck." Too frequently, the spouse will also develop neck pain because of the constant stress of dealing with the narcissist's outbursts.

Not only is the narcissist's life force inhibited by such tension but these people breathe from the neck up. The high-pitched voices of some attest to the restricted flow of oxygen caused by tensed muscles and constricted air passages in the throat area. This condition becomes chronic when a person is constantly under stress.

Image is everything to narcissists. Their vulnerability is hidden from others and even from themselves because they are out of touch with their own fears, sadness, and pain. Their carefully crafted persona conveys the image of someone who is a strong, independent, decisive, even powerful person. The truth is that narcissists are often irresponsible and tend to avoid making personal decisions whenever possible. They are always about to do something and may be totally convincing in their declarations of intent. Narcissists need and seek power to compensate for their real, but disowned, vulnerability. The persona, without strong feelings to support it, is, after all, only a facade.

Narcissists lack self-acceptance because the loving and nourishing capacity of the Feeling function is crippled. To compensate and keep their ego inflated, they come to *need* the approval and admiration of others. It is their ego they feed, not the Self. Peter, for instance, spends an inordinate amount of energy on anything that helps influence how the public will view his success as an influential businessman. This one-sided development and lack of feeling information affects his judgment and eventually produces high anxiety and panic attacks as his confidence wanes. Such responses are nature's way of sending strong distress signals from an unbalanced psyche. In the narcissist, both the Self and the ego are damaged.

IDENTIFYING NARCISSISTIC CHARACTERISTICS

Self-Aggrandizement

The narcissist's deepest fear is to be labelled a failure or not to be seen as in charge. An accomplishment can even be interpreted as a failed enterprise if others did not notice or pay homage to it. Peter's perfectionism causes him to obsessively plan and scheme so that his peers will recognize his expertise, even if this means "borrowing" junior staff members' ideas and neglecting to give them credit where it is due. Each single-minded pursuit leaves Peter ever more selfish and self-serving. His work has become a glorified form of self-aggrandizement. The image he portrays in the business world preoccupies his thoughts. Peter would stoutly deny this preoccupation, however. His rationalization is delivered in a pompous tone: "I'm working hard, of course, strictly for the benefit of my family."

Specialness

In Peter's family, excellence was *expected*. His parents made it crystal clear very early on that Peter was special, an "exceptional child." They indulged his every whim, tolerated his willful determination, and rarely disciplined him. Peter mirrored their idealization and built up a carefully crafted persona that broadcast the success, prestige, and power that were expected of him and by him. He believed that he deserved only the best and always aimed to reach the top. "All this came quite naturally to me," he explained. Since negative feedback conflicted with Peter's perfect image, any criticism was quickly dismissed. Peter *was* his image. From his point of view, he could do no wrong.

Impression Management

As is typical of narcissists, Peter monitored his clothes and appearance closely to project a certain style. He was meticulously well-groomed and spent much time, effort, and money towards this end. His shoes were always highly polished. He wore expensive suits and the latest in fashionable ties. He often spent Saturday afternoons at his favourite menswear shop, where the owner fussed over him and treated him like an important customer, which indeed he was. This "impression management" was designed to provide the visibility, upward mobility, and aura of success he desired. He joined the right clubs and made sure he was immaculately dressed at all social functions.

Other narcissists may choose a style that is the opposite of Peter's. Some have a studied casual air. Others are labelled eccentric for their unique brand of image-making.

As narcissism takes its toll and self-doubt and self-loathing surface, a reversal often takes place. Although Peter still dressed well for work, at home he wore the same old shirts and rumpled pants, until Sally threatened to set fire to them. Unconsciously, Peter wanted people close to him to feel sorry for him. He dropped his club membership in case others accused him of being pretentious. Peter made excuses in order to avoid business functions, preferring to stay at home in a safe shell where he could still exercise some semblance of control.

Centre of Attention

As a child, Peter played a game with his mother. He called himself "Number One Son." She humoured him by playing along, even though Peter was her second son. Later on, Peter loved it when Sally sent him cards addressed to "my debonair, sophisticated, charming, witty, and intelligent husband." Because he performed exceptionally well at school and rose so quickly up the corporate ladder, many others took the opportunity to single him out for praise, thus unwittingly contributing to his growing arrogance. Peter loved it when waiters or the maitre d' recognized him and called him by name. He therefore was loyal to a few good restaurants that fed his ego as well as his stomach. Occasionally, he would get quite irritated and sharp if he was seemingly ignored by the waiter or indeed taken for granted by anyone. One bad evening and that restaurant ceased to exist, at least in his universe. Peter didn't like to be kept waiting and refused to line up for anything, as he told me, "based on principle!"

Selfish Takers

Achieving one's goals, getting from point A to point B, having one's own way, always being right – that is what really matters to the narcissist. Success brings not gratitude but a hunger for more impressive accolades. Narcissism and gratitude rarely coexist.

Because narcissists are out of touch with their feelings, they find it difficult to truly give of themselves in relationships and shy away from being personally involved or committed. They almost never say "I love you," unless prompted or compelled to do so. They "love" only those under their control. Spouse and children are seen as extensions of their own personality and therefore are expected to think the same way and do what is expected. Sadly, the narcissist's offspring are rarely accepted or loved unconditionally and many spend their whole lives trying to get the approval and attention that the narcissistic parent is unable to give. One exasperated woman whose father and husband were both narcissistic workaholics exclaimed, "I've spent my whole life trying to get blood out of a stone. When am I ever going to smarten up?" This phenomenon is apparent in the rash of books written by the children of famous people, such as movie or television stars, depicting their own tragic personal stories of unmet needs and neglect. Ironically, narcissists see themselves as generous. Yet they depend on the generosity and vicarious warmth offered by others. They tend to marry warm, caring, nurturing people and then take, take, take. One wife's lament says it all: "My husband took all my love and gave it away." Their generosity is saved for public display. Many give large donations that are well-publicized or demand naming rights in exchange for being a benefactor of some important institution.

Dependency

Narcissists pride themselves on their independence, yet, unsure about how they *should* feel, they depend on clues from others about what is appropriate. This is especially noticeable when relationship-related issues are raised. They may be observed watching their spouse for signals that tell them whether what they just said or did is acceptable. Their eyes are on the spouse, not on the person with whom they are talking. Yet, moments later, they may be heard publicly putting down their spouse over some petty issue. Sadly, narcissists resent their increasing dependency and as a result often punish those closest to them.

Duplicity

The contrast between private and public behaviour is often startling and can be very hurtful to the spouse. In public, narcissists can be most charming. Outsiders cannot imagine that their wonderful doctor or minister neglects his own partner's need for love and attention. His wife receives glowing reports from outsiders, often with disbelief but also with pain.

Narcissists are master manipulators of others' resources and know how to get what they want. Somehow they manage to convince others to work hard and be enthusiastic about getting involved in their pet projects or schemes, while they themselves remain emotionally detached and aloof. They could teach Tom Sawyer a thing or two!

Arrogance and Ingratitude

Arrogance and taking others for granted seem to go hand-in-hand.

Peter, inflated with a sense of his own importance and having been labelled special, eschewed mundane tasks as beneath him. As Sally phrased it, "Peter seemed to think that all he had to do was show up for family functions. He didn't have to do a thing! It was as if we should all be delighted that he made it!" It would never occur to Peter to be involved in menu-planning, shopping, or cleaning up. When guests were there, however, he was the model gracious host and would even take credit for the success of the party. Sally told me he almost never acknowledged her hard work and certainly never praised her publicly.

Occasionally, though, when he wished to impress a special guest, Peter would decide to make what he called "The specialty of the house." Much fuss was made by all, since the family wanted to encourage his participation. This rarity was "special" indeed!

Denial

Denial is like a psychological wall that protects these people from harsh reality. Narcissists cannot love an imperfect Self, so when things start to go wrong, they don't wish anyone to know. Secrecy and privacy become vital habits to ensure that their perfect persona remains untarnished.

Narcissists need support, but "help" is a word rarely uttered. Others' words of encouragement carry little weight because words are an expression of feelings. Without feelings, only action is important. Peter often told Sally that it didn't matter what she said; it was what she *did* that was important. Despite the veil of secrecy around his work, Sally knew that Peter's business was in serious trouble. But her probing questions brought only angry responses from him. Peter heard only criticism in Sally's questioning, not her loving concern. His business failures were his business, and none of hers.

Peter was shamed by his failures but also remained in denial about his part in what went wrong. Even though shame is largely unconscious, Peter's gut was aflame. Shame can manifest itself in self-abuse or in punishing behaviour towards others. Peter was eating too much, drinking to excess, and had started smoking again. He was excessively picky and argumentative with Sally. Such behaviour typically follows the loss of integrity or professional failure that occurs when a person is entrenched in denial. Anything to avoid feeling the pain and remorse that healthier people would feel in a similar situation.

Inflated egos and a false reality usually lead to the misuse of power. Narcissists exaggerate their own abilities and remain unaware of their own limitations. They overlook personal flaws and even turn them into virtues. For example, Peter had his own timing, his own schedule, and showed no insight into the chaos this often caused others. Peter would rationalize, "I know I'm always late, but that's all right! The meeting can't start without me anyway!"

Sadly, through all their bravado, narcissists show almost no awareness of what their behaviour does to others. At work, they overestimate their capabilities, and as a result their plans become too expansive or diversified. Reality checks are avoided because only positive outcomes are considered. Not willing to be seen to be dependent on anyone, narcissists avoid delegating or consulting others in favour of a climate of secrecy, privacy, and closely held power. Typically, they make unilateral decisions.

Ironically, the more narcissists *need* to depend on others, the less they are willing to admit that their own judgment can no longer be trusted. It is excruciating for them when the independence they pride themselves on dwindles.

The Diabolical Laugh or Sneer

There is a mocking tone of disdain, a chilling quality to a narcissist's laugh. It bursts out when a healthy person would ordinarily express an emotion. As Lowen explains in *Narcissism: Denial of the True Self,* "A patient appears to be on the verge of tears, but instead of crying, this laugh occurs. An emotional response would show that the person has been affected by the experience. The laughter denies any feeling. 'I won,' it declares. 'I am more powerful than you. I can resist you'" (120). One-upmanship laughter strokes the ego.

As one of my clients so eloquently described her response to that laugh, "I can literally feel a dark dread rise up in my stomach as we talk about this. It makes my scalp crawl!" Then she added, "I was always terrified when I heard that diabolical laugh because it usually meant more put-downs were to come!"

Punishing Behaviour

Opinions that differ, questions that challenge, and decisions that interfere are not to be tolerated. The confronter is considered the "enemy" who must be controlled or, should that person make repeated challenges, someone to be punished. Punishment may be meted out in the form of refusing to go to an event or canceling plans to go on a holiday that the spouse had arranged months before. Or a junior at work may be passed over for advancement, demoted, or let go.

A perfect example appears in Andrew Kazdin's book, *Glenn Gould at Work: Creative Lying.* The recording engineer for Gould tells how he was suddenly dismissed in a telephone conversation on the eve of a planned recording session. "Does this mean our association is over?" he queried. Gould replied hurriedly, "Yes. Now don't be a stranger ... Maybe I'll see you if I ever get down to New York. Look, I've really got to go. Goodbye." Kazdin adds, "I never heard from him again. This ended our 15-year relationship. No regrets, no emotion, no thank yous" (163).

Similarly, a family member who dares to stand up for her own rights is discarded as no longer useful. I hear many tragic tales of wives who have been left with few resources after years of tolerating a narcissist's emotional abuse and neglect. The withdrawal of financial support or initiating a blatant or clandestine affair are favoured ways of punishing a rebellious spouse. If a separation or divorce ensues, many narcissists fight bitter battles to ensure that they get to keep their "hard-earned" money. "I want to see you crawling across the floor begging me before I give you a cent," was how one vindictive husband threatened to abandon his responsibilities.

Once the narcissist moves on, the spouse is out of the picture, even after long years of marriage. It's not hard to let go when emotional involvement is at a minimum. Some avoid seeing their ex-spouse at all, and too many fail to keep in regular touch with their children. This is especially true if the children have sided with the other parent. Remember, dissociation is a well-used defense mechanism.

Narcissists tend to think that societal rules are for other people. Their arrogance puts them on a plateau above the norm. Robert Fulford in his column "Rediscovering Frank Lloyd Wright" in *The Globe and Mail,* quotes from Anthony

Alofsin's book, *Frank Lloyd Wright: The Lost Years, 1910–1922*. Wright had left his first wife and six children to live with the wife of a neighbour. He held a press conference at which he announced that his genius gave him special rights. "The ordinary man," he declared, "cannot live without rules to guide his conduct ... It is infinitely more difficult to live without rules, but that is what the really honest, sincere, thinking man is compelled to do." Fulford comments that "Wright's hypocrisy operated on a colossal scale, like his genius and his ego."

Deceit

Lies, lies, lies! Promises, promises, promises! Narcissists are *always about to do something*! They make unrealistic promises based on what they think others want to hear. Then they fail to follow through. In fact, neglecting to tell the truth becomes a chronic habit. Peter had the greatest difficulty acknowledging that his avoidance of telling the truth was lying. When Sally accused Peter of withholding information from her about the very real threat of his company going bankrupt, Peter's twisted, off-the-wall response was, "I'm too diplomatic to call Sally a liar." It was his projection that twisted the truth. Peter told lies with ease. Sally did not.

Lack of Insight

Narcissists are dangerous people simply because their ego boundaries are so hopelessly blurred. *They see people, but don't truly experience them.* Narcissists have little respect or empathy for other people as distinct, separate, and unique individuals who have different points of view and special needs.

Peter shows little appreciation for what his family does for him. Sally has put so much effort into being supportive and helpful to Peter, often at the expense of her own emotional and physical health. It's therefore painful for Sally to hear Peter say, "Well, what do you do for *me?* You've never been there for me either!" Yet he commands their attention and insists that Sally and the children respect him. Unless their lives revolve around Peter's needs and his timetable, there is trouble. The children are expected to greet their father. He rarely seeks them out when he comes home.

Although narcissists have little insight into their own failings, they have an uncanny ability to home in on others' vulnerability. Because Sally's friends were extremely important to her, she always took great care to keep in touch and be loyal to them. If she was talking on the phone when Peter came home, he would resent her paying attention to someone else. So when Peter wanted to wound Sally, his favourite retort was, "Well, you have no friends. You're too selfish!" Stunned and hurt, Sally would withdraw. The truth, of course, was that it was Peter who had no friends. He was the selfish one.

Fear of Aging and Death

Surprisingly, narcissists tend to be youthful looking, and their faces often remain remarkably unlined. This is partly because avoidance allows them to remain relatively free from the stress they create by not problem-solving. Untouched by others' emotional pain, they stay aloof and uninvolved. The spouse is expected to look after any problems that the children have. Sadly, this is true even when children become seriously involved with drugs or theft, or are acting out sexually trying to find love and attention elsewhere.

Narcissists dread old age and death, and lack the deep feelings necessary to mourn. Unfortunately, emotionally unavailable narcissists also lack patience or understanding for those who do suffer. This is especially painful for the partner who must mourn alone for lost loved ones.

Narcissists are fatalistic, rather than proactive. They block out sadness and pain lest they be left vulnerable and weak. By failing to deal with unwelcome realities, however, they leave themselves wide open to the whims of fate. Typically, narcissists become increasingly cowardly as uncertainty begins to overwhelm their fragile ego.

Outbursts and Rage

Narcissists may remain without insight yet be remarkably resilient. That is, until too many failures or rejections crack their thin veneer. At such times, repressed self-loathing and contempt are likely to surface periodically and the narcissist's reserve will give way to temper tantrums or rage. These episodes are quickly forgotten, at least by the narcissist. Peter would be enraged if Sally brought up a situation again to try to get the problem resolved. She had no wish to experience his fury again. A typical response from Peter, however, would be total denial. "Nothing of the sort happened! You must be losing your mind!" he would bark.

As Lowen reminds us, it is important to note that narcissists have a deep unconscious fear of going crazy (100). This may explain why severely narcissistic personalities refuse to go for help: the threat of someone challenging their version of reality is too scary to contemplate.

Loners

Some narcissists manage to keep up appearances and are able to keep their careers intact. They maintain power, often doing so through fear and intimidation. They can be cold, callous, and calculating in their control but seduce others with grandiose promises and perks. They hire hard-driving Type A personalities who, like them, are not easily intimidated.

Motivational rewards are just enough to keep employees "hungry." Their spouse is kept in the background, especially as age takes its toll.

Many charismatic narcissists surround themselves with attractive, enthusiastic, but naive people who want to please. These loyal employees respect their boss, so they make excuses for his intermittent outbursts of anger. Sometimes other people use the narcissist. Picture the movie magnate whose office is full of young, beautiful, and equally ambitious assistants. I'm told this is called the "babe factor."

These hard-core power brokers who carve out their own reality often become increasingly unwise about, and vulnerable to, the real world. Assessing people solely on their "usefulness," narcissists often are poor judges of character. They refuse to check with others to confirm whether their choices are indeed wise. Subsequently, they can become easy prey for younger, equally manipulative people who use them, both emotionally and financially, to serve their own career ambitions.

Many less charismatic narcissists lead provisional lives and become loners as they age and their power erodes. They run out of people to manipulate and reality comes crashing in with business and professional failures. Nowadays, many are deserted by their long-suffering families, who cannot cope with their erratic and destructive behaviour. Spiritually bankrupt and emotionally empty, these loners experience depression or chronic psychotic breaks. Many escape into alcoholism.

Narcissists of this type want you to feel sorry for them. They will drive older cars, let others pick up the bill in the restaurant, and cry poor. Often, they are quite wealthy, but keep this secret from their family and won't discuss finances. Not surprisingly, though, if *they* want something, they get it! Increasingly needy, they crave instinctual pleasures and creature comforts. It is okay for them to indulge in an expensive meal, but if their spouse wants to go out with a friend, he or she is chastised for spending too much money at a trendy restaurant. Soliciting sympathy may be costly, as this is often the last straw for a long-suffering spouse.

The narcissist's world shrinks, growing ever smaller. Peter will go to only one restaurant now. If a show isn't on at the local theatre, he refuses to go. His circle of influence has also narrowed as colleagues whom he has offended or manipulated in the past avoid contact.

Entitlement

Entitlement, the arrogant illusion that one is above the rules of society, spells the downfall of many well-known public figures. We read about their fate after they've committed some daring or fraudulent act or lost their integrity by taking part in some other criminal act. Then there are others such as the chess genius Bobby Fischer, whose superior attitude of entitlement led him to become a cheerless recluse who "lapsed into a strange and contrarian solitude." In *The Globe and Mail* obituary entitled "Enfant Terrible of Chess Won a Battle of the Cold War, and with It the World," Bruce Weber writes about this hugely demanding personality. "For much of his life, he fought imperiously on behalf of that entitlement, demanding uncompromising loyalty from his supporters, concessions from his opponents, special treatment from tournament organizers, and unalloyed respect from the world at large." This outlook became ever more skewed, and Weber concludes that Fischer's self-involvement isolated him and was his ultimate undoing. He alienated his fans and left no immediate survivors. Unfortunately, this regrettable tale describes the fate of many fallen narcissists.

HOW DOES THE NARCISSIST AFFECT THE FAMILY?

It is one thing to damage oneself and to live out the consequences of narcissism in one's own life. It is quite another tragedy, however, when narcissists wreak havoc in the lives of those closest to them. No one can predict this. Trusting mates who were initially attracted to their charm and youthful good looks were won over by their habit of telling others what they wanted to hear. Their children may have been inflicted with the narcissistic wound at a time of naivety and innocence when it was impossible to foresee the damaging consequences that living with a narcissist might have on their own future development and happiness.

In chapter 6, we will explore the family dynamics in which one parent is, or has become, highly narcissistic.

6

The Narcissist's Family

The Birth of Narcissism and Its Generational Legacy

Narcissism and gratitude, like oil and water, don't mix.

DANGER – NARCISSISM IS CONTAGIOUS

The children of a narcissist are likely to inadvertently copy their parent's self-serving behaviour and thus develop a skewed value system. This same parent may reward and foster certain personality traits and talents that encourage a child to feel special and set apart from other children. Often a narcissistic individual will project his or her ideal image and single out one child as a favourite. Thereafter, that child can do no wrong.

THE NARCISSISTIC WOUND

Let's explore how narcissism begins to develop within the family circle. The most severe narcissistic injuries are inflicted in childhood. Surprisingly, there are two seemingly opposite dynamics that wound a child and facilitate the development of narcissism. There are also degrees of injury, depending on the source and the length of time a child is exposed. One dynamic has its history in parental idealization and/or indulgence; the other, in ongoing emotional or physical abuse, or neglect. In Jungian terms, the adult narcissist is referred to as the "eternal child," the *puer aeternus* in males, and *the puer animus* in females. The emotional level of such individuals remains stunted at the adolescent level unless a midlife crisis forces inner growth.

Narcissism is all too prevalent in today's family. Christopher Lasch, in *The Culture of Narcissism,* suggests that because our society lacks a belief in the future, it therefore neglects the needs of the next generation. Today's parents attempt to make children feel loved and wanted, yet there is "an underlying coolness in the remoteness of those who have little to pass on to the next generation and who in any case give priority to their own right to self-fulfillment." Lasch concludes that this emotional detachment, coupled with "attempts to convince a child of his favoured position in the family is a good prescription for a narcissistic personality structure" (101–2).

THE NARCISSIST AS PARENT

Narcissism affects one's ability to be a good parent. The narcissist's parenting skills are warped by feelings that have been deadened by their own parent excessively indulging yet manipulating them, or acting out some form of abuse or neglect. In turn, they may repeat the same pattern with their children.

Neglectful or Overly Protective Parents

Many parents who neglect their children do so because they themselves have been damaged and left emotionally crippled. As children, they were psychologically ill-equipped to handle the pain of their own childhood. Often traumatized by ongoing physical or emotional abuse, or witness to other family members being abused by a chaotic parent, these children block off memories that are too toxic to bear. Thus, they remain unaware, yet chronically anxious. No wonder some choose to compensate by overprotecting or idolizing their own children one minute, yet find themselves repeating abusive patterns when stress levels climb and suppressed rage erupts out of control. Modelling is a very powerful teacher!

Another common dynamic in these families is the child who becomes overly responsible because the non-abusive but victimized parent relies too heavily on this child for emotional support. By responding to the frightened parent's need, the child is unwittingly robbed of a carefree childhood. Inappropriate adult roles are thrust upon such a victim prematurely. No child has the emotional maturity to handle the often bizarre power-plays acted out in these disturbed families. The child becomes overly responsible for others but shut off from his or her own instinctual needs and happiness. Personal pleasure can make these children feel uncomfortable and guilty.

In contrast, the parent who was indulged and overprotected as a child often fails to recognize that any emotional damage has been done. These people may have learned to deny their undesirable negative feelings, attempting to live up to the unrealistically high expectations of a narcissistic parent. As parents, they too want their child to make them proud. Because this is a less obvious form of abuse, this group is not likely to question their own parenting skills. After all, aren't they and their family perfect?

Ongoing Deception in the Next Generation

Chronic anxiety becomes a perpetual state of mind for a child living with the fall out of abuse, high expectations, or some manipulative action used as a means to control what the child does and thinks.

As in all dysfunctional families, eventually things start to unravel. One crisis begets another. Denial becomes a necessary but largely unconscious habit that protects family members from feeling disoriented, crazy, or simply less than perfect. It becomes less painful to pretend or lie, to guess what others want to hear. This is how Bruno, a client, justified his form of deception. "By lying or keeping silent, I covered up all my mistakes. It was the only way I could hide my weaknesses from Dad." He paused, and then added thoughtfully, "Little lies helped solve my problem of avoiding the attention, or sometimes rage, I otherwise would have received when he discovered what I had done. Now that I'm on my own, I'm still telling lies. I just can't seem to stop myself. I hate to admit this, but honesty is not one of my best traits." Old habits die hard.

Since chaotic feelings are uncomfortable and even painful, children learn to resort to reason and logic to determine the actions best suited to their own self-preservation. They crave positive attention and will do anything to ensure that they get it. Their "impression management" strategy becomes "look good, no matter the cost." Demands that children be strong, good, right, and perfect can be a powerful motivator.

Tragically, the long-term cost of denial is typically the loss of integrity and respect.

The Shamed Child

A subtle emotional abuse occurs when children are shamed by being repeatedly put down by an arrogant parent who has the narcissist's inflated view of self. Children are told they are "stupid," "slow," "no good," "inferior," and so on. Their self-esteem plummets, yet the humiliation of carrying such labels is shut off from consciousness. Instead, others hear in their response a certain heady cockiness, a show-offish retaliation. Shame is often the source of narcissistic denial in the next generation.

In other cases, the child takes on the shame of a parent. Many workaholics, for instance, seek control of their lives after a parent has been publicly humiliated by business bankruptcy, divorce recriminations, accusations of sexual impropriety, or imprisonment. The seeds of workaholism are often planted at such times because the child is determined to be fully in charge and totally independent, and seen to be a respectable member of the community. No one is going to crack this perfectly constructed persona. Control thus becomes essential to emotional survival.

The Idealized Child

A more subtle wound is inflicted when the children of an anxious parent are not disciplined fairly but instead are spoiled, overprotected, and indulged in a material or permissive sense. This idealized child has a special set of problems.

Certainly Peter was such a child. In spite of his parents' good intentions, Peter grew up amidst emotional confusion. He bounced back and forth between his mother's strong overprotective, sometimes hysterical reactions and his father's laidback, cool detachment. His father prided himself on being a good provider so he gave the children whatever they wanted, but took little responsibility for discipline or guidance. If anything went wrong at home, he would either withdraw into a mood of stony silence or burst into a fiery rage. No one could predict which it would be. Blind to his own faults, Peter's father was all too aware of others' foibles. He got extremely annoyed if there was any trouble at home. The trouble apparently had nothing to do with him. Someone else was always blamed.

Peter, like his father, devalued everyday, simple pleasures and responsibilities. He discovered early on that "home work" received no recognition. So his energies were channelled into more lofty ambitions, ones that would be publicly recognized at school and thereafter. One goal would always lead to another quest. But nothing was ever enough to fill up a haunting inner sense of emptiness.

Secretly, Peter never believed his own myth. Low self-esteem and self-doubt plagued him until harsh reality eventually threatened to dismantle his crowning glory, the business for which he had sacrificed his family life. In one of our sessions, Peter went back to search for the roots of his workaholism. He explored the reasons why he never felt fully involved in what he was experiencing and why success had left him still numb and empty inside. As he explained, "It goes way back, really. Even when I first got that Industry Achievement Award, I felt like an impostor. It was as if part of me was watching at a distance as I walked across that stage. That award gave me no pleasure. I just couldn't relate to the whole scene." There was a wide split between Peter's experience and his own detachment from it all. Nothing seemed to give him joy.

"Way back," for Peter, was still recent history. What Peter hadn't realized was that the seeds of this detachment were deeply planted in early unfulfilling interactions with his role model, his self-absorbed but influential father.

THE THIRD GENERATION – ONE FAMILY'S STRUGGLE WITH NARCISSISM

Unfortunately, a similar, potentially tragic dynamic is being played out now in Peter and Sally's own family. As we have learned, the child who is singled out for special attention and spoiled by a narcissistic parent is likely to develop narcissistic traits. And so the cycle continues.

Initially, Peter's father idealized his son because he saw in him an extension of his own perfection. He had high expectations for Peter, and Peter knew it. In spite of this idealization, his father was so absorbed in his own inner world that he remained aloof and was a poor listener. His neglect stemmed from a packed, goal-oriented schedule that left him little time alone with Peter. It would never have occurred to him to take Peter to places a child would appreciate. Instead, he would occasionally surprise Peter by taking him to the office on a Saturday morning. He rationalized that it was part of Peter's grooming to see his father in action, surrounded by pomp and power. He would leave Peter in an empty office to sit and draw while he busied himself with paperwork or talked on the phone. During lunch afterwards in *his* favourite restaurant, he would initially ask Peter questions but would soon become distracted and lost in thought.

Peter was now overcompensating for the conditional love that left him emotionally scarred by giving his youngest daughter special attention. He was motivated to indulge her every whim. No one was going to accuse him of neglect!

As I worked with Peter and Sally, it became clear that their marital problems were only the tip of an iceberg. It was Sally who alerted me to this when she was complaining one day that one of her biggest problems was Peter's refusal to discipline the children. Worse still, he didn't support her discipline. This was especially true with Penny, their youngest, teenaged daughter.

Unwittingly, young Penny was drawn into her parents' struggle over how they would share personal and parental responsibilities. Although Peter was ultra-responsible at work, at home it was another story. Because he worked such long hours, Sally found herself, by default, solely in charge of discipline. She didn't relish this role at all; being nurturing and supportive were her best traits. Peter hated it when Sally let off steam about something one of the children had done. He always defended their misbehaviour, and played down her real concerns. Occasionally, he would promise to speak to one of them, but would never quite get around to it, citing work-related pressure as his excuse. Or, more frustrating still, he would tell Sally that he "just forgot."

Sally was becoming increasingly alarmed for Penny. According to Sally's description of events, Peter sometimes behaved like an adolescent boy with Penny. He flirted with her, fussed over her clothes, and would make admiring comments on her appearance as she left for school each day. Sally was surprised at this because Peter never commented on what Sally wore, even if it was new. He would spend time in Penny's room with her, looking through fashion magazines. Penny's door would be closed. If Sally came in, she was made to feel unwelcome. He would cut into conversations Sally and Penny were having and turn the conversation around so that the focus was on him. He would use a seductive tone with Penny but not with the other children.

In turn, Penny could twist Peter around her little finger. Anything she wanted, she got. Peter would drive Penny wherever she wanted to go, and he seemed to take a vicarious delight in hearing about the intimate details of her sometimes stormy relationships. Penny would say quite outrageous things about her friends. Her mother, in a negative tone, would suggest that Penny was being unkind, but Peter would laugh. He seemed to get a real kick out of whatever Penny did, good or bad.

This indulgence, seduction, and refusal to discipline, carried to extremes, can be a form of emotional sexual abuse. Sally had every reason to be fearful: Penny's future development would be greatly affected by Peter's inappropriate attentions. The other children would not go unharmed by this situation either. Peter's son badly needed his father's attention. His other daughter could not help but be affected as she watched her father's obvious devotion to her sister. Her self-esteem and confidence in her own femininity would suffer. Puberty is an especially critical time for a daughter to be emotionally seduced by a father or to be ignored by him.

Peter initially saw nothing wrong with his actions. He explained to me that when the children were young, he was over involved with his work. His career advancement meant everything to him; and, yes, he was away a great deal. In later sessions, Peter was able to admit that he had been jealous of the closeness Sally had with their children. The family had their own routines and schedules and Sally was orchestrating it all because she was always there, always dependable.

Peter, who was used to being the centre of attention at the office, felt left out. When his business was well-established and prospering, he resolved to plug back into the family and exert his influence. "By the way," he assured me once again, "everything I did at work, I did for my family."

His re-entry into the family occurred when Penny was twelve, a critical stage for her. He began competing for the children's attention by interrupting and then dominating the children's conversations with their mother. If they asked Sally a question, as they were used to doing, Peter would answer. Soon Sally was getting pushed aside and told not to interrupt. Her opinions were trivialized or discredited. The children, too, started to put her down. This sudden attention from their absent father was a welcomed change.

At puberty, it is normal and natural for the daughter to become critical of what her mother wears, how she speaks, or what she does or does not do. A typical complaint might be, "Why don't you wear your hair short like Trina's mother?" Teenagers, as we know, can be totally insensitive and scathing in their spontaneous comments or sometimes purposely cruel.

Healthy Resolution

In a healthy family, the father would understand his daughter's rebellious need to challenge her female role model. Such challenges are the way she defines herself and begins the process called individuation – discovering the essence of her Self, different and separate from her mother. At the same time, the father will recognize that his present attraction, from his daughter's point of view, lies in her new fascination with the opposite sex. He needs to be sensitive to this and respectful of these early sexual stirrings.

The father needs to be sensitive to his daughter's vulnerability but offer firm guidance, as well as appropriate affection and encouragement. His most important role is to be supportive of his wife as she weathers her daughter's rebellious criticism and complaints. If the daughter goes overboard, he must intervene and challenge the daughter's inappropriate behaviour. He might say, "I understand that you are upset and that is okay. However, what's not okay is for you to talk to your mother like that! Would you please apologize to her right now." He might also explore with his daughter how she might feel if someone spoke to her that way.

Her mother, buoyed up by her husband's support, will be better able to maintain her composure and position of authority. She is firm but refrains from lashing back emotionally because she is able to remain objective and not take the daughter's criticisms too personally. Resolution comes eventually when the daughter makes the connection that, "even though I'm obnoxious and miserable, Mother still loves me – I must be okay!" As she learns to accept herself and her own foibles, she will hopefully come to terms with her *real* mother, not the idealized one she longs for. A more equal, adult relationship based on mutual understanding and respect can help the daughter establish a clear sense of Self and be able to resolve her own issues around femininity.

Family communication is vitally important at such times. If even one family member is upset, all will suffer. The future relationship between mother and daughter hangs on the individuation process following healthy lines.

Unhealthy Resolution

The narcissistic father who needs his own immediate instinctual needs satisfied will be less focused on what is in the best interest of the child over time. Like Peter, he neglects to discipline the children and support the mother. He wants to be admired, so he takes the adoring daughter's side in arguments, laughs at her when she is cheeky or rude, and refuses to discipline her. Instead, he makes excuses for her. Then he tells his wife, "She doesn't mean anything bad. Stop being so childish!"

Unconsciously or not, this husband is using his daughter to punish and dominate his disapproving wife. He may be angry because she no longer seems to show him the respect that he believes is his due. Like Sally, the wife may have been complaining about her husband's lack of emotional involvement and his excessive work schedule. Once the wife ceases to mirror a positive image for the narcissist, she is no longer of value. Only he must be in control. Everyone must pay attention to him.

THE PEDESTAL DAUGHTER

"Pedestal daughters" like Penny have too much power in the family. However, underneath their veneer of self-confidence and arrogance lies a deep insecurity. There is a part of Penny that believes she really is "special." Yet another part strives for perfection and is filled with self-doubt. Penny's anxiety takes the form of her becoming obsessive about her school work. She spends an inordinate amount of time studying late into the night. She bites her nails, worrying about her grades.

Unbeknownst to Penny, her anxiety may cover an unconscious fear of incest or a conscious threat of possible humiliation or rejection should she return her father's overtures. When these girls do respond to their father's flirtations, such titillating or ambiguous situations may make both father and daughter feel uneasy and anxious. Over time, the daughter's sexual feelings may be repressed or even disowned as a result. A pseudo-sexual relationship with her father makes it difficult for a daughter to relate to other males, especially sexually. Her father is idealized and admired. Awkward, self-conscious, bumbling adolescent boys cannot compete with these charming, youthful-looking narcissistic fathers. Young men may ask her out but her arrogance and disdain throw them off. Often these girls are admired and attractive to boys, yet they don't get asked out because they convey a sharp edge or a brittle quality. This superiority masks a critical, and often sarcastic, one-up nature. Relationships tend not to last because these girls lack the warm nurturing qualities and empathy necessary for true intimacy. Faced with constant rejection, they lose confidence. Some become "boy crazy," trying to find the elusive male who will make them feel desirable and loved.

Linda Leonard, in *The Wounded Woman: Healing the Father–Daughter Relationship,* suggests that a daughter like this sees the "eternal boy" father as someone her own age, someone she can manipulate through his fascination for her. "The daughters of these eternal boys grow up without an adequate model of self-discipline, limit, and authority, quite often suffering from feelings of insecurity, instability, lack of self-confidence, anxiety, frigidity, and in general, a weak ego" (12).

Power and performance become important to these girls because they have identified with the masculine traits of the idealized father. They are cut off from their own feminine instincts because they have devalued the rival mother. As a consequence, the masculine side of their personality develops; the nurturing, gentle side does not. They may "perform" sexually by intellectualizing but are cut off from their own sexual instincts. Daughters who become rivals of their mother for their father's attention are robbed of the normal resolution of the mother–daughter struggle. Without an intervention to correct this dangerous family dynamic, Penny will stay stuck at this adolescent stage of development. Her father will remain her White Knight and everything her Black Mother does will be wrong. Because repressed feeling and nurturing qualities fail to moderate Penny's harshly critical judgments, she will continue to have problems in her relationships.

The roles of masculine and feminine, of husband and wife, are skewed in this family. The mother, by default, has had to assume the role of disciplinarian. Because her weak, indulgent husband has abdicated his responsibilities in favour of being Mr Nice Guy to the children, it is she who must establish the values, authority, and traditions of the family. Absolutely no one wins in this human tragedy. Future relationships for girls such as Penny will be deeply affected by their own budding narcissism. Anxiety and obsessive behaviours signal their confusion around appropriate role models and values.

Tragically, the narcissist's communications may confuse a child's reality further. Narcissists can be very charming and convincing. Their certainty about being right and their arrogant pronouncements overwhelm the insecure child who is trying to discover truths in the increasingly crazy family system that the narcissist creates.

The narcissist's children know instinctively that one does not challenge a narcissist without consequences. Narcissists are not good listeners, although this is sometimes not readily apparent. Because they see things in black-and-white concrete terms based solely on their own experience, they quickly direct conversations back to their particular point of view. Different ideas go unacknowledged or are fiercely argued. Remember that in the narcissist's world two people of differing views cannot both be right. Worse still, if a child disagrees, the self-referencing narcissist thinks that "the child thinks that I am wrong!" Such an affront cannot go unchallenged. These intolerable games can go on endlessly, unless the need for help becomes starkly obvious.

THE ACCEPTANCE OF HELP

Knowing when to ask for help is wisdom! Fortunately, it is not too late for Peter and Sally to turn their family around. Peter's business failures and Sally's depression have forced Peter to take stock of where he is headed. After all, he had agreed to come for psychotherapy, even if it was "for Sally." Hardcore narcissists rarely agree to seek help or stay long enough to develop the insight and strength necessary to break through their incredible denial.

Initially, Peter kept aloof in the sessions. He avoided answering questions or voicing his opinion unless asked directly. He waited for Sally to speak, and then would twist her words around until he looked good and Sally bad. His diabolical laugh at such times was chilling. Sally would cringe, as if struck. No wonder she was afraid of him.

Very slowly, Peter became fascinated with the process of self-discovery and eventually the sessions actually became a priority in his week. The fact that he was emotionally crippled had never dawned on him, but Peter did recognize that his family was in serious trouble. His carefully crafted persona did not include a separation or divorce. He did "love" his family, although at present he really didn't know what real love was.

Even though Peter had committed himself to this journey, getting in touch with his feelings was an uphill struggle. For example, one day I asked Peter whether he was interesting and fun to be with at home. He looked annoyed. When I explored the joylessness between the couple, Peter replied that he could certainly relate to a story I told about a wife who had complained that as soon as she and her husband married, he stopped taking her out or even talking to her. Peter's comment was chilling: "As soon as we got married, I no longer had to fight for Sally. I had conquered her, and she was off limits to anyone else!" Then he added, "I got my mind back to business, and she ceased to be a priority."

Although Sally looked visibly shaken that day, Peter was telling the truth. As yet, he had little awareness of the impact of his words. When I asked him the following week about his reaction to the previous session, he told me that his mind went blank on the way home. He couldn't listen to the radio or talk to Sally. He was numb and couldn't remember anything that had gone on in the session.

When I reminded him of what he had said the week before, Peter looked sheepish and remarked, "That's not very nice, is it?"

Although the didactic focus in this story is an unhealthy relationship between a father and his daughter that seriously affects the marital relationship, other triangles can also form when one parent is narcissistic. A narcissistic mother can be overly involved with a son or daughter and freeze out her husband. Or a narcissistic father can be connected to a son in an exclusive relationship that leaves the mother out of their interaction.

Starting the Journey

By now, you may have some idea about whether depression, anxiety, or narcissism is presently signalling that your feeling side has shut down.

It is now time to begin the three-stage journey that teaches people to *Internalize* – a process I have developed and used for over thirty years to help individuals rediscover their feelings and to learn how to problem-solve effectively.

Chapter 7 describes how to become aware of the signals your body is sending to alert you to shifts or changes in your feelings and emotions (Identification); how to process and interpret this information (Justification); and how to feel the feeling, stay with it, and experience it fully (Experiencing). Finally, a review of defense mechanisms reveals the different ways people react in order to protect themselves against negative emotional reactions.

The Journey – Stage 1, Awareness

Learn to Internalize Your Feelings

Changing attitude is relatively easy; changing behaviour is not!

I SEE YOU, I HEAR YOU

Imagine that you are sitting in my office. Your feelings are flat, and you're not too sure just how you feel at this moment, or how you *should* feel.

You may have been the "good kid" in your family. You always fit in, performed well at school, and rarely rebelled, except maybe to skip a few classes or smoke behind the garage. Or perhaps you grew up in the midst of the family's Battle of Waterloo. You're not sure if anyone actually won any of the skirmishes, but you do know that you "run for the hills" and hide if anyone starts up with you.

Or perhaps you were a "seen-but-not-heard" shy child who was left out of a lot of things, like conversations. People around you seemed just too busy to notice what you were feeling or doing.

Or perhaps you are a Feeler who grew up in a family of Thinkers who either didn't listen or, if they did, would often distort what you said beyond recognition. "Don't I speak loudly enough?" you wondered.

Whatever the reason your feelings have been squashed, ignored, or discounted, the following techniques can transform your world!

Peter's journey through this process I call *Internalizing* was difficult because he was such a strong Thinker. At first, he always had to *think* through how he felt. Later his Feeling function became more independent, and this translation process became less necessary. Sally, a natural Feeler, was able to restore her Feeling function relatively quickly. However, her uphill struggle began when she had to learn to catch herself *before* she lashed out in anger or withdrew into an ugly mood. She had to take the time to monitor and analyze her negative thoughts, and ask herself *what positive Thinking would do* in this situation. This transformational process allowed Sally to regain inner control and problem-solve more effectively. She kept her independence by resolving to be responsible for her own response, not Peter's, and learned to remain objective as she calmly thought through the situation.

ANGER, YES, BUT WHAT ARE THESE OTHER FEELINGS CALLED?

Our goal is to know immediately how we feel, at any given moment. We want to be in enough control that we can decide when it is best to *act on our feelings* and when it is best to *delay action*. In either case, it is important to be fully responsible, to problem-solve using a combination of wisdom and empathy.

Feeling, as distinct from the complex called emotion or affect, is the way we subjectively decide the value of something or someone to us. It is a way of making decisions and problem-solving. It is rational, unless some powerful emotion overwhelms Feeling. When our emotions are activated by strong feelings or thoughts, our heightened response tends to distort the other functions. For example, people can't think clearly when they are upset or when their reaction to a situation is coloured by a dark mood.

Emotions vary according to the *intensity* of feeling. Anger may range from mild irritation to violent rage. As intensity increases, the danger is that the emotion, be it positive or negative, may capture us within its grip. Various levels of tension are created that either cause us to irrationally act out our emotions or allow us to experience our feelings internally without a strong need or desire to take action.

Feelings vary according to *quality* on a continuum from pleasant to unpleasant. The intensity of the feeling will affect its tone and determine how it will be perceived. Fierce rage is distinctly unpleasant for all involved, while the titillating fear of a roller-coaster ride may well feel pleasurable.

We are going to attempt here to get in touch with the major broad feelings: happy–sad; love–hate; warm–cold; admiration – jealousy; joy–grief; pride–shame, and so on. The four negative feelings of *anger, anxiety, fear,* and *pain* will be treated separately. Under their influence, we become overtly emotional and tend to lose control more quickly. By doing so, we end up negatively affecting others and ourselves.

A high degree of psychological and physical tension is associated with these four primary feelings because the situations that evoke them are often intimately involved with some goal-striving activity. Although the essential condition for arousing *anger* may be the blocking of goal attainment, *fear* can itself elicit an emotion of avoidance. We wish to keep power and to be competent when handling a threatening situation, yet we fear "losing it." One can name a fear, as in "I'm afraid of the bear," or "I'm terrified that I'll fail my exam!"

Anxiety, on the other hand, is fed from a number of sources, some of which are conscious but many of which remain repressed. Anxiety is amorphous, free-floating, and thus more difficult to pinpoint. *Pain* is a complex subject, but at high levels of intensity, we may experience acute emotional agitation and muscle spasms. Sometimes pain is referred from other locations. What we call heartburn, for example, may actually be an irritant located in the digestive tract. There are also strong differences in how people handle pain, based on age, life experience, psychological and personality factors, social class, ethnic group, and so on.

The earlier we can recognize these four significant feelings, the more chance we have to stay in control. Hopefully, this recognition will also result in a lowering of the intensity of our reactions. Full control is possible only up to the point where powerful defense mechanisms come into play and take over. Remember, the role of our defenses is to cover up, compensate for, or block out unwanted negative emotions.

THE PROCESS OF EXTERNALIZING

Before I can teach you to *internalize* your feelings, it is helpful to understand what you presently do when you process information. Most people I see in my practice have learned to *externalize* their feelings. When something happens, they go into their thinking mode and figure out how to react by second-guessing what the other person wants them to say, think, do, or feel. They may have learned in their dysfunctional family that it's smart and adaptive to say what others want to hear and do what others, especially parents, want them to do. They thus learn to anticipate, and eventually to manipulate others to gain some advantage, some power over outcome and possibly over their own destiny. They are survivors, or at least they try to be.

Unfortunately, by doing this, they learn to *react*. By reacting too quickly before they've had a chance to think through *why* they are feeling a certain way, they not only short-circuit the information coming from their Feeling function but also lack the ability to stay objective and consider the other person's unique and separate reality. Feelings, when they remain largely repressed, work slowly, if at all. These people realize they are angry five minutes later, an hour or two later, or even the next day. At that point, it is necessary to go backwards in time to problem-solve.

Retreating typically spells trouble. Here is Vivian explaining her reactions after-the-fact to her sister Francine: "Francine, remember when you told me about what Aunt Lillian said at the party the other day? How she never phones you any more, and how you're writing her off?" (Remember, this version of the story is Vivian's *"projection"* of Francine's conversation.) Vivian recalls all the feelings this conversation stirred up in her. At first, she felt a mixture of disbelief and criticism towards her sister. Then she felt concern for her aunt. But now Vivian is startled by a deep-seated anger bubbling up inside that stems from her own issues with Francine. She then goes off on a somewhat irrational but invasive triangulated tangent. "Well, Francine, I don't know why you expect to hear from Aunt Lil when you don't even bother to phone your own sister!"

At this point, all hell breaks loose, because Vivian's adaptation of what her sister initially said doesn't jibe with Francine's recollection at all. Francine proceeds to set her straight about what she actually did say. Tempers flare. Soon the bickering escalates to a level at which both women are shouting to make themselves heard. It has become an argument about "who said what." For Vivian, it's about the distortion of her own words.

Sooner or later Vivian learns, usually after many such unhappy experiences, that trying to solve problems after the fact rarely works. "Things will only get worse if I say anything," she concludes. So, guess what? For the sake of harmony, she rationalizes, it is best to do nothing! Instead, she becomes passive-aggressive with her sister. She blocks her feelings and blithely lets troublesome conversations flow by her. She ceases to react, at least visibly, and eventually even to listen.

Unfortunately, all those pent-up feelings one day explode like firecrackers on the Fourth of July! She and Francine pitch their flags and have another rumble.

"I've had it up to here with your selfishness!" Vivian bursts out. "You expect everyone to run circles around *you*. Well, I for one am giving you notice! I have no intention of stooping to that level!"

Anxiety is the result when unresolved distress lurks just below the surface, waiting to explode. Excess adrenalin is produced to fuel any arousal state, but anger is especially lethal. As our bodies prepare for "fight or flight," our blood pressure rises because the heart is forced to work harder to keep on the alert. Our blood cholesterol level also climbs above normal. As well, there is an increase in acid secretion because the body demands extra blood to provide food as well as the extra energy needed to perform when, or if, it becomes necessary. Increased muscle tension in all parts of the body takes its heavy toll. Our head aches, our back stiffens as if frozen rigid from ongoing fears. This state of arousal becomes too frequent a visitor. Sleep becomes increasingly disturbed and fitful if stress is prolonged over time.

Problems, unfortunately, don't seem to disappear after "fight or flight" warfare. People who externalize have a lot of "unfinished business." They also tend to be worry-warts and to fuss endlessly about past or future events. They are like chameleons, reflecting back whatever is going on around them. These *reactors* are affected by the weather, other people's moods, and what people think about them. They have no centre and are forever shifting, blown by the current wind. Unwittingly, they have given over their power to others.

What to do instead of externalizing becomes the big question. Learning to do the opposite, to *internalize*, will not be an easy task. Habits die hard. Be patient. Your hard work will pay off by expanding the narrow range of feelings you now live in. A wide range of feelings allows you to respond with pure joy but also to fully ache with sorrow when life's circumstances send grief your way. Instead of walking through life like a zombie, you will *experience* every person and situation fully.

THE PROCESS OF INTERNALIZING – AN ILLUSTRATION

I am now going to explain this process called *Internalizing*. But first, let me tell a story. Each part of the story represents a step in the process.

Step 1 – Identification

One Monday morning I woke up feeling "yucky," out of sorts, but not knowing why. Since it was only 6:45 a.m., I couldn't figure out what was wrong.

Normally, I would ask myself three questions: (1) <u>What</u> *has just happened?* (2) <u>Who</u> *said what?* and (3) <u>Specifically,</u> *what am I reacting to in this situation?* But since it was close to dawn and my day had not yet begun, I asked a fourth question: (4) *What did I* <u>dream</u> *about that still might be affecting me?* I remember my dreams pretty well, but last night there hadn't been anything in them that would upset me.

I started to make breakfast for everyone and promptly forgot about my bad feelings. A half-hour later, alone at the table, I suddenly noticed how I was sitting. I was *bent over,* felt very *heavy,* and was aware of *tears welling up* in my eyes. Over the years, I've become aware that this is how I react when I experience sadness. (By the way, you will have your own unique combination of reactions to sadness.) With this recognition came a flash of insight!

Step 2 – Justification

As soon as I was aware of my own sadness, I recalled some *"unfinished business,"* an image from the night before of my daughter's face, looking sad. Then I remembered. On Sunday night, as I was bustling around the kitchen, getting dinner ready for some guests, one of my daughters entered the kitchen with a long, sad face. She was upset and wanted to talk.

My hurried response was, "Sweetie, would you mind sitting on the stool here so we can talk while I'm finishing this salad?" I was listening, albeit going from cutting board, to fridge, and back several times. The door-bell rang, and I went out to the hall to greet our guests, who had arrived a half-hour early. Somewhat frazzled because I hadn't finished dressing, I forgot completely about my daughter back in the kitchen. I quickly welcomed our guests, got them comfortable, and then dashed back to the bedroom.

Not my version of being a good mother! The choice between getting dinner ready on time and listening to someone who is upset is usually not a hard one. The guests' early arrival apparently jumbled my priorities. It was apparent that this present disappointment with myself was a delayed reaction.

My sadness had another source, however. A close friend was dying of cancer so periodic feelings of sadness would wash over me whenever I thought of her plight. Three years before she had asked me to go through her death with her. Time was ebbing away for her, and death was imminent. I was aware that through association, my sadness this day was only heightened by my ever-present grief.

Step 3 – Experiencing

Now that I had justified two valid reasons for being sad, I gave myself "permission" to be thoroughly sad.

I also knew that I had to take special care of myself. I needed time to work through all the reasons for my present sadness, and anticipate the future loss of my friend. At my office the next day, I made sure that my clients left on time, that I had a few minutes between sessions. Also, at lunch break, I had to decide whether I felt like going for a walk or wished to feel pampered with a large pot of tea and comfortable service. I chose a quiet restaurant and just relaxed. I let my thoughts run through the mixture of feelings I was experiencing and let that be okay.

By evening I was still feeling down, so I decided to simplify my plans and have a "peace-and-quiet" evening at home. Accordingly, plans to go to a movie had to be changed. Instead, I'd relax, take a long bath, and go to bed early. Emotions can be draining and exhausting when you're running on empty. It takes an extra effort to remain effective at work when personal issues demand your attention.

If the next day had been my "writing day," I would have lowered my expectations about what I hoped to accomplish. I'd promise myself to not only monitor my level of sadness that day but also take the time to fully experience this powerful emotion. I might play soothing music in the background while I worked, music that fit my current mood.

After working through the reasons for my heightened reaction to disappointing my daughter, it was time to act. I knew what I wanted to do.

Step 4 – Problem-Solving

Only at this point was I ready to make amends. There was no use trying to rectify the situation while I was self-absorbed, felt empty, and had nothing to give.

I sought out my daughter and apologized for my thoughtlessness. I asked her if we could talk some more now that we were both free from interruptions. I also phoned my friend at the hospital and asked her what was going on there today. I was now more able to be supportive and sensitive.

This whole process forms a Gestalt, a finished package. However, even though I'd let go of some sadness and tried to make up for my insensitive shortcomings, there was still some unfinished business. I wanted to learn from my mistakes.

Step 5 – Seeking Wisdom

Sometimes we learn from others, and sometimes others learn from us. When a number of things are making me anxious, I imagine each one as a building block, similar to the ones we played with as children. In my mind, I pile each stressor on top of another and ask this question: "Of all these problems, which can be resolved *only by me*? And which absolutely *has* to be done today?

Then I do the one or two things that are best done immediately. Taking action, however small, usually eases distress. Problem-solving brings a sense of accomplishment and raises self-esteem. I know from experience that other tasks are better left until another day when I'm feeling more "up." With added energy and clear thinking, I handle troublesome issues much better. When people are drained of all energy, they tend to feel defeated and helpless. Hopelessness, by the way, feeds depression.

Remember, it is rarely wise or efficient to do things poorly, be in a rush, or act under excess pressure!

HOW DOES THE PROCESS OF INTERNALIZING WORK?

Within this story lies the process you will follow to begin to *Internalize*.

Step 1 – Identification

What you feel depends on what is happening in your body. To cue into your feelings, pay attention to which particular muscles and nerve endings are being triggered as your body automatically reacts and sends signals to your brain. You may be reacting to something that is occurring in your immediate mental or physical environment. Or, through association, your unconscious mind may be bringing some past disturbing memory or unresolved experience up to the surface. If you are fully aware and connected to your body, you will *experience* the resultant feeling, be it excitement, pleasure, anger, or discomfort. Hopefully, your response will be appropriate to the situation. If you are upset, you have a choice of whether to take corrective action at the time of awareness or decide to delay resolution until a more appropriate occasion when you are in control. How to delay action and reschedule will be addressed later in chapter 8.

1–1. AWARENESS   You'll notice from my initial story that I suddenly became aware while sitting at the kitchen table that it was sadness that I was feeling. I already knew that something was not right with me. Insight came only when I recognized that my upper body was bending forward, I was experiencing a feeling of heaviness and my eyes were filling up with tears. In short, I was bent over, feeling heavy, and slightly teary.

Three distinct channels brought the feeling of sadness into my awareness: a change in physiology (*teary*), a change in energy level (*heaviness*), and a change in body position (*bent over*). Let's explore each channel in more depth.

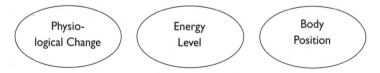

1–2. PHYSIOLOGICAL CHANGE   Physiological changes are complex and varied. They are not only unique to each individual; they may also be specific to each person's

experience of that moment in time or that particular circum-
stance or place. External influences – such as unusual situations, others' reactions or moods, or even the weather – may
affect these bodily changes.

Clients often tell me that their first warning of *anxiety*
is a tightness of the muscles in their stomach. For others, it
is an acidic taste from bile secretions. Some people notice
their shoulder muscles tensing, hunching up towards the
neck. Others reveal anxiety by fidgeting, gesturing with their
hands as they talk, or biting their nails, and so on. What
are your signs? Do you jiggle your foot? Are your ankles or
upper thighs tense? If so, are your legs tightly crossed? Do
you feel tension in your arms? Are you, by any chance, fold-
ing your arms across your chest and thereby limiting your
oxygen intake? Is your forehead creased in a frown, or is
there pressure behind the eyebrows or at the sides of your
temple? Do you have a permanent frown line etched between
your brows?

The jaw and chest areas are especially important because
breathing is easily obstructed here. How does this happen? A
tensed muscle is short and fattish. A relaxed muscle lies flat
and is more elongated. As anxiety escalates, tense muscles create a constriction in the air passageway. Listen to your voice.
Like a pitch pipe, its tone will rise as you grow more upset.
Blocked passageways mean that much-needed oxygen is cut
off from the brain. One cannot think. When people say they
are confused, what is often happening is that their brain is cut
off from its life source, precious oxygen.

Is your jaw tight or are your lips pursed? If you experience
any pressure in the chest area, chances are that the muscles
surrounding the trachea and esophagus are also tight. Can
you feel any constriction in your throat? Is your voice higher
than normal? Or has "normal" for you become a high,
squeaky tone?

I've noticed combinations in my own reactions to stress.
When I'm fatigued towards the end of a busy workday, even

ordinary background noise suddenly becomes annoying. At the same time, I'm aware that my right ankle is bent upwards, signalling tension in my right leg. I've also become aware that typically my shoulders will be hunched up as well. These insights make it possible for me to start rotating my ankles and, simultaneously, do relaxation exercises like making circular motions with my arms to release the tension in my shoulders. If noise is irritating me, I can turn off the radio playing background music in the waiting room. Usually, I don't even hear it.

If you recognize ankle and/or neck stress, take a moment to try this: Hang your arms at the sides of your chair, and let your head fall forward towards your chin. Imagine there is a great weight attached to your wrists that is pulling down, making your arms feel heavier and heavier. Continue until you experience a tingling in your fingers. Feel the muscles across your back and shoulders. Are they stretching out and elongating? If so, keep your arms hanging at your side but raise your head and let the relaxation continue to spread. To release ankle tension, rotate your ankle at the same time. This way you are simultaneously reducing the tension damage done to both areas..

Incidentally, any time you are aware of fatigue, slow down! While you are working, take a long, deep breath and then extend your exhale slightly longer than usual. The next breath will go even deeper. Only through awareness of these physiological reactions will an immediate remedy be possible.

For *each of the major emotions*, try to zero in on *where* you feel muscle tension and which nerves are signalling your distress.

1–3. ENERGY LEVEL   This one is relatively simple.

Heaviness describes a decrease in adrenalin that occurs during sadness or depression. At such times, there is a change in the chemical reaction in the synapse, the space between the body cells. Here the dendrites, the receptor membrane of a neuron, receive the stimulation. Ordinarily, the axons

conduct nervous impulses away from the synapse to produce activity in the distant parts of the organism where other
nerves, muscles, or glands are in turn stimulated. However, in
this case, the electrical charge flowing through the body cells
is slowed down as it hits the changed chemical reaction in
the synapse. As a consequence, we feel sluggish. When people
are depressed, they move their eyes more slowly, speak with
more hesitation. Their reflexes are slowed down and their
co-ordination may be affected. Their digestive system churns
and, being uptight, people often become constipated. Over
time, *everything* moves more slowly.

Lightness describes an increase in adrenalin. When "fight
or flight" responses are appropriate, the adrenal glands work
overtime, digestion is speeded up, and other hormones are
released into the bloodstream. The heart adjusts to an "emergency" by changes in rate, force, and contractions. As Archibald Hart points out in *The Hidden Link Between Adrenalin
and Stress*, the heart has "no direct connection to the nervous
system to receive signals from the brain, but it is designed
to respond to signals from the complex chemical messengers
circulating in the blood – including the adrenalin hormones"
(16). Unfortunately, these same messengers, when out of balance over a long period of time, can literally cause irreparable
damage to the heart.

Remember that stress can remain hidden. We adapt to situations that are harmful to us. What's more, good things can
also create stress. We may feel excited by our work and be
happiest when challenged by a new idea. Or we may become
energized when we're faced with a crisis or emergency in our
latest project. Yet, despite feeling exhilarated, we may still
experience panic reactions, irregular heartbeat, ulcers, or high
blood pressure. The heart does not acknowledge the difference between "good" and "bad" stress; it responds only to the
excess of adrenalin.

When you experience a strong emotion, ask yourself if your adrenalin is up or down. *Do you feel heavy, or light?*

1–4. BODY POSITION Body language is complex. When you feel assertive or angry, do you lean or move forward? When on the defensive, do you sit back or withdraw physically from the situation? When anxious or agitated, do you tend to become restless, get up and down frequently, or move around in your chair? Do you tap your feet or drum your hands on the desk? Do you go to the washroom more frequently? Do you look down and slump forward when you are sad or discouraged? When you've taken a remark personally or have otherwise been offended, do you find yourself crossing your arms and legs as if to protect yourself?

One day one of my workaholic clients, an ambitious executive, was sitting slumped in his chair. His head was resting on his chest and he was staring at the floor. I asked him to freeze and then imitated his slumped position. After a few moments, I commented, "I can hardly breath now, can you? I have a suspicion that part of you doesn't want to be here!" Gordon laughed and told me he had no idea he was sitting like that. This gave us a chance to discuss whether he was here for himself or to please his wife. He was used to being in charge, and he admitted that being in a "learning" position was not easy for him.

When I was writing my book on workaholics, I wrote only on Mondays. Each week I found it hard to get back to where I was the week before. I could tell I was anxious because I would start to write and then suddenly remember that I hadn't checked in with my answering service. I would start to write again and then remember that I needed to put the wash in the drier.

At this point, I would toss my pencil up in the air and then make a wide sweeping circle with my arms. This motion served to open up my chest area so that I could breathe properly once again.

Circles plug us into the nurturing, feeling side of ourselves. Thinking, which is goal-oriented and linear in its processing, is best represented by a straight line! Pretending to conduct a symphony when you're upset isn't such a bad idea.

Make notes to record the information you are gradually discovering about yourself. It's like detective work! Try to become aware of your body position when you notice a shift or change in emotion. Note physiological changes and your energy level for each feeling. Later on, this information will hopefully jump to your attention and automatically be recorded in your mind.

1–5. LABELLING   By attaching a label, I mean *identifying and giving a name* to the feeling. Sometimes we recognize our body's reactions but we don't know what to call the feeling that is summoned. At other times, we can name it but have to work backwards from there to become aware of our typical reactions.

Jenny, a social worker, told me that she knew when she was angry. "This is ridiculous. No one has to tell me I'm angry!" When I asked her what was happening inside physiologically when she was angry, she admitted, "Well, I don't know that!" I suggested that the next time she found herself angry, she pay attention to her body to see if she could figure it out.

The following week, she burst into my office and said with glee, "Guess what I found out about myself this week? The other day, I was *really* angry. I found myself turning purple. My fingers dug into the palm of my hand, and I locked my jaw. I could even hear my teeth click!" Then she looked surprised. "I never knew I did that." Later, we'll find out what was happening in Jenny's life when she gained this insight.

1–6. ACHILLES' HEELS   Watch for *situations that typically trigger* certain feelings. In other words, learn which situations tap into your weaknesses or sore points. If you are able to problem-solve right away, this may help reduce your stress. Quick action, however, will only make the situation easier to handle if you manage to remain in control.

Let's say your father was a perfectionist and he criticized you unmercifully when you were growing up. Your stress level around criticism is apt to be sky-high, so you may need to react sooner than others when faced with *any* criticism. Say, for example, that someone has just reprimanded you and is about to continue. You may need to intervene and inform that person, "I don't handle criticism that well." (You don't need to burden the listener with the Family Saga.) You might add, "I'll think about what you just said, and get back to you. I'd like to discuss it further then."

If the other person respects your vulnerability, he or she will stop. If not, you may have to take a stronger stand. "I don't think you understand the significance of what I said. I'm leaving now, but I'd like to continue this discussion when I feel calm and better able to listen."

1–7. HOMEWORK   You might well ask: "How can I get in touch with my physiological changes, my energy level, and my body position, all at the same time?"

Try this exercise daily until it becomes a natural process. At least six or eight times a day, stop and ask yourself these awareness and labelling questions: How do I feel *right now*? *What do I call* this feeling? *Where in my body* am I noticing a reaction? *What muscles or nerves* are sending messages letting me know about this feeling? *Has my body position just changed*? Am I sitting, standing, or moving?

You will tend to remember to do this when there has just been a shift or change in emotion. Our minds process information in a steady stream. Unless there is some significant change in the tone of a conversation, a harsh unwelcome criticism, or we suddenly become aware of a toxic stimulus in our environment, there is little reason for awareness to dramatically shift.   .

Step 2 – Justification

As soon as you can identify and name the feeling, it is time for some *reality-testing*. Ask yourself, *"Is this emotion a valid one*, considering what is actually going on right now? If not, *what might be causing me to react* this way? And do I think my response was *appropriate and sensitive* considering the circumstances?

It is necessary to explore what is going on at a conscious level, but also important to go further. From a deep, unconscious level, *what memories of past experiences may be aroused* to elicit this particular emotional response?

2–1. CONSCIOUS AND UNCONSCIOUS DATA   Reflect on what is happening in your *immediate* experience that might have triggered the identified feeling.
Conscious Data. Ask yourself:

1. *What* just happened?
2. *Who* said what?
3. What *specifically* am I reacting to in this situation?
4. What did I *dream* last night that still might be affecting me?

Unconscious Data. Ask yourself:

5. Am I *overreacting or acting impulsively* because of a *layering* of old feelings over present ones?

Remember to search for information from your day, as well as any "unfinished business" from the past few days or weeks – or sometimes even years, right back to childhood if necessary. Stories often have long histories! In my story, there were two justifications for my feelings of sadness. One was the incident from the night before involving my daughter. The other was the ongoing but impending death of a close friend.

Let me relate another personal example. This time the experience occurred on the same day as my recognition of it. One day, some years ago, I was returning from a dental appointment, and was stopped at a traffic light near a McDonald's outlet. A little old lady dressed in layers of beige-coloured clothing was going through a nearby garbage bin. Her threadbare coat with its frayed hem covered bulky sweaters and a woolen dirndl skirt. A tattered green scarf was wound round her neck. Her wizened face was framed by a lopsided bonnet tied around her chin, and she wore wire-framed spectacles. I can still feel the pathos I felt as I watched her fumbling deep inside the waste bin for what seemed like forever. Her grocery bags were propped up against the bin. Was she looking for discarded hamburger, cigarette butts, or half-eaten buns?

I had observed street people in New York, but this was the first one I had seen in this neighbourhood. I was naturally upset by what I saw. As I drove back to my office, I wondered where she slept, where her family was, and how circumstances had led her to this.

Back at the office, I got involved with clients and forgot all about her. That is, until my five o'clock client was late. For no apparent reason, I suddenly felt overwhelmed. What in the world was troubling me? The previous sessions had gone well, and there had been no telephone interruptions. All at once I "*saw*" her and, through association, figured out that my feelings of pathos needed to be dealt with further. I needed to learn a lot more about people like her, and what was being done for them in our community.

Awareness after-the-fact occurs because immediate problems take first priority on our energy. The mind has a way of determining priority and ordering our experiences, temporarily submerging troublesome information until it finally resurfaces during a lull in activity.

2–2. HOW THE MIND STORES INFORMATION   The next step, which involves getting in touch with information about feelings from the unconscious (*question 5*), is not an easy one. At this point, let's digress a moment.

The mind stores information in bits and pieces. The corner of the desk in my office, for example, has a number of attributes – it is triangular-shaped, grey-coloured, made from Formica, one-inch thick, and is called a desk top. The mind gathers all this information and stores it separately and as a whole. To retrieve a person's face from memory, a number of facial features must be recalled. Often, we remember that someone's name starts with an S, but we must wait until further information clicks into place. Then we might recall that the person's name is Shelley. A poet, a writer, or the name Percy may have been the association needed to provide us with the clue, the missing piece.

W. Kintsch, in *Learning, Memory, and Conceptual Processes*, reports that Donald Hebb, a researcher interested in learning and behaviour, postulated two kinds of memory. Long-term memory is "based upon a structural trace and is permanent except for interference from other long-term traces; and short-term memory, [is] based upon an activity trace" (146). Information that is rehearsed out loud for more than sixty seconds goes into long-term memory, and its capacity is essentially unlimited. Forgetting is relatively slow and, according to Kintsch, takes two forms: "actual loss of information and inability to retrieve information which is nevertheless still in storage" (142).

Short-term or trace memory, Kintsch further explains, is the information we remember, like a seven-digit telephone number, that fades within fifteen to twenty seconds. This memory has a limited capacity, "although it may be retained in primary memory for more extended periods through rehearsal" (142). Obviously, the more easily one learns to repress certain information, the more difficult it becomes to retrieve such unconscious memories.

Much of our memory does lie within the unconscious, and our psychological growth often depends on uncovering such repressed information, both from early childhood and from the recent past. Only then is it possible to gain the insights necessary to transform unhealthy thoughts and actions into mature and positive behaviour.

In the 1950s, Wilder Penfield, a brain surgeon in Montreal, stimulated the brains of his patients during surgery in order to determine what functions the various parts of the brain perform. His research team was able to map correspondences between areas on the surface of the cortex and subjective experiences. A. Lazerson, in *Psychology Today: An Introduction*, describes one finding. By "applying a tiny electric current to points on the temporal lobe of the cerebral cortex: One woman heard a familiar song so clearly that she thought a record was played in the operating room" (315).

I remember hearing about an investigation in which one lobe of the brain was triggered during surgery. The patient had a memory of a picnic many years before. This person apparently could smell the food at the picnic, feel the sun, hear the birds, and remember conversations he had had previously with classmates whom he hadn't seen for years.

This type of research led to the "computer" theory of memory. Before it was done, researchers had no idea of the scope of the information stored in the unconscious. As a student, I remember being delighted to learn that all I had to do was figure out how to retrieve that information through the processes of association and/or recall. In association, an object or person is linked to another through mental connections or bonds between ideas, memories, or sensations. In recall, stored information that we have learned or experienced in the past is retrieved or remembered at will.

2–3. UNCONSCIOUS MEMORIES   In order to understand our feelings, we need to *sort out* <u>what</u> *we are bringing in from the past*, as distinct from what is actually happening in the present. It is important to *look for layering of old feelings over present ones*. When a couple fight over money, for example, it is likely that residual emotions from past related quarrels will flood up and colour their present feelings.

Imagine you have just met someone who makes you feel anxious, although you're only mildly aware of this. Your conversation is going well, but suddenly this fellow says something sarcastic, and you find yourself getting *really* angry. An *overreaction* to a situation or to a person is often a signal that the unconscious is working overtime. At this moment, you realize that this man looks like a kid in your Grade 6 class who used to hammer you with sarcastic, stinging comments. He is not that person, however, and your anger is *out of all proportion* to what is actually going on.

If you are able to recognize this association immediately, you can take responsibility for your inappropriate response. You might explain to the man that he just happens to resemble an old school chum, who, by coincidence, also used sarcasm to your great discomfort. "I guess you triggered some ghosts there. I apologize," you might add.

Jenny, a client mentioned earlier, whom I'd asked to monitor her responses when she became angry, gave me a wonderful example of the unconscious at work. After completing high school, she had gone across the country to attend university. During her second year, she fell in love with her university professor. They married after her graduation and things went well until she decided to return to university to get a master's degree. This training helped Jenny develop her own thinking and professional expertise, and she became more vocal about her own opinions and creative ideas. Concurrently, she also became more assertive and complained to Simon, her husband, about how unfair it was that he did not share household responsibilities.

The marriage eventually did not survive the tensions that Simon's scathing criticisms and neglect created. Jenny's self-esteem was badly shaken by her experience, and she returned to her parents' home to rest and recharge. She told me about a letter she had written to Simon requesting that he send on her belongings. What arrived one day on a truck, c.o.d., was all her books, the long, heavy boards from her bookcase, and the bricks that propped up its shelves. Nothing else – none of her files or records, no clothes, make-up, or treasured knick-knacks. A very angry statement from Simon, it appeared. She was absolutely furious!

Jenny recalled that she didn't sleep very well that night, so she got up about five a.m. and went downstairs to her parents' den. "I walked through the door, and all of a sudden, I felt extremely angry. At the time, I had no idea why. Then I remembered you suggesting that the next time I felt angry, I take some time to learn more about my reactions."

Jenny continued, "I sat myself down. As I did this, a book on the couch caught my eye. It must have been from the pile of books that arrived the day before. Maybe Mom or Dad had been reading it." When Jenny entered the room a few minutes earlier, she had not "seen" the book because she was lost in her own thoughts. However, her brain "*saw*" it, and *through association*, registered the rage she experienced after the truck delivered its unwelcome contents.

It was only after Jenny actually "saw" the book that she was able to locate the source of her present anger. Her response made perfect sense now. As Jenny put it, "It's frustrating that it takes me so long to figure it all out! But hopefully, if I can learn to *Internalize,* I just might clue in sooner."

If we become aware of how an association or recalled memory is affecting our response early enough, we have a better chance of handling the situation while the person is still present or the event is ongoing.

2–4. ESTABLISHING THE LEVEL OF FEELING When exploring whether your feelings are appropriate, it helps to imagine the feeling (for instance, sadness) on a perpendicular line. To the left of this line, there is a stress curve running on a 45-degree angle to the top. The top is the point at which your defenses take over.

ESTABLISHING THE LEVEL OF FEELING

You can handle moderate levels of sadness with little obvious discomfort. However, both ends of the stress curve cause equal discomfort. The lower end – not being able to express sadness – is stressful. As an example, have you ever attended a funeral and worried that you might sob uncontrollably if you let yourself go? To prevent this, you force yourself to tune out of the service, to think about something else. You do manage to get through it, but this blocking off effort has taken its toll on your energy.

Near the upper range of the curve, your sadness level is elevated to the point that you are obviously experiencing discomfort and even pain. Tears are spilling down your face, and there is a choking sensation in your throat.

2–5. SOUNDING THE ALARM   The crucial question to ask at this point in the internalizing process is, am I still comfortable and in control or am I becoming overstressed?

I know when I'm not okay because I get a "jiggly" or agitated feeling, and I can't sit still. I call this sensation "feeling yucky." *Naming the reaction* helps me take responsibility for it and sends a signal that I better start problem-solving right away. Otherwise, my defenses will mobilize and complicate or block my ability to seek solutions. Words such as irritated, perturbed, antsy, or "hyper" may better describe your distress signals.

Before you are ready to problem-solve, however, there is one more step. Take time to fully *feel* your emotions.

Step 3 – Experiencing

When we fail to do our best, or we lose something of value, or things don't go our way, we suffer mini-losses. Our response to these losses I call "mini-grieving." Such a response is usually of relatively short duration.

Major losses may result from the death of someone close to us, the break-up of a relationship, an illness or accident, or the loss of a job. Whatever the reason, time and energy must be devoted to working through and grieving that loss, however long it takes.

We must *feel the feeling* once we identify what it is, *stay with it*, and allow ourselves to *fully experience* its impact. And then we need to think about how and why we react to certain things this way. Remember, from the original story, how once I recognized that I was feeling sad, I plugged into that sadness and fully experienced it. Those fearful of "going down that path" might bang pots and pans instead or distract themselves by jumping back on their personal "Gerbil Wheel," and running themselves ragged. Or they may sit comatose in front of the TV and give in to their despair. They can't think and they won't feel, so no solutions surface up to consciousness.

One of my clients, Dino, told me that one day he found himself going downstairs when it suddenly hit him how anxious he was. "I sat down on the middle stair, then and there. For the next few minutes, I stayed put and pondered all the reasons I had for being anxious." Then he grinned. "I felt like a kid discovering what was in Pandora's box! And surprisingly, at least to me," he added, "the stuff I came up with wasn't really all that bad!"

People who are prone to severe depression are often terrified of letting themselves experience deeply painful feelings. Who is going to pull them back up if they sink? Ironically, when I accompany a client by listening empathically to his or her painful story and agree in response that things are pretty bad, something remarkable happens. The person starts to tell me why *everything* isn't terrible. Some story about a positive event typically emerges into consciousness. Once this has happened enough times, people realize that they can pull themselves back from the brink of despair. Suddenly, these awful moments don't last quite as long. And they don't happen so often!

This sorting-out process takes time and energy and therefore drains your resources temporarily. Often the immediate solution is to *simplify, simplify, simplify*. Lower your expectations about what you hope to achieve that day. Make sure you get extra rest and relaxation time during this period to help sustain your strength.

3–1. NURTURE YOURSELF Stay alert and let your strongest sense, be it sight, sound, touch, or smell, fill you up. If you like music, play one of your favourites. If you love colour, leaf through one of your treasured art books. Or step outside and watch the clouds drift by. Take time to smell a flower and savour the fresh air.

At this point I often use humour to improve my disposition. One morning last fall I was stopped at a red light on my way to work. Two cute twin girls, about eight years old, with pigtails hanging down their backs, were crossing the street in front of my car. I noticed that around each twin's waist was a bright red skipping rope, which effectively tied them together. The twin in front looked to be in charge of these antics. I watched as they waited to cross at the light to head off to school and wondered if the same little imp would take the "lead." Sure enough, she did, and away they marched.

As I continued my journey, I entertained myself wondering if being twins motivated these girls to play this amusing game. My mind wandered to a radio program my sister and I listened to as children. Every morning, Happy Hank would tell us when we were supposed to put on our underwear, skirts, blouses, socks, and shoes! I laughed as I contemplated whether the "Happy Hank" show would survive our modern-day censorship.

As I neared the office, I thought I saw what looked like two workmen playing patty-cake! Drawing closer, I realized the men were installing fence posts. Each was pushing back against the drill handle as it came round to his side. By the time I got to the office, my "mood" had been transformed.

If you share this muse, you can go out any time of the day or night, and play with what is happening before your eyes. It's a wonderful gift to help you lighten up.

3–2. EXCEPTIONS TO STAYING WITH YOUR FEELINGS
It was mentioned earlier that there are four negative feelings

that will be dealt with separately. Don't stay long in the *Big Four – Anger, Anxiety, Fear,* and *Pain.* These feelings quickly escalate, and, before you know it, you are likely to exceed your stress limit, and lose control. Try this exercise: Divide a piece of paper into four squares, and at each quadrant's upper left-hand corner, write:

1. *Anger,* 2. *Anxiety,* 3. *Fear,* and 4. *Pain,* respectively. Then, as you monitor your feelings each day in the upcoming months, record your reactions.

You may discover, for instance, that among your *physiological* responses to *anger* are one or more the following:
- My cheeks flush with pink.
- My stomach tightens and feels cramped.
- My forehead creases as I frown, and so on.

Your *energy level* will be up, activated by a surge of adrenalin preparing you to take action.

Your *body position* may reveal a defensive stance:
- I fold my arms across my chest.
- I straighten up, and my body goes rigid and stiff.
- I lean far forward as I speak, and so on.

After working on this list for six to eight weeks, ask yourself this important question: *Which one of these responses happens first?* In the future, your *first response* will be the one you pay special attention to. This gives you the opportunity to reduce the symptoms of stress *before* muscle spasms, chest pains, or headaches cause further stress damage. Your well-being depends on prevention. Don't wait until more extreme reactions signal your distress. By then, it's usually too late to maintain inner control. Defense mechanisms have a way of "taking charge" of your life.

3–3. DEFENSE MECHANISMS   It is important to take corrective action as soon as you are aware of being overstressed.

Otherwise, emotional control will evaporate and your defenses will take over. You risk finding yourself locked in the grip of a mood or overwhelmed by rage.

We use defense mechanisms every day and, to a degree, they are adaptive and protect us temporarily from feeling the pain of insecurity, low self-esteem, and threatening circumstances. By "fooling" ourselves and remaining oblivious, however, we leave ourselves exposed to the manipulations of others who recognize our vulnerabilities and know how to exploit them.

If our defenses remain unconscious, they work against us. They block out reality and disorient our decision-making functions. These disruptive dynamics can leave us emotionally crippled, and soon neurotic behaviours threaten our stability and even sanity. Eventually, we may put ourselves at risk of experiencing episodic psychotic breaks with reality or suffering a nervous breakdown.

The mind has an incredible capacity to block out incidents we cannot handle, for whatever reason. This blockage may be adaptive at some point in our lives, but haunt us later when associations break through the layer of denial. A child whose ego strength is inadequate to handle abuse may block out a painful memory from consciousness altogether. That is, until years later some incident triggers a distraught feeling or terrifying childhood recollection.

The following brief descriptions of the key defense mechanisms are adapted from R. Campbell's *Psychiatric Dictionary* and A. Lazerson's *Psychology Today: An Introduction*.

Projection.   One's own attitudes, feelings, or thoughts are ascribed to others, especially if they are considered undesirable. We use innocent people as scapegoats, and lash out and blame them for *our* shortcomings or mistakes. We thus free ourselves from pain by denying responsibility.

Obsession/Compulsion. In order to avoid experiencing anxiety when an idea, emotion, or impulse *persists* in forcing itself into our consciousness, our thinking becomes obsessive. We distract ourselves and narrow our focus, and our thoughts *fixate* on something such as one particular idea or one aspect of another individual. Over time, the fixation may enlarge to encompass the pursuit of an ambitious goal. At pathological levels, the sufferer loses conscious control of his thoughts. Any attempts to manoeuvre or block repetitive thoughts typically fail to divert attention away to something or someone else and anxiety increases.

Compulsions are obsessive behaviours that come from a *strong impulse to act*, contrary to one's will. A person leaving for work may have to return to the kitchen four or five times to check to see if she turned off the stove. Only then can she lock the door and leave. Such rituals can become extremely complicated when the routine no longer eases anxiety and a number of extra actions must be added. Failure to perform the trivial or stereotypical act generates acute anxiety. Sadly, only temporary relief is gained from each repetition.

Eventually, obsessions and compulsions develop a life of their own and dictate behaviour. The person gradually loses self-control, feels powerless, and becomes neurotic. A psychotic breakdown reflects a complete loss of reality wherein the obsession or compulsion becomes totally irrational or bizarre. The individual is relentlessly driven to perform the compulsive act or thoughts of going crazy will surface. Such thoughts become torturous as fear grips the psyche and will not let go.

Rationalization.   An act or idea is *justified* or made to appear reasonable when, in fact, it is irrational and illogical. "I decided not to go to her party because she is so immature and dresses like a teenager," was one excuse used by an insecure client who was terrified of group interaction. Rationalizing is a cognitive cover-up, an explanation that preserves a person's self-esteem and helps him or her avoid anxiety when there is a threat of criticism or conflict. False but plausible reasons are given to justify the person's conduct. Rationalization usually involves a web of explanations and if one fact is challenged, several more are held in reserve to support the claim. Deluded self-justifications eventually become so convoluted and complex that the person fails to problem-solve altogether and becomes caught in a tangled web of shifting stories.

While excessive intellectualizing protects the person from dealing with the emotional aspects of a problem that they often have created, the effects on others who are exposed to their manipulation is totally disregarded. Empathy and compassion take a back seat to opportunistic escapism.

Dissociation. This is the act of *separating or disconnecting* oneself from conflicting attitudes, impulses, or even parts of the personality. One part of consciousness splits off. Troublesome people and things are simply ignored. In a more pathological form, they cease to exist, removed from consciousness. One chronic workaholic who had become very abusive with his family never saw them again after his wife left with the children. He quickly moved to a different city, soon remarried, and refused to answer any calls or mail from his children. The most extreme form of dissociation occurs in cases of amnesia or multiple personality, where two or more distinct, but not autonomous, personalities are present in one individual.

Isolation. Isolation or *compartmentalization* is the fragmentation of the psyche. One part of the personality is kept separate from the whole. A man who declares emphatically that he is a good husband and father, yet neglects to mention that he is having an affair with his secretary and rarely comes home before the children are ready for bed is compartmentalizing his life. Each compartment is kept separate and distinct.

Repression. The repressed person *remains oblivious* to anxiety or guilt-producing impulses or fails to remember deep emotional or traumatic past events. One naïve woman I know takes pride in always having a smile on her face. Negative situations rarely touch her, and she refuses to watch the news or read the newspaper. "There's too much going wrong in the world," she protests. Repression may or may not be deliberate, but it is not forgetting. Intensive psychotherapy, hypnosis, or drugs are often necessary to recover the lost memories or painful conflicts that triggered the original response.

Reaction Formation. In this defense, conscious traits and behavioural patterns are developed in the ego that are *opposite to those that have been disowned.* Extreme empathy may cover sadistic impulses; exaggerated manners may conceal disdain. The intensity of the exaggeration is a clue as to whether or not a person's motivation is truly well-intentioned and genuine. Dan, a university student, lavished praise on his competitor and told a fellow student how much he admired him. When out of earshot, however, he let slip a caustic and disdainful remark about his "hero." Later, Dan denied anything but admiration. His envy was completely disowned.

There are other defense mechanisms, such as regression, that may involve a temporary return to an earlier stage of adaptation when the person is threatened or under stress; and sublimation, where instincts or impulses are redirected or modified to meet the conventional standards of society.

We all need to *be aware of our own defense mechanisms.* Unfortunately, denial makes this difficult. It's best to remember that these mechanisms are adaptive only to a point. After that, *beware!*

PITFALLS ON THE JOURNEY

The next step in our journey towards inner balance is, oddly enough, learning when *not* to problem-solve! I cannot promise that *Internalizing* will teach you to always be in control. All of us get upset. My hope is that you will learn to identify when you are starting to "lose it," thus giving yourself enough time to avoid costly mistakes.

Chapter 8 is about establishing inner control. To be both effective and wise, we need to know not only what we think *and* feel but also make an effort to understand the thoughts and feelings of the other party. Be patient. It takes time and energy to seek workable solutions, to reach consensus, or decide to agree to disagree. The mutual satisfaction of all concerned is the goal.

Not an easy task certainly, but let's begin.

8

The Journey – Stage 2, Rescheduling

Problem-Solving. Now or Later, That Is the Question!

Slow and steady wins the race.

INTERVENTION – TIMING IS EVERYTHING!

Like Sally and Peter, you are beginning to be super aware of your body. When something happens, you monitor its reactions. You tune in to exactly which muscles and nerve endings are registering your present emotional state by automatically sending signals to your brain. You then label the emotion by naming it. Take anger as an example. You might say to yourself: "Wow, am I ever fuming inside my gut! My shoulder blades are all hunched up, and my blood pressure is rising fast." There may be other sites affected in your body, but for now this information is good enough.

You then use your *Thinking problem-solving* function to ask yourself these five key questions:

Conscious Data:
1. *What* just happened?
2. *Who* said what?
3. What *specifically* am I reacting to in this situation?
4. What did I *dream* last night that still might be affecting me?

Unconscious Data:

5. Am I *overreacting or acting impulsively* because of a layering of old feelings over present ones?

Whatever you determine is the cause of your upset, NOW may or may not be the time to take some action, especially if your anger is approaching a boiling point. However, without some form of intervention, you're liable to start projecting blame or otherwise go off the deep end using one of your other defensive tactics.

Listen to your intuition. Is an inner voice warning you that your stress level is already over-the-top? Or is it telling you: "Better not feel all that confident about being able to stay in control right now."

The basic dilemma becomes the question "Do you problem-solve now – that is, let the other person know that their troublesome action is not okay with you – or make a decision to *reschedule* your intervention to a later time?" If you are to make a wise choice and handle the situation well, your intervention must be fair and appropriately timed for *both* parties.

If you are still in control of your feelings and able to think clearly, there are two further considerations before you continue. One concerns timing and the other explores whether the action you choose to take is appropriate to the situation or place.

Timing

Your escalating stress level may shout *hurry up*, you'd better problem-solve *now*, *before* you do lose control. At this point, an *important question* becomes, "But what is going on with the person I need to speak with?" Sensitivity is essential when other people are involved in *your* efforts to seek some sort of resolution.

1. IS THE OTHER PERSON ABLE TO LISTEN? Sally has been aware all day that her anxiety is sky-high. She and Peter had a tremendous blow-up on Monday morning. Sally had been worrying about Peter's health for some time. During much of the weekend, Peter was irritable and short with Sally. She watched him pacing up and down in agitation. His face looked flushed and puffy.

Sally, the proverbial "fixer," decided to "help" by saying, "Peter, how about sitting down and having some breakfast with me this morning? You need to relax and start out your day with a full stomach. You were like a caged lion all weekend." Sally's invitation may have been well-intentioned, but it sparked a flame in Peter. He heard only criticism. Peter no longer wanted *anyone* to tell him what to do, even if it was good advice.

Peter lashed out at Sally, sneering, "I'm sick and tired of your nagging, whiny voice! You've got time to sit around all day, drink coffee, and read your newspaper. It must be nice!" Then he added an all too familiar dig: "Why don't you get yourself a decent job, and I'll be glad to retire!"

Sally was devastated. Peter's cruel jab hurt deeply because Sally had tried to get herself back into the workforce. Two years earlier, she had taken several small business courses and had begun a commercial venture with a friend. At first, Peter was amused, but this gave way to stubborn resistance. Sally was frustrated at every turn because Peter continued to put demands on her time. He refused to baby-sit when Sally needed to work late. He still expected Sally to entertain his clients and to accompany him to business conventions. Peter belittled her efforts, in truth, because it took attention away from him.

Any time the kids complained about the extra work they had to take on, Peter would use the opportunity to nitpick, usually about some mundane matter. To add fuel to the fire, he would accuse her, in front of the children, of not being there for any of them! Sally finally caved in and resigned herself to staying home to keep the peace.

This particular day, rather than spend all day fretting, Sally made a decision to remain calm. She resolved to speak to Peter when he came home that evening. Then, she was able to let go. At six o'clock, Peter walked in the door and announced to one and all that he had the flu. "I'm going straight to bed."

If Sally had decided to go ahead with her plan to let Peter know how she felt about his recent tirade, she would have been fighting a losing battle. Both parties must be *fully present* if lasting solutions are to be found. As we will soon learn, Sally's best course was to let Peter know she did wish to speak with him but was willing to postpone what she had to say until Peter was feeling better.

2. TIME OF DAY   Some people are best in the morning. Others don't truly wake up until noon. They shine at night, so staying up late is no problem for this group. Keep in mind your own and others' biological clock when you next decide to speak about an unresolved issue with someone you know well.

Typically, we suffer periods of low energy some time during the day. For many, about an hour after lunch is deadly. Chuck, a client, told me he realized that the quarrels between himself and his wife, Shirley, occurred most often between the time he got home from work and supper time. I queried whether he might be experiencing some hypoglycemia and be irritable because of a drop in his blood sugars. To test this out, Chuck decided he would have a snack and go for a walk before dinner. Then he added, "I won't speak to Shirley about what I'm upset about till after supper."

About a month later, I asked Chuck how his new plan was working. He looked somewhat sheepish as he explained, "I've been waiting until after supper, as I said I would." Then he confessed, "The problem is, though, quite frankly by then I can't remember what it was I was going to talk to Shirley about!"

I was not surprised by his discovery because Chuck and I had been working on the Myers-Briggs typology and he had scored as a Feeler. It's somewhat unusual for a Feeler to go into engineering, unless it involves human engineering. Chuck admitted he had gone into engineering to please his father. He hated his job and did not feel at ease with his co-workers. He often felt like the odd man out, especially when his feeling values and language were misunderstood. Unfortunately, Shirley had found herself on the receiving end of Chuck's frustrations when he walked in the door at night. "Miraculously," Chuck assured me, "things seem to be getting better between us."

3. COMPLICATIONS   Sometimes alcohol or drugs complicate an already difficult situation. Betty and Kent, another couple I worked with, resolved to go out regularly for "romantic evenings," as they called them. Inevitably, they would end up quarrelling, and their relationship remained rocky. I asked them whether they were drinking too much, and both vehemently denied any such thing.

Intuitively, I still suspected alcohol might be a problem. One day, after another distressing tale, I asked this couple if they would be willing to try something. "If one of you is still angry about something, would you be willing to promise yourself that you won't drink any alcohol that night? The other person is free to do whatever he wishes." This was reluctantly agreed to and over the next month, they did have some good times together.

Then one day I got a frantic phone call from Betty. "There's no way I'm staying with that man! Last night was the last straw." She proceeded to launch into an angry litany of her husband's faults, until I finally stopped her.

"By the way, Betty, did you have anything to drink at the restaurant last night?" There was a long pause, and then a high, squeaky voice drifted over the phone. "Well, as a matter of fact I did," she reluctantly admitted.

I laughed. "Sounds to me like you blew our agreement!" Betty hesitated, and then she laughed, too. "I did, didn't I!"

"Well, try again," I encouraged and then added, "I think we'd better have a serious chat about whether you two just might have an alcohol problem." Many months later, Betty and Kent enrolled in an Alcoholics Anonymous program and agreed to quit drinking altogether. Betty told me that the day she phoned me was a turning point for her, an "ah-ha" experience.

As she put it, "Never before had it really dawned on me that alcohol leaves me with no self-control. I can't communicate the way you taught me when I have even one drink." In chapter 9, we will find out how individuals can communicate so that their partner is truly able to listen, without becoming defensive and counterattacking. In other words, how such couples learn to avoid destructive power struggles.

Appropriateness

As well as the timing of any problem-solving intervention, the appropriateness of the situation must also be considered. If you become upset, consider the following *before* you proceed to act.

1. DO YOU LIVE OR WORK WITH THIS PERSON? Problem-solving takes a great deal of energy. It is important not to waste our resources fussing over a situation or something that, in the long run, is not a major issue. In other words, the question becomes, "If I problem-solve right now, will I be spending my energy wisely?"

Now, ask yourself these three questions. First, can the other person handle my intervention? Second, will it do any good? (For example, is the person I'm angry with unwell? Is he too young to understand the significance of my upset? Is she too old, not very bright, or too confused in her thinking?) Lastly, is this someone I have to interact with again?

If you live or work with the person, then it is important to invest your energies in improving communication, rectifying a misunderstanding, or correcting an injustice. If not, *let it go*. When a store clerk or gas station attendant is rude, it's easy to get mad. But instead of verbalizing your annoyance, just mutter to yourself something like "What a jerky thing to say!" Take a deep breath and let go. Few similar situations truly merit pumping unnecessary adrenalin into your already overloaded system.

2. WHAT TO DO IN A GROUP SITUATION WHEN YOU BECOME UPSET   If your spouse, partner, or friend says something upsetting in public, an important question to ask yourself *before* you decide to respond is whether *now* is the right time. No one else need be embarrassed or, for that matter, involved in your upset.

Let's say you and your spouse are at a friend's dinner party. Your wife tells a story about an embarrassing episode from a recent trip. You find yourself becoming increasingly alarmed as she finishes. Rather than relaying this information directly while both of you are surrounded by fellow guests, signal your displeasure right away. You might make eye contact and frown, or even cough. Then, when you leave the party, say something like, "Did you notice earlier in the evening when you were talking about our trip that I was frowning at you? I'm very upset that you even mentioned that trip because some of my co-workers were there. You know how important privacy is to me." This lets your spouse know why you are upset and gives her the opportunity to explain why she brought up the topic of your holiday.

Otherwise, you're apt to let your anger simmer for a couple of days before you do something. Then you'll have to recreate the whole scenario to pinpoint what was said and when it was said. An inflammatory version of such a conversation might go something like this: "Remember last Saturday when you were telling that story to the Browns about our trip to Texas? Why did you have to go *on and on* about it? I can't believe you *had the gall* to tell them I thought it was a good idea to move to the States because our health system here is deteriorating so badly?" You then launch into your own long-winded explanation of all the reasons this was supposed to be kept secret. "I can't believe that you would *jeopardize my career* here for a cheap laugh at my expense. You just *don't think* sometimes!"

During your rant, your wife feels threatened by this harsh attack on her judgment and proceeds to justify her actions. She vehemently disagrees with your version of what she actually did say to the Browns. And soon, the two of you are off to the races, arguing about *who said what*, what is secret or not secret, etc. Sound familiar?

Another scene finds you in a business meeting. One of the board members says something you think reveals an unethical practice on his part. You have to work with that person on a committee, so it is important that you share your concerns and differing views. However, the board meeting is probably not an appropriate time to do this.

As soon as you are aware of your own dissonance, let the other person know by quietly stating that you would like to speak with him after the meeting. There is no point in confronting or embarrassing someone when all the facts and explanations are not in. When you leave the meeting together, you might say, "I spoke to you about getting together now because you and I are both on that rules and regulations committee. I have an ethical problem with Rule 1." There is no personal attack here but an objective statement about what you see as possible ethical issues that may arise. The two of you can take the time to share your divergent views and strive to come up with some kind of resolution. This respectful approach avoids misunderstandings caused when one person criticizes or comments on his own interpretation of someone else's position or values.

Reconstructions of conversations are rarely accurate and arguing about "who said what" is seldom productive.

Now that we have considered the timing and appropriateness of our intervention, it is essential that we know when to choose to *not* problem-solve but still remain responsible. Your initial reaction to this suggestion may be: "What's this? How can I be a responsible person if I don't solve problems when things happen?"

Rescheduling

Our true responsibility is to keep our own integrity intact and to treat others with respect, empathy, and dignity. Pride is a foolish emotion that compels us to worry about how things appear to others. *Dignity*, on the other hand, is vital to our self-esteem. If one remains ignorant of the dark Shadow side of the personality, it is apt to erupt into a temper tantrum or cause us to withdraw into a poisonous, stony silence. Each time this happens, our personal integrity is eroded further.

1. THE BOILING POINT   Our task is to know when our stress level becomes problematic, to recognize the moment when our defenses begin to rule our behaviour. The process of *Internalizing* alerts us to our degree of discomfort. If you can feel your face turning pink, before rage changes it to a purplish hue, then you may still be in enough control to act in a responsible fashion.

Rescheduling is appropriate when your anger, anxiety, fear, or pain gets the better of you. None of us is capable of being in control all of the time. When you feel confused, chaotic, or caught in the grip of a mood (for example, you feel bitchy, sulky, stubborn, morose, or overwhelmed), cancel all thoughts of immediate conflict resolution. Knowing when to call *time-out* is important. Let's say a teenager has just confided to her parents that she has been taking drugs. Dad's anxiety soars and Mom's imagination goes wild. At this point, neither is capable of listening.

If Mom and Dad have the presence of mind to know they are temporarily not in control, they may tell Janet that they are too upset right now to talk coherently about this. Father then says, "Your mother and I better take a walk to get ourselves calmed down. This is distressing news." Mother adds "But when we get back, the three of us will sit down and try to figure out what needs to be done!"

Janet sees her parents depart for their walk. Instead of feeling abandoned, somewhere deep inside she feels a sense of relief. She knows, from past experience, that when her parents are really upset, Mom usually cries and Dad typically shouts. There is some hope in the air, instead of despair, as Janet calmly awaits their return.

2. LEAVING A SITUATION   "I'm great at this part," boasts Henri as I teach him how to reschedule. My response to this is, "I know. That's why you're here!" We both laugh since Henri now understands that leaving a situation is a passive-aggressive way of showing anger. This form of anger creates *unfinished business*, as nothing gets resolved when people withdraw to avoid responsibility.

If you have to leave a situation because you are overstressed, always say *why* you are leaving, and *when* you are coming back. Fear of abandonment is a basic emotion inherent in us all. When someone walks out on us, slams a door, or otherwise deserts us, an instinctual fear rises from the depth of our being. Our response may be an outburst of anger, a sinking feeling in the stomach, tension in the neck, or just plain angst.

Say <u>why</u> *you are leaving.* If you admit that you need to withdraw because you're feeling too upset to be rational, that is being responsible. You are not abandoning that person but giving yourself time to think about what the other person said and to figure out what is really going on between the two of you. Hopefully, he or she will feel flattered that you care enough to devote your time and energy to relationship issues.

Don't forget to say <u>when</u> *you are coming back.* Try to arrange a mutually agreeable time that gives you sufficient opportunity to collect your thoughts. Mull through all the reasons behind your reaction and consider how best to solve the problem. You might say, as you leave, "Let's sit down after dinner tomorrow night when the kids are in bed. I want to talk about this when I'm calmer. Okay?"

Or if tempers are flaring on both sides, "Maybe the two of us need some time-out right now. Let's both think this through, and see if we can figure out what in the heck this is all about. Could you let me know when you're ready to talk and where it would be best to meet? I'd really appreciate that!" Underlying key problems are rarely recognized without the objectivity that distance often brings.

Non-verbal communication, such as leaving a scene, is ambiguous at best. This passive-aggressive behaviour fosters further misunderstandings and confusion. The ego-centered part of us is quick to feel that the world revolves around us. "Your behaviour must be a response to something I've done!" is the assumption. Some martyr-victims go even further. "It must be *my* fault that you left."

The Triangular Pattern

If I know that I've lost it and can't think clearly any more, how do I get back my "cool"?

Think of a right-angled triangle.

THE TRIANGULAR PATTERN

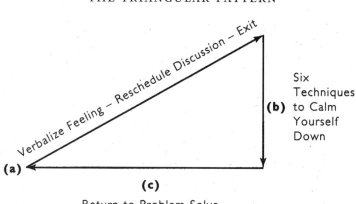

a) You make a *conscious decision to exit* because you recognize that you are overreacting. You *verbalize* this insight, and then proceed to *reschedule*, i.e. arrange another time when both parties are free to discuss the situation.

b) You now attempt to *regain control* by performing one or several of the calming techniques that follow.

c) When you do feel calm again, *follow through* on your promise to return to problem-solve. Be sure you really are thinking clearly so that wisdom will guide you towards solutions that satisfy both or all parties.

Regaining Control

ACTION-ORIENTED IDEAS   If you are free to move about, plug into some *activity* that helps reduce your stress to a comfortable level. No pumping of adrenalin, please!

- Go for a walk or a slow jog. Watch the scenery. Look for interesting distractions.
- Do stretching exercises to help tense muscles elongate and free up stored tension.

- Take a long warm but not hot bath. Set a candle on the side of the tub and watch the colours in the flame.
- Sit in a rocking chair and slowly rock until you feel some release.
- Build a fire in your fireplace. Watch the flames and enjoy the warmth.
- Play your favourite music while you sit in an easy chair by a window. If you feel energetic, dance or just move around until you feel like laughing!
- Phone a friend and let off steam. Choose only friends who *don't* problem-solve for you. Empathy alone is just fine!
- Use your imagination to develop new ways to calm down. Continue this list, adding ideas as they come to you.

PASSIVE-ORIENTED IDEAS   If you must stay where you are, if it is awkward to leave, or to escape the upsetting situation, the following six techniques may be helpful in calming yourself down.

1. SLOW DOWN AND DEEPEN YOUR BREATHING   Because you are experiencing stress, chances are you are cutting off your breath. Try this: *Breathe in* for one count. *Hold* for one count. Then *breathe out* slowly for two counts. On the next breath, your inhale breath should be slightly deeper and your exhale slightly longer. Follow this pattern, but do so in small incremental steps. You don't want to take in too much oxygen at once and start hyperventilating and end up feeling faint. Make sure your shoulders are back and you are sitting tall. Try to relax.

After about five minutes, your breathing will become slower and deeper. Your brain will receive more oxygen to help you think with more clarity. Are you feeling calmer and more in charge? Keep practising throughout the day. And remember to breathe this way any time you start to feel tense.

2. MEDITATION   The point of meditation is to achieve the state of "no-thingness," the *absence of thought*. Robert Campbell, in his *Psychiatric Dictionary*, explains transcendental meditation: "It appears to be a natural process, perhaps a fourth physiologically and biochemically definable state of consciousness (the others being sleeping, dreaming, and waking), that does not require any mental or physical system, nor does it involve hypnosis or suggestion" (660–1). The end result of meditation is reduced activity in the autonomic nervous system, which can lead to a lowering of tension and anxiety, and an increase in contentment and tolerance for frustration.

I cannot teach you to meditate here, but I can help you determine which type of meditation might work best for you. Dr Richard Bandler and John Grinder, two researchers who studied communication in the seventies, developed a system called Neuro-Linguistic Programming. In *Frogs into Princes*, they report that they observed effective communicators, such as therapists Virginia Satir and Fritz Perls, in order to discover what techniques, cues, and responses worked or didn't work in communication.

As they watched the interactions between therapist and client, Bandler and Grinder noticed that some people *looked up* a lot, others *looked to the side*, and others *looked down*. Three channels were named Visual, Auditory, and Kinesthetic. They theorized that we each have a dominant channel.

Visual people, when they are trying to remember an image, will look up to the right. When they want to create an image, such as "What would I look like with purple hair?" they will look up to the left. *Auditory* types look to the right side, or down to the right, when they are remembering sounds or words. They look to the left side, or down to the left, when constructing sounds or words. *Kinesthetic* individuals apparently look down to the right when they are experiencing feelings, smells, and tastes. According to the researchers, there is some variation, depending on whether a person is right-handed or left-handed, but there seems to be a consistent pattern within each individual.

To explain further, suppose a Visual person attends a ballet with friends. On returning home, she tells her husband about the beauty of the ballet. Her eyes often dart up to the right as she speaks. Her Kinesthetic spouse listens, but his wife notices that he is looking down at the newspaper in his lap. She gets increasingly angry and finally shouts, "You haven't heard a word I said!" He looks up, startled, and assures her that he has heard every word. Halfway through her description, he wished he had gone with her. He had slipped into his feelings of regret and lost eye contact.

Not only can this theory help relationships, it can also suggest which type of meditation will work best for you. Some time ago, I was trying to decide whether my visual or auditory channel was stronger. One day my son and aunt were having a discussion about whether they would rather be blind or deaf as a result of some injury. Both agreed that they would rather be blind. I shot back, "Heavens, I'd rather be deaf!" Their choice made perfect sense, as both are singers. My choice helps explain why, if I do attend an opera, I spend a great deal of time with my eyes shut. My visual impressions overpower my hearing. Similarly, on a guided tour of an art gallery, I get frustrated when I look at a painting and try to listen to the guide at the same time. My dominant visual function drowns out the auditory information. There is too much competing stimulation, so I prefer to look at paintings on my own.

Visual Meditation. To achieve a meditative state, if your dominant function is visual, focus on a single *object*, such as a vase. It is best if the object is off by itself, rather than surrounded by other distracting things. A lovely thing to meditate on is a candle, but the flame must be steady, not exposed to drafts. Place a candle on the edge of your bath tub.

Let the warmth of the water calm you at the same time that your meditation creates a peaceful mind space. If a competing thought interrupts your gaze, *refocus*. Practise until your mind is cleared of all distractions and you are able to rest.

Auditory Meditation. People with a dominant auditory function find the repetition of a word or phrase, called a mantra, the easiest way to meditate. The word mantra itself is sometimes used. Or, elongate words like *still, peace, warm*. Repeat the word over and over until you feel a calming effect. If interrupting thoughts intervene, simply refocus.

People who are obsessive often have problems with the mantra. They can't seem to empty their minds to free themselves of unwanted thoughts. To rectify this, when you find yourself becoming obsessive, make a loud, preferably low, *buzzing sound*. This jars your thoughts and interrupts the obsession. Then try the mantra again. If others are present, put all your thoughts into an imaginary salad crisper and spin the handle to make a word salad. Now resume the mantra exercise.

Kinesthetic Meditation. If emotions are dominating your thoughts, try *stomach breathing*. To learn this, lie flat on your back with your hands folded on top of your stomach. Now breathe in, but instead of breathing out, try to push the air further down into your stomach. Your stomach should inflate like a balloon, pushing your folded hands up with it. Hold your breath as long as you can, and then exhale. Keep doing this until it becomes easy. Now try visualizing your breath going into your mouth and arcing down to your stomach, ending up somewhere near your belly button. Reverse this arc and exhale through your mouth. Follow your breath as it goes out into the room.

When you first practise stomach breathing, do so in a horizontal position. Your system is not used to the extra oxygen that is inhaled, and you may feel light-headed. Before you stand up, sit for a few moments until your heart rate stabilizes. As well as the benefits of introducing more oxygen into your system, visualizing your breath as it follows the arc can be somewhat hypnotic. This meditation is excellent if you wake up in the middle of the night and find yourself brooding over some troubling thoughts. Your thoughts are preoccupied as you visualize the journey of your breath in and out, back and forth in a rocking motion. You will begin to relax, likely yawn, and soon slip back into sleep.

3. VISUALIZATION   Another excellent technique to calm yourself down quickly, anywhere, anytime, uses *memory and imagination. Imagine a scene*, somewhere you have actually been, where you felt totally relaxed and peaceful. Now *place yourself in that picture*. What are you doing? What are you wearing? What time of day is it? Is there a wind? Is the sun shining? Are there any sounds? Are you alone or is somebody else in the picture? Add any details that make the picture more complete. *Keep rehearsing that same scene* until you can recapture the peaceful feelings you originally experienced.

The memory I use is of a day when my sister and I were rock collecting on the shores of Lake Huron. It was twelve noon, and I had sat down on the edge of the lake with my feet in the water. Beside me in a small puddle were tiny pebbles, like jewels of many hues. I was fascinated by the intensity of the colours and could feel the water lapping gently at my ankles as the waves reached the shore. My sister was off in the distance, busy at her task.

I have only to think of that scene for a few seconds and I feel my shoulders relaxing. It feels as though the wave as it recedes from the shore is releasing all my tension with it. Practise your picture until you can recapture its calming affect and remember to celebrate the beauty or powerful impact the experience had on you.

4. HUMOUR   What a wonderful gift it is to be able to laugh, especially at ourselves. My PhD dissertation was the first empirical study on humour in psychotherapy. Presenting this work in a paper titled "A Shift to a New Perspective," I introduced what I called *"verbal picture painting."* The following story will illustrate how this technique can introduce *objectivity and distance* when feelings overwhelm us.

A very agitated client, Matthew, was telling me about a new boss who was driving him crazy. This boss turned out to be a neatness freak who was totally obsessive when it came to having his office look well-organized and "perfect." Yesterday, Matthew had come back from lunch to find everything on the surface of his desk jammed into his top desk drawer. As he described his fury, Matthew became red in the face and talked faster and faster. I stopped him. "While you've been talking, I've got this Harry guy all dressed up! You and your buddies have just gone out for lunch and, soon after, Harry goes to his coat closet. He brings out an old khaki army uniform with brass buttons, epaulets, breeches, jodhpurs, and spurs and proceeds to put them on. To top it all off he wears a large plumed hat set at a rakish angle. As an old army man, he's in his glory." I continued the saga. "He snaps to attention and starts to strut around your office looking very important. He comes to your desk, and it is a total mess. 'Ah-ha!' says Harry, with a big smile on his face. He lurches forward and in one fell swoop jams everything into your desk drawer. He straightens up, puts his hands on his suspenders, puffs out his chest, and utters a grand sigh!"

Matthew laughed as I explained. "You're never going to be able to think about Harry doing his number without thinking about that silly story. It's like a film screen overlaying that particular memory."

Humour, used in a creative way, can give you a *new, fresh perspective.* A word of caution, though. The kind of humour used here is exaggeration. No sarcasm or black sadistic humour, please. Take some ludicrous aspect of an upsetting situation, focus on it, and use your imagination to *play* with the image. You can dress people up, have them say or do something silly or ridiculous, or anything that will somehow distort the reality of the situation. It's as if you are a fly on the wall, looking at yourself as victim, but with new eyes. Such objectivity momentarily provides the distance needed to gain a fresh perspective on a troublesome incident.

Humour can be developed. It needs only time, energy, and lots of imagination! It can take many forms. Sometimes I suggest to clients that they *draw cartoons* of painful situations and place words in the "balloons" above the characters' heads. The cartoon titles are often quite revealing. One young student who was suffering high test anxiety was asked to draw a picture of someone who might help him. Sam drew a picture of himself on a throne with a crown on his head, and a scepter in his right hand. He titled his drawing King "Wish-All." Then he commented, "This king looks happy, he's enjoying his false realism! If he can take away exams, I can stop worrying about them." Sam laughed in relief. When humour surfaces, the insights that emerge are sometimes unexpected, but always creative.

5. TOUCH   Touch is a powerful force for healing. In fact, the *Therapeutic Touch* movement is entering new territory each year. There is usually no direct touching involved. Instead, the technique uses the *energy field* that surrounds each person and object. Daniel Worth, in "Non-Contact Therapeutic Touch and the Healing of Wounds," in the *Journal of Subtle Energies*, describes an early controlled study that examined the effect of therapeutic touch on the healing rate of wounds in human subjects. By the eighth day, this group had an average wound size ten times smaller than the untreated group. By the sixteenth day, thirteen of the twenty-three subjects were completely healed, while as yet none of the control group had healed.

Energy fields appear to be very powerful. *Try this*. Hold your hands about an inch apart in a praying position for some minutes until you feel a slight heat build up. Then move your hands very slowly apart, until you feel a cooling. Then again move your hands together, very slowly. A resistance will be felt in the space between your hands as contact is made with the energy field.

Self-touching is healing. Watch people who are very upset. Often, they rub their hands across their skirts or pant legs. Or they cross their arms and hug themselves. When I worked at the hospital, the schizophrenic patients who were waiting outside my office would often rock to and fro. Try sitting in a rocking chair when you're agitated. Rock yourself until you feel calm. It really works. Your energy is focused within the body and soon your mind is distracted by the motion.

Next time you find yourself in pain, cup your hands under your chin, as if you were comforting a small child. It helps make you feel cared for. Remember, if you do hug yourself for comfort, take care to release your arms so that you can resume breathing between hugs.

Be aware that the pads of our fingers are ultra-sensitive. Self-touching done gently and with great care can be therapeutically healing. It is a way of nurturing ourselves whenever we are undergoing undue stress.

6. SPIRITUALITY   If you are in touch with your spirituality, *letting go unto God* is a powerful tool to restore inner peace. You may pray to ask God to carry a burden you find too painful to bear. Or you may ask that you be protected from harm by being surrounded by His love. Be still and try to imagine yourself encircled by a warm, soft glow of white light. Those with a strong spirituality will understand the power of such a request.

For those of you who resist or do not believe, I have a joke to tell. There is an atheist hanging by his fingertips from the branch of a tall tree. He just can't hold on any more. Sounding quite frantic, he looks up to the skies and calls out, "Is there anybody up there?"

There is a long pause, and then the booming voice of God calls out, "I am here, my son!"

"I'll do anything, I'll do anything!" the poor man shouts.

"Then *let go,*" God orders the man. There is a pained, frightened look on the man's face. Then he looks up beseechingly in the opposite direction.

"Is there anybody else up there?" he asks in desperation.

It is very difficult to let go when you do not have enough faith to believe that you won't fall into an abyss. Workaholics, for instance, must keep control at all costs. I warn my clients that their journey back to health will likely lead them to a search for their authentic Self. Since the centre of the Self is the soul, recovery often leads the workaholic to find, or in some cases rediscover, his or her spirituality – the inner connection between humanity and God's higher power. It is a journey many of us are on, either consciously or unconsciously. M. Scott Peck's book *The Road Less Travelled* sold millions of copies for this very reason. It is the story of his own odyssey, and people relate to his inner search.

These six techniques to calm yourself are useful tools to help you re-establish control. You will find some of the techniques better than others, especially in specific situations. Obviously, meditation only works if you take the time to learn it and build it into your daily schedule. Fantasy pictures, on the other hand, may be evoked at any time and in any place. Practise the ones you feel most comfortable with until you can use them freely at will.

When you are calm and back in control of your emotional response, return as promised to problem-solve. Be ready to communicate your thoughts and feelings about the initial situation, and then reach out. Ask the other party to describe their views so that there is a fair and shared exchange of information.

ABOUT LISTENING AND RESPECT

In chapter 9, we will learn how to say what we need to in such a way that others can hear and understand us, without getting defensive. I call this technique, *non-controlling communication*. We will also discover why ego boundaries that are ill-defined get us into a pile of trouble. Controlling and manipulative behaviour and language cross the ego boundary line, and leave both parties hopelessly enmeshed. Power struggles, agitated confusion, and chaos are guaranteed when we invade other people's space and privacy. We will also learn why second-guessing what another person feels or thinks is fraught with error.

9

The Journey – Stage 3, Non-Controlling Communication

Unplugging Our Ears and Staying on Our Own Side of the Fence

I know you better than you know yourself!

A workaholic's remark to his wife

Our journey so far has shown us how to *identify our feelings* through the signals our body sends us at the time an incident occurs. We then use our *thinking* to *analyze* our reaction by making use of the answers to five questions, the last of which asks whether we may or may not be overreacting because of some past-related experience.

The next step is to *communicate our feelings and thoughts* with sensitivity and respect. We remain fully present, and refuse to withdraw or lash out even when the other person invades our space. We are now *Internalizing*, in control, and ready to problem-solve.

Effective problem-solving involves us in taking some action that, it is hoped, will transform a negative situation into a mutually agreeable resolution. This resolution comes about for two reasons: first, we choose to be responsible; and second, we have the where-with-all – the knowledge, skills, and maturity – to carry it off. Statements such as "John is such an effective communicator" or "Sheila solves her problems with such tact and wisdom" quite often reflect the integrity of the people being admired.

Following the *Internalizing* guidelines, we try to problem-solve at the time a situation occurs. On occasions when we are not in control of our emotions, we know enough to reschedule and then follow through as promised at a later time.

ASSUMPTIONS

Let's start the process of problem-solving with two assumptions. Both are based on the dual premise that we must be *fully responsible* for our own behaviour and feelings, and that we must be careful *not to second-guess* what is going on with someone else. Neither position takes the arrogant view of one insecure man who insisted on being one-up on his wife. In smug tones he declared, "I know you better than you know yourself!"

The *first assumption* is that people find it difficult to listen if they suspect that someone is trying to control them. Therefore, if I want to communicate so that others can hear me, I need to *respect ego boundaries* and not cross over. Instead, I will concentrate on making sure *my* response is clear, honest and non-threatening. I will let the other person know what I *feel*, what I *think*, and if it is appropriate, what my *needs* are. However, I must also *leave that person free to respond* to me *if* he or she can, *when* he or she is able, and *in the way* he or she chooses.

After all, individuals need the freedom to approach others in a way that fits their personality. My version of how things should go may not be theirs. The truth of the matter is that the odds are less than even that you will be right about how someone else thinks or feels. But more about that later.

The *second assumption* is that, as an adult, I am responsible for *communicating information about myself* to others. People should not need to "fish" in order to discover what is wrong. In other words, if I don't give other people enough information about why I'm upset, I'm acting like a child who goes around pouting, hoping her mother will notice that she is out-of-sorts. "What's the matter, dear?" is the hoped-for response to such passive-aggressive behaviour. The choice to *not* respond is a covert control tactic that has no place in healthy communication.

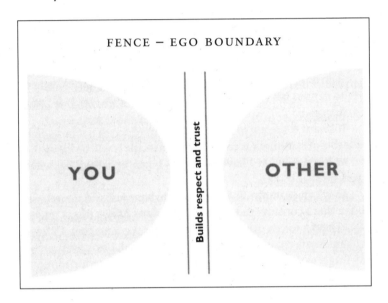

FENCE — EGO BOUNDARY

YOU   Builds respect and trust   OTHER

Imagine that there is a line between you and another person. I call it the *fence,* but it is really your *ego boundary.*

The clearer you are about *where your responsibility lies,* the healthier you will be. Unhealthy families, in contrast, are *enmeshed,* like two hands with the fingers intertwined. Its members regularly problem-solve for each other because there is no clear demarcation line that distinguishes each member as a separate and unique individual. In healthy families, where ego boundaries are intact, people respect each other's individuality, and trust that other members will not invade their space. *Only when invited to do so* will one member offer his thoughts to another. As we will soon learn, "crossing the fence" not only shows a lack of respect, it also undermines trust and encourages dependency.

We are now going to learn how to communicate without crossing this imaginary fence.

THE "I" MESSAGE

Something upsetting has just happened. Someone has just been rude to you. An appropriate response would be to let that person know how his behaviour has affected you. However, deciding *what* to say and choosing the *way* to communicate this information is your responsibility. You cannot be responsible for how that person will respond back.

Remember that your message must be non-threatening, and leave the other person free to express his views, *if* he can, *when* he is able, and *in the way* he chooses.

If I want someone to listen to me, first of all, I need to tell the person *how I feel*. This sort of statement is called an *"I" message* because it is natural to start with the word "I" when expressing a feeling. It is much easier to listen to someone trying to explain his or her feelings, rather than listening to opinionated hostility.

Here's an example. Imagine that I'm furious because you have just said something to me that I consider extremely rude. If I tell you what I *think* first, I might say, "That's a rotten thing you just said!" At the same time I'll likely lean forward in my chair, raise my voice, and even point my finger at you. Notice that I used the evaluative term "rotten" and there is no feeling language to tone down my knee jerk reaction. It is, in fact, a retaliatory attack.

Your response may be either to "run for the hills," psychologically speaking, or to lash back at me.

Now, let me begin with an "I" message: *(Feeling)* "I'm really upset right now! *(Thinking)* I consider what you've just said to be quite rude. (*Needs*) Being polite is very important to me, so I would appreciate it if you would respect this." Notice that there are no evaluative terms like "rotten" involved. It is simply a description of how I feel at the moment. However, I did have to identify specifically what it was about the conversation that upset me. In this particular case, it was rudeness.

When delivering an "I" message, it is important to let others know what our *needs* are, if this is appropriate. In the previous example, I explained my need for politeness. However, we must always resist the temptation to tell the other person how to fulfill that need.

To illustrate, imagine that you feel lonely and isolated from your partner. You might say, "I really miss having some romance in our relationship right now!" The temptation now is to suggest just what the other person should do about this. "I wish you would send me some flowers or something" might be the broad hint, but your partner may resent having to follow through on your request. It is better to compliment your spouse on something you consider romantic that he or she has already done.

For example, "Remember at that party at the Smiths' a month ago? We were standing talking to Pat and Eric, and you put your arm around me." The important part follows: "I felt so special when you did that!"

The spouse is left to be creative, yet is affirmed and complimented on something he or she has already done or said.

"I" Messages Must Be Brief

Try to be brief and to the point. *You do not need to defend how you feel!* This is where people so often go wrong. They send an excellent "I" message, and then they blow it.

Back to the example in which you were rude to me. I start to tell you how I feel. However, instead of stopping there, I go on. Here are some ways I might defend how I feel:

- "You're *always* rude" or "You're *never* polite" are
  statements that will likely raise your ire. What's more,
  "always" or "never" statements are rarely true.
- "You were rude to George last week at that cocktail
  party" is a good "elephant memory" message. Try to stay
  in the present, and resist being historical.
- "The kids think you are really rude, too," enlists the
  troops to your side. Ganging up on someone is a bullying
  tactic.
- And the clincher, "Your mom told me you were a really
  rude teenager!" That last one usually elicits an explosion, and no wonder. We like to hang on to the idea,
  or the myth, that our mom, at least, thought we were
  great!

All the above are examples of *dirty fighting*. I call them the
soldiers. And I really do deserve to be "shot down" for using
any one of them.

"I" messages are very effective, even with difficult people.
Alice, one of my clients, told me that she had gone home to
talk to her mother about something that had always upset
her. She decided to use an "I" message, and then stop. Her
mother had been very critical of her as a child, and their relationship was quite tense.

Alice described what happened. "I told my mother what
was upsetting me, and I didn't defend what I had to say.
My mother waited for me to go on, because I always
did," admitted Alice. Then she added, "When my mother
realized I wasn't going to continue, she looked surprised,
sat back, cocked her head to one side, and looked me in
the eye. 'Well, dear, I never knew you felt that way!' is all
she said."

Alice was quite pleased. "You know," she laughed, "I think
it is the first time we ever really heard each other. That "I"
message thing really works!"

Stay in Your Own Territory

On your own side of the *fence*, within your own ego boundary, you have a great deal of power. You can *stand up for yourself* and *be assertive*! By keeping your "I" message concise, you increase the chance that you will be clearly understood. Messing up what you have to say with confusing, extraneous information is not helpful. Communication overload usually makes it impossible to follow, let alone to really hear.

Unfortunately, we have no power to change others. If you forget to use the "I" message and, instead, challenge someone else to do or say something, this individual may withdraw into silence and refuse to answer, or walk out. Most people resent being told what to do.

Many people who cross the fence do so to keep power. They tell their version of what *they* think the other party wants to hear, instead of the truth. These passive-aggressive types promise to follow through and then choose to do nothing. Procrastination is a wonderful way of looking good while getting away with murder! *Pleasers*, people who can't say no, also use this tactic to avoid responsibility. Keeping harmony at all costs is their justification for misleading and manipulating others.

A Safe Atmosphere

"I" messages create a safe atmosphere and make listening possible. Because no blaming, judging, or interfering is involved, and there is no talk about who is right or wrong, the listener has no need to become defensive and prepare a counterattack.

In using an "I" message, people are simply trying to convey, in purely descriptive language, their experience as they react to what is being said or done by others. The "I" message will leave you feeling confident that you are being responsible and, at the same time, standing up for your own rights and freedom of speech.

CROSSING THE BOUNDARY – USING "YOU" MESSAGES

Recognizing *how you control and manipulate* others is a crucial but daunting self-confrontation. Most of us fail to recognize the subtle or blatant ways we do this.

Unfortunately, "*you*" messages, unlike "I" messages, do not always begin with the word "you." Covert "you" messages include someone raising his eyes in disbelief, or saying something like "Nonsense!" or "You've got to be kidding!" or "Oh come on!" In overt "you" messages, someone is clearly telling another person what he or she should *do*, *say*, *think*, and *feel*. Quite often, people point an accusatory finger as they pronounce their "should" message.

Ironically, *finger-pointing* may help you identify when you are controlling others. For example, Kelly discovered she was a finger-pointer par excellence. Every time she did this in our sessions, I would articulate my "I" message. "Sorry, I can't hear you right now. I'm too busy watching your finger!"

Kelly got quite good at "I" messages. However, one day she was so upset about something her husband, Ken, had done, that she started in on him early in the session. Wagging her finger, she warned Ken, "You shouldn't have said that to the kids. You were being totally irresponsible! There's no excuse for ever doing that."

As she spoke, Kelly became aware of her outstretched finger. She reached out, grabbed it, and drew it towards her body. We watched as she struggled with her thoughts. Finally, she came out with a perfect "I" message, and we all laughed in relief. She had caught herself, once again, trying to control her husband.

Kelly went on to explain to me that she had been to her family home twice since she had started to use the "I" message. "You won't believe this, but my mother still wags her finger at me all the time!" I laughed, and assured Kelly that I could very well believe it. If we come from a family where there is a lot of controlling going on, guess what we learn to do?

When angry, hurt, frightened, or enraged, we can become nasty or even vicious. It is then that we often resort to name-calling, insulting, putting others down, or being sarcastic. "You" messages fly up from our unconscious whenever our Shadow side is activated by negative emotions. As you yourself will likely discover, one must be in control in order to use "I" messages.

Typically, such dictatorial tactics cause the other person to launch a counterattack or make a hasty exit. Soon the problem has escalated into a power struggle that no one will win.

The Teeter-Totter Power Struggle

One of the major ways to *escalate a power struggle* in any relationship is to use the "you" message.

When you interfere in another person's business, you take on responsibility for what happens to them thereafter. If someone else tells you about a personal problem and you proceed to tell them what to do, or suggest some possible solutions, you are robbing that person of taking ownership of his own experience. At the same time, you eliminate his or her chance to build self-esteem. Ultimately, both parties will resent each other.

"What's wrong with helping people?" you may ask. Or, "Why shouldn't I protect my kids from making mistakes?" Then you might add, "I don't want them to suffer as I did!" Oddly enough, *"helping"* and *"protecting"* are rationalizations for manipulating and controlling. But let me explain.

Imagine that I'm holding up a pencil in the horizontal position. On the right side is the person who has a personal problem. We'll call her Helen. Helen is telling her husband, Mario, on the left, about some difficulty she is having at the office with a co-worker. As soon as Mario jumps in to tell Helen what she should do about the situation, the pencil tilts down to the right. Mario, by intervening in Helen's problem, has tipped the balance of power in his favour. If Helen follows Mario's advice, she no longer "owns" her own solutions. It's like helping your kids with their homework the night before a test. If the child does well, he can't take credit for his marks. He certainly can't take you to university with him! If he fails the test, he can project blame outwards and neglect to learn from his errors. Finding out what we are *not* good at is an important lesson in life.

The implicit message here is that the other person lacks the ability to handle his or her problems. As soon as we offer solutions, the message is one of dependency – *you need me!*

The irony in Helen and Mario's interchange is that Helen is a Feeler who needs to talk through her own solutions. When Mario problem-solves for Helen instead of simply listening, he unwittingly takes away her independence. Often, as a result, she loses her initiative and self-confidence. Helen is left feeling like a child who needs to be told what to do. No wonder she doesn't feel good about herself.

The power struggle between Helen and Mario resumes when Helen attempts to regain her own power. She resents Mario's interference, yet in a way she wonders if she set him up by telling him about the office problem. But, she ponders, "Surely I can talk to my own husband about things that bother me!"

Mario isn't happy either. Although it temporarily feels great to have broad shoulders, and know that others depend on you, this situation eventually gets tiresome. When you have too many problems of your own, the last thing you need is to be responsible for the happiness of another person. As a consequence, Mario ends up resenting Helen.

The *teeter-totter balance of power* tips again. Helen gets back at Mario by using the silent treatment. She withdraws and quietly steams at his suggestions. Or she retaliates and decides that the next time Mario has a problem, she'll be sure to tell *him* what he should do. "After all, fair is fair," fumes Helen.

Nobody wins in this or any other power struggle. Now, instead of just the original problem, there are many other serious issues. Mario's suggestions feed into Helen's insecurity because her talents don't lend themselves to his solutions. She is left confused about just how to proceed. Mario, instead of feeling good about his involvement, experiences the heightened tension hanging in the air. He stays on the alert for a backlash and goes on the defensive. His own trigger-happy anger sits ready to pounce.

If you wish to be in a *peer relationship* with someone, neither person should be in a power position. The pencil should stay on a horizontal level. Mario needs to simply listen to Helen. He might offer empathy and support for her predicament. No problem-solving allowed! The magic question for Mario to ask Helen, if he wants to relate to her on a peer level, is, "What do you think you want to do about this?"

Helen is left with her own dignity, and the implication is that she is quite capable of handling her own affairs. This is a message that feels good and boosts self-esteem. If I problem-solve for somebody else, the message is the reverse. "You can't handle your own problems." I put you in an inferior position by inferring that you are not capable of doing your own problem-solving. The inference is, "You need me, or others like me, to help you." Nobody feels good about these messages.

By the way, parents who problem-solve for their children, instead of *consulting* by asking them what their own solutions might be, are robbing these children of the chance to develop self-confidence, make their own mistakes, and learn from their errors.

Be patient. It's not easy to switch to a whole new approach.

GOOD LISTENING

Good listeners usually have many friends. People love being able to discuss problems with a friend who simply offers empathy and support.

Remember that good listeners *do not give advice* unless their opinion is requested. To this, I would add a warning proviso. I believe that this should read: "unless their opinion is requested about an *impersonal* problem only." If somebody asks me what I think the stock market is going to do tomorrow, I might hazard a guess. I'll then return the question by asking that person about his own prediction. This *reciprocal exchange of information* keeps us on a peer level.

Now, if someone asks me a question about what she should do about a *personal* matter, it is best that I refrain from answering that question. Instead, I need to serve as a *sounding board*, someone who encourages others to elaborate. Often it is helpful to bounce ideas off others while you are in the process of developing them.

I believe it reveals our arrogance when we problem-solve for someone else. Our history, our sources of knowledge, our sexual orientation, our morality and ethics, and our opinions are unique to each of us. It is presumptuous to think that what would work best for us would be suitable for another person.

Here's an example of this process of good listening that involves young people. Let's say my eighteen-year-old daughter asks me, "What do you think I should do this summer, Mom?" My best response would be something like this. "Gee, sweetie, I don't know! What are you thinking about?"

She tells me about three possible summer jobs. The first one she appears to know a great deal about. She has talked to many people and found out important details about the company itself. This job option is obviously an important one to consider. She is setting priorities as she describes her feelings because she is stressing some things and leaving out others. She mentions certain feedback from the other people she has spoken with. In fact, she is doing her *own* problem-solving as she speaks.

The second job she is considering happens to be at a lodge I'm familiar with. While she is telling me about this place, I become somewhat uncomfortable because I'm thinking about the tipping system they use for employees. I also wonder if she knows about the bus schedules changing at the end of August. However, I remain quiet while she tells me about her third choice.

This particular job I know nothing about, and the company is new to me. She also seems pretty vague about what it is the company sells and what would be expected of her.

She finishes, and then asks again, "Well, what do you think?" At this point, I have to be very careful *not* to go over onto her side of the fence. Instead, I might comment on the process of her thinking. "You seemed to know a lot about that first job. You sound excited about it." You'll notice that I used the word *seemed*, as it is best not to presume you know for sure how someone else feels. Then I might add, "I know very little about that company, so I don't have any thoughts to contribute, one way or the other."

I do have some relevant information about her second idea. However, I must respect her space in the way I deliver that information. I must first *request permission,* be invited over *before* I offer it. To let her know my thoughts, I might say, "As I was listening to you talk about that lodge, I remembered thinking while we were vacationing there that their tipping system was not fair to the staff." Then comes the important question: "*Would you like me to tell you about it?*"

She agrees, and I now have the invitation I need to describe the details of the tipping schedule. I also mention the change in bus schedules at the end of August, but she already knows about that. The bus schedule is important because the staff is expected to work the September weekends and also Thanksgiving. Otherwise, they don't get their summer tips. My daughter is attending university quite a distance from the lake district. Getting back to school for Monday-morning classes might be a problem next fall.

Her third job idea was so vague that I would simply say that I had a hard time following her description. In *consultation* I may ask, "Do you think it would be worth your while to find out more about that job before you make your final decision?"

The conversation may end on this note. "But sweetie, which one of these jobs would be fun for you? Which experience might be good to have on your curriculum vitae?" She will "*own*" her own decision and will be totally responsible for whether it works or not. At no time did I take that responsibility away from her. Her self-confidence will develop as she explores her options. She will discover many of her own strengths and weaknesses and a great deal more about herself, whichever job she takes.

In my family psychotherapy practice, I meet many children who have not been allowed to make their own decisions. Then, when they turn twelve or thirteen, their parents decide that these children should suddenly be responsible. One typical complaint is that the children are not doing their chores around the house. I may ask the parents what jobs they wish the children to do, and then ask them to please remain silent while I consult with the children.

"Now that you guys know what Mom and Dad want done, try to negotiate with each other about how best to divide up the jobs." Eventually the three children agree on who is going to do each chore, and I make notes for future reference.

When this family returns two weeks later, I enquire about how things are going. Mom tells me that George isn't doing what he agreed to do. At which point, I may turn to George and ask him, "How come?"

George's response: "I want to do what Michael is doing!" I say, okay, and then suggest that the two of them work this out here. I proceed to tell them a bit about mediating, about "getting to yes," and then I, too, stay out of the conversation. When the boys reach an agreement, I ask, "Are you two both okay about this now?"

George rarely has been treated in this peer fashion. I didn't bawl him out when he changed his mind. By leaving the two boys to solve this problem, I respected their space. The solution will be theirs, and it is up to them to succeed or fail at it. George is very co-operative after this show of confidence. He feels important. Finally someone is willing to listen to him, without commenting on whether his ideas are good, bad, or indifferent. He is left free to be responsible or not.

Good listening is respectful and leaves the other person with his or her dignity intact. One more point, however, needs to be made about good listening. It has to do with second-guessing what others feel and think.

Why Second-Guessing Is Unwise

Be careful not to second-guess what is going on inside another person's psyche. Instead, make it a rule to *always ask, instead of tell*! If the situation does not allow for this, then plan to check out your perceptions later with that person.

A story best illustrates this. Years ago, a fifty-year-old woman was referred to me by her general practitioner. Valerie was barely functioning and had taken a three-month leave-of-absence from her job. We worked together on her journey towards being able to *Internalize*. She was starting to feel much better.

Valerie decided to ask her Aunt Mildred over for tea. It was the first company she had had in months. As she told it, "We were sitting at the dining-room table, laughing and talking. I felt like my old self again. It was wonderful!"

In the middle of this, her husband, Bert, came in from the backyard. As Valerie described it, Bert glared at her and looked disapproving. "My heart sank, and I started to cry," she reported.

"What did you do?" I asked.

Valerie explained that at this point she and Bert had to withdraw to another room. Valerie was furious and let loose a torrent of feelings. All thoughts of "I" messages went out the window. "I told him he always looked that way, that he had spoiled every good time in my life!" Apparently, this attack was the last straw for Bert. Inside, he was boiling mad, because for months he had been pussy-footing around Valerie, respecting how fragile she'd become. But now that he had witnessed signs that she was starting to recover, he decided to let her have it.

Valerie recalled the terrible things they had said to each other. Their arguing apparently had grown increasingly destructive. I asked Valerie, "How did you know how your husband was feeling when he came in from the backyard?"

Valerie, quite incensed, shot back at me, "Don't tell me I don't know how that man feels! I've been married to him for twenty-eight years. I know him like a book!"

I laughed and replied, "I have some trouble believing that." And then I explained to Valerie why this was so. During the 1960s and early 1970s, efforts were made to train people to rate certain aspects of behaviour in psychological experiments. One study had to do with measuring the ability of people to guess what others were feeling. Researchers tried all sorts of techniques that involved pictures, actors, and real people. They could not get even close to a reliability score of 35 percent (Krech et al., *Elements of Psychology*, 468). This finding suggests that our chances of being wrong when we second-guess are likely to be 65 percent or more.

This finding is not surprising when you acknowledge the many permutations and combinations of *physiological responses, energy levels, and body positions* that different people experience during the same emotion. Bert's facial expression looked to Valerie like someone glaring with anger. I told her that if a wife in one of my sessions tells her husband what he is thinking or feeling, I typically ask that wife to rephrase what she did say by putting the same thoughts in the form of a question. When the husband replies, it often becomes clear that the *projection* was not accurate at all. In fact, it often says more about the speaker than about the person who is being described.

I then suggested to Valerie that we replay that scene again. "Your husband has just walked in the back door, and you get upset at the look on his face. Would you allow me to role-play a bit here?" Valerie agreed.

"This time, you might say to Bert something like, I looked at your face when you came in the door, and I thought you looked angry." The important *peer-relationship question* follows: "*What was going on with you?*"

As we soon learned from Bert, he had developed ulcers during this stressful time in their lives. While the ladies were having tea, he was in the backyard raking leaves. Suddenly, he began to suffer terrible stomach cramps. As he approached the house, he heard laughter, something that had become scarce in their home. When Valerie saw him, he was tiptoeing through the dining room, trying not to disturb them. He was on the way to the medicine cabinet in the bathroom where his medication was kept. Tiptoeing requires a focused concentration that may have resembled a frown or grimace.

The whole thing had been a disaster. They could never take back the awful things that were said. Yet, in the long run, it proved to be an important lesson for the couple. They began to see how they *projected* all sorts of misinformation onto each other when they were angry. They also agreed to test out the accuracy of their projections to prove to themselves that, more often than not, they actually were wrong. Valerie and Bert soon became experts at *asking, instead of telling.*

Why "You" Messages Are Dangerous

People have to be in control to use "I" messages. If you can feel your cheeks flush pink long before you turn a purplish hue, then you have lots of time to problem-solve. When you eventually are able to *Internalize*, you will be strongly aware of your feelings and the signals your body is sending. You will be able to communicate at the time, or close to the time, that something has started to make you anxious or upset.

Unfortunately, when feelings escalate and flood up unbidden from the unconscious, "*you*" messages tend to pop out unannounced. This happens because we cannot be in control of emotions that are repressed or underdeveloped. The Shadow, as we learned earlier, dwells in the unconscious. Its dark aspects are responsible for much of our negativity, and our subsequent destructive and vindictive behaviour.

Because so much of our Shadow is hidden from our awareness, we often fail to take responsibility for poor behaviour. We "*forget*" by dissociating anything negative we do not wish to own. Or we compartmentalize and keep certain information quite separate and removed from the rest of our reality. Either way, the dark side of the Shadow spells trouble for us. For those we affect, it is especially problematic. In this case, "What you don't know can't hurt you!" is a dangerous denial of reality.

Remember, "I" messages are healthy and responsible communication. "You" messages are manipulative and controlling.

THE JOURNEY MOVES ON

The three stages of the journey – (1) *Awareness: Learn to Internalize your feelings*; (2) *Rescheduling;* and (3) *Non-controlling communication* – involve a long, slow process of change. You may encounter inner resistance because unwittingly you may have been *Externalizing* most of your life. So be patient. It won't happen overnight.

Remember to stop yourself, get in touch with your feelings through your body awareness, and then ask those five questions about *why* you are upset. Persevere until you know the answers, as close as possible to the time of the situation. The key is to learn the *earliest signs of each of your emotions*.

The encouraging news is that once you're able to use the "I" message more naturally, people respond positively. You, in turn, will become a much better listener, and likely be surprised at how much you can learn from other people. After all, being right and having your own way all the time does not encourage growth.

And, the best news yet, friendships are formed through *peer relationship interactions*. The *"new you"* will not be a Dr Jekyll one day, Mr Hyde the next. *By learning to show respect, you build trust.* Others, in turn, can then respond with new attitudes and behaviour towards you.

Seeing the Results of Your Efforts

In chapter 10, we will explore the differences between Feeling and Thinking *language*. You will discover how to distinguish Feeling and Thinking *behaviour* and learn how to *rephrase* things using Feeling language. As well, you will be able to *recognize* when you are on the *negative or positive side* of both functions.

Don't worry! You are not going to give up your best function. If you are a Thinker, you are going to *add* the Feeling function and its language to your repertoire. In doing so, you will discover many new facets of your personality that lead to exciting new challenges and a higher level of maturity. Feelers will affirm their best function and make sure it is working well. They will need to concentrate on developing the best aspects of Thinking to counteract their own negative Inferior Thinking, which takes over whenever they are upset.

Once you go through the hypothetical door to open up your opposite function, there is a whole new world to explore. Stored there are fresh and surprising revelations that offer excitement and joyful renewal. Push the door open, and see where it goes!

10

Feeling and Thinking Language and Behaviour

"I Thought We Spoke the Same Language!"

You can't grow if you don't know what is holding you back.

A young medical doctor and his wife came up to me after my lecture on understanding the addiction of workaholism and its devastating effects on the family. "After reading your book," the husband said, "we realized that we were pretty good at complimenting and rewarding our two children for their accomplishments." This, apparently, was quite easy for them to do.

Then the wife joined in: "But after we talked it over, we decided to make a conscious effort to reward our kids for their 'being and feeling' side as well. Unfortunately, what we soon discovered, to our great discomfort, was that we don't really have a language to do this!"

I've often thought not only of this couple's eagerness to do the best for their children but of their choice to model a value system that honoured both the "*doing*" and "*being*" sides of their personalities. It is quite amazing, when you think about it, that two bright, well-educated, and articulate people could suddenly realize that their language is inadequate, that the imbalance in their own Thinking and Feeling functions was inhibiting their ability to perform such a task.

DISCOVERING A DIFFERENT LANGUAGE

Feeling language is scarce when someone is numb and flat much of the time! Sometimes the Feeling function has been repressed to avoid intolerable pain experienced during a chaotic childhood. Such an imbalance of functions can leave an individual vulnerable to dysfunction in adulthood.

Workaholics also become emotionally crippled during the predictable breakdown syndrome that this addiction follows. Jon, a forty-year-old accountant, was increasingly aware that he now functioned at two speeds. As he put it, "I was either low as a submarine and zombied my way through each day, or I was supercharged. I would pump adrenalin as if it was going out of style." Increasingly, Jon lived in a state of emotional greyness, and he was suffering frequent bouts of rage. If there was any disorder in the home when Jon returned from work, he would simply go berserk. His erratic behaviour and verbal abuse had reached crisis proportions. His wife, Tania, was unable to overcome her depression because of the ongoing trauma, and the children were chronically anxious. Stefan, their six-year-old, showed signs of regressing. He was wetting his bed frequently, and his father's outrage at this only made the situation worse. In contrast, Alec, the older child, stood up to his father and his aggressive outbursts only added to the family's turmoil. Tania was at a breaking point.

Tania gave Jon an ultimatum. Either he get his act together or she was initiating separation proceedings. At this point, I asked whether Jon might consider withdrawing to their cottage for a week. Barely functioning and feeling totally numb, Jon needed to somehow remove himself from the situation for everyone's sake. His stress system was overloaded. Any aggravation, however slight, set him off.

On his return from the cottage, I saw Jon alone. "What were some of your thoughts while you were away?" I asked. "Well, I feel much better," he began. "I went for a long walk every day, and I worked on the steps at the cottage."

"Yes, but what were your thoughts about how you've been treating your family?" I prompted.

"Well, I didn't think too much about that!" was his reply.

My heart sank. It was apparent that Jon was still totally out of touch with his feelings. His Feeling language was minimal, except when his anger forced negative emotions to the surface. He couldn't afford to let in any more pain for fear his fragile Self would be totally destroyed. He was stuck. In retrospect, though, this week did prove to be a watershed. Jon began an earnest plunge into the therapeutic process. It was as though his life depended on it.

Some weeks later, the couple were sitting in my office. There had been no outbursts at home. On the contrary, Jon was able to stand back and objectively rationalize about why for example, the fort the children had built in the middle of the living room was really okay.

Jon and I were discussing the overwhelming amount of anger that had surged up to the surface in our sessions in the previous few weeks. As he spoke, Jon's arms were stretched in a circle in front of him, his hands clenched, not quite touching. Every muscle stood out on his arms and his shoulders were hunched over and tightly locked. He was busily analyzing past injustices. "No one was allowed to be angry in my family. It never would have occurred to us to even think of building a fort in our living room. Children were to be seen and not heard. That much was crystal clear!" Jon was intellectualizing his insights.

"Would you please stop for a moment?" I asked. I imitated Jon's tense arms and their circular position. I asked him to assume that stance again.

"What does that position make you think of, Jon?" I asked.

Jon hesitated. "It looks like a dam. I feel like I'm holding in this torrent of rage. If it ever gets through that hole between my hands, then all hell will break through!"

I pointed out that, up until now, Jon had been intellectualizing. I wanted him to just feel how much stress he created in his body when he was expressing the historical reasons for this rage. "Just hold that position for a few moments. Try not to think. Just feel. Now, exaggerate your tension!" I instructed. We both held that pose. My shoulders ached as they arched forward. The muscles in my arms hurt as the tension across my back spread through to my fingertips.

After a few minutes, I said, "Now, Jon, try shaking out your arms. Just let go, like this." I watched as he intently followed these instructions. "Just imagine all that negative energy flowing out in concentric waves, washing away from your body."

Finally, Jon sat quietly. "This is the first time I've been aware of the difference," he said thoughtfully. When I asked what he meant, he explained, "I know that I intellectualize all the time. I've been aware of that for a long while. But," and then he looked pleased, "until this moment, I didn't know what the alternative would be!"

Jon, Tania, and I laughed together, partly in relief. Jon had finally got out of his head and into his body. Nothing disastrous happened, as he had feared. His feelings didn't overwhelm him. His anger didn't explode. At the end of the session, Jon summed up the experience: "I really did feel those waves take my anger away! Thanks for stopping me. I think I'm finally on to something."

THE RISK OF OPENING UP PANDORA'S BOX

Changing is scary! As Jon had put it at the end of our first meeting together, "Promise me, Dr Killinger, that at the end of this journey you've been describing, I won't end up hating myself!"

"On the contrary," I replied, "I think you'll be quite proud. When your Feeling and Thinking functions are better balanced, the decisions you make will be wiser and better-informed. And, you'll likely be more effective and compassionate in the way you seek solutions to problems."

I believe that people like Jon act out their repressed Feelings because they are unable, or sometimes unwilling, to free up deeply entrenched, painful memories. The challenge becomes first one of *exploration*, and then *transformation*. Often, lasting change is accomplished through revisiting stressful childhood experiences and viewing them from the adult's perspective. Remember that the child sees things from a uniquely egocentric focus in which everything revolves around his or her experience. Past fears and trauma were often too difficult to handle at the time each incident occurred because of the child's age and stage of development. Unacknowledged hurts can cripple future growth.

Knowledge is the key to unraveling the mysteries contained within Pandora's box. As adults, we have the advantage of objectivity and life experience when we review the past. We must factor in the personalities and histories of our parents. They are *real* people, not the ones we once idealized or resented. Their behaviour too was motivated by unmet needs and deficiencies, and influenced by previous generations and times.

Sociological factors such as war, the Depression, unemployment, the addictive behaviours of alcohol, gambling, gaming, smoking, and so on — all must be considered. As children, we often remain largely ignorant of the complexity of such factors.

Through confronting our conflicts and searching for meaning, we progress towards balance and maturity. The paradox is that growth does not come without journeying *through* our pain.

RECOGNIZING PATTERNS OF DESTRUCTIVE
BEHAVIOUR

A first step towards self-knowledge is to *recognize signs* in your behaviour that signal that the dark, Shadow side is becoming powerful in your personality. Watch for changes in the *language* you use. Do you find yourself talking down to people or saying things that humiliate or punish others? Do you hear yourself swearing or using abusive language? Do you *act out self-destructive behaviour*, such as overeating, excessive drinking, or smoking, and then belittle yourself for it? Do you *ignore signs of body distress* and remain numb rather than seek help? Do you *experience a sense of alienation, isolation, or depression* and feel your self-esteem plummet further? Or, do you have an *obsessive need to be in control* and insist on telling others what to do? It is important to recognize that fear underlies these manifestations of anger and abuse.

When you are able to master the process of *Internalizing*, a broader range of feelings will break through to the surface and be available to you. Listen to their *intensity*. What shades of meaning do these layers of feelings convey? Is this anger I'm experiencing mild or extreme? Am I overreacting or do I really care that much about this particular issue? Both positive and negative feelings must be acknowledged before inner balance is possible. Recognition allows you to nurture yourself, instead of continuing to punish yourself and others, albeit unconsciously. Welcome your dark Shadow side into consciousness because, as Carl Jung reminds us, only then will you be safe. Each time you become aware of one of your flaws, acknowledge its presence. It is time to do some growing!

As new shadows surface into consciousness, set each fresh "insight" aside for present or future analysis. Some people like to make a journal entry. The next time you slip up and repeat old habits, reprimand yourself. Your impatient response may be something like, "For Pete's sake, I just did it again!"

Old habits die hard. Keep trying, and don't be discouraged. If you don't remain vigilant, resistance and laziness will win out.

The couple we are calling Sally and Peter each opened up a Pandora's box. Through self-exploration and learning new skills, they transformed the negative energy that was poisoning the atmosphere in their home. We will now return to their story.

New Behaviour and a New Language

SALLY   As you may recall, Sally scored as a Feeler on the Myers-Briggs Test Indicator. When I first met Sally, though, she was depressed and largely unaware of how deeply angry she had become. She didn't hear the snap in her voice, nor did she realize how much she lectured her family.

Sally progressed quickly through the process of *Internalizing* because she was restoring the Feeling side that came naturally to her. Also, she became super aware of the times when *Inferior Thinking* was distorting her normally sensitive reaction to a troublesome situation. She would grimace every time she became aware of her sharp, short delivery and her acid tongue. "Surely that wasn't me!" she protested.

Keeping harmony had cost Sally a great deal. Her naivety and depression blocked out the painful reality of how much her personality had changed. Her fear of confrontation, along with Peter's threatening disapproval and rages, kept Sally trapped in her own trauma.

Sally's energy was renewed as her depression lifted. She was now ready to develop the *positive* side of her less-developed Thinking function. She purposefully read the editorial section of her newspaper to become better informed about the thoughts and ideas of others on the important issues of the day. She learned to be more critical of what she read and tried to analyze why certain things were happening. She also attended lectures on current affairs. Entering this fresh world of ideas and thoughts was very exciting. Understanding issues took on added meaning.

Eventually, Sally made a decision to go back to school. Through re-establishing her Feeling side and encouraging her positive Thinking, Sally developed new confidence. She was able to articulate her own ideas clearly with both grace and assurance.

Sally grew from the trauma of what she called "The Terrible Years." Peter's bankruptcy had been the catalyst for change in this family. Bankruptcy is about as concrete as things can get. Denial and naivety have difficulty surviving that cruel reality. "It was the worst of times. It was the best of times," as the saying goes.

Sally soon realized, with some awe, just how much there was to learn about the rational, logical, analytical, and pragmatic side of her Thinking function. Freed from depression, she found her new "growth journey" both exciting and highly stimulating.

PETER   For Peter, a natural Thinker, the journey towards Feeling was much more difficult. For a long time, he would have to translate his thoughts into feelings. "I had to *think* about how I felt all the time" was how he described this struggle.

Eventually Peter was able to acknowledge that he had indeed become emotionally crippled. Sadly, his distress was compounded by the shame of lost integrity. As he put it, "I recognize now the real reason I came to see you. Something in me was crying out. I can see that my Shadow was pulling me further down into disaster. I couldn't stop myself." Shady business practices, secrecy, deceit, and greed had led him away from his former idealism. Bankruptcy woke Peter up. His pride, however, took an awful tumble.

The jolt of pain he suffered when his business failed suddenly made the need for psychotherapy more relevant to Peter. Survival was something Peter did believe in. He battled through his airtight denial and his strong defenses of dissociating and compartmentalizing. Peter had *forgotten how to tell the truth.*

As new insights broke through to consciousness, Peter became more open to revelations about his childhood, and these shed light on his present situation and the drastic change in his personality. Surprisingly, instead of the pain that he dreaded, relief flooded in. "No wonder I did that!" became a frequent exclamation.

I knew that Peter was ready to take a further step because he was showing real concern for the damage he had done to his family. Tears spilled whenever he realized a new aspect of the turmoil he had caused in Sally's life. Nowadays, his face appears softer and gentler, a sure sign that Peter's feelings are working.

"I never used to cry," Peter explains. "It always hurt me physically because there was such a block in my throat. I could only choke." Then he added, "I was watching a movie the other night and I could feel tears spill down my cheeks. I reached over to Sally, and we just held hands for a while. It was just a great moment!" He laughed in relief.

Some time later, Peter hesitantly asked me if I could write a "cookbook" or something like that to help him. He needed more insight into how he could change his surly, brusque behaviour. He was still offending people, but didn't know why. Would I help him learn some different ways of saying things? Peter's request indicated a need for more concrete direction. Peter could experience his feelings now but had no language to express them.

PETER'S COOKBOOK   Changing an attitude is one thing. Transforming behaviour is quite another challenge. It certainly isn't easy. Thinkers and Feelers phrase similar thoughts in very different ways. Peter and I worked together on some of the key changes he wished to make.

It is important to remember that Thinking and Feeling are *ways of making decisions.* Thinking has a *focused awareness* that concentrates on getting from goal A to B. It works best when dealing with things one at a time and follows a logical process aimed at an impersonal finding. Ideas and goals are formed through the Thinking process. This function also checks for flaws or errors in decisions based on emotion and intuition. When Thinking is *obsessive*, its focus narrows and becomes one-tracked as it *fixates* on something or someone.

Feeling, on the other hand, uses a *diffuse awareness* that is directed outwards. In fact, it is often too other-directed! Feelers may disregard what matters to them simply because they wish others to be happy. Even their own body signals may be ignored when the early signs of illness should be alerting them to health problems.

The Feeling function can concentrate on a number of things at once. Feeling considers the person's own thoughts but also is open and receptive to cues and feedback from other people and from the surrounding environment. Feeling bestows a personal, subjective value on things. Feeling decisions, therefore, evolve from one's personal value system and are influenced by *what one appreciates and values.*

Feeling opens us up to wait, watch, and wonder. The *key concepts* of Feeling are openness, receptivity, and reaching out to others. It is our thoughtful, sensitive, empathic, tactful, gracious, loyal side. It values harmony above all. People and relationships are of special interest, so sharing and intimacy are important values.

The following tasks may help you to nurture and develop your own Feeling side. Expect to feel awkward and self-conscious when you first exercise your Feeling "muscles," especially if you are a Thinker. Eventually, as Feeling works independently, its expressions will seem more natural and genuine. You will not have to translate, to Think about how you Feel.

A. Better Listening and Healthy Communication

"How can I be a better listener?" Peter asked. Awareness is key. In time, Peter learned to recognize the moment when he turned himself off and switched to his own inner dialogue. "I'd hear myself rehearsing what I was going to say next," he observed. "I realize now that there was no way I could do this and listen at the same time. I would simply have lost track of what the other person was saying." It took discipline for Peter to refocus back to the initial conversation. He often found that he had to ask the other person to repeat what he or she had said.

Peter also learned to re-examine his own communication after a conversation. Had he said what he intended to say, and was his message easily understood? To do this, he reviewed some of the *negative aspects of Thinking* that Carl Jung warned lead to poor communication: (*Psychological Types*, 380-7)

a) Thinkers tend to *clutter up their communications* with adjuncts, qualifications, retractions, saving clauses, or doubts, and fail to convey the essence of their message.
b) They *don't give enough information* and sound blunt, sharp, or abrupt.
c) They *talk far too long, are too intense* about their idea, and neglect to focus on the listener or relationship issues.
d) They bore the listener by *lecturing or preaching and not exchanging* views.
e) They *fail to personalize and own what they are saying*, talking instead in generalities and using theoretical logic, etc.

f) They *become "historical,"* bringing up incidents from weeks, months, or even years before to support their point of view.

It took awhile, but Peter gradually understood that his style of communicating was not only off-putting but could lead to confusion, misunderstanding, or serious misinterpretations.

HOW TO IMPROVE YOUR COMMUNICATION

1. *Go beyond your own subjective viewpoint.* In order to be other-directed, you need to develop *diffuse awareness* in addition to your focused-awareness. Practise by watching for feedback while you are talking. *Observe other people's reactions and facial expressions,* especially the eyes. Talking and watching at the same time is not an easy task for Thinkers.

2. *Observe and question without judging.* As you are speaking, *watch to see if the listener shows loss of interest, restlessness, boredom, confusion, a blank expression, or loss of eye contact.* Try to curb your naturally skeptical nature. Remember, the negative side of thinking tends to be judgmental, critical, and pessimistic. Ask yourself: How might I be turning that person off? Am I lecturing, or going round in circles? Am I arguing rather than discussing, or is my logic difficult to follow?

3. *Comment on your own communication.* At first, when Peter realized he had somehow lost contact with the other person, he would blurt out, "You're not listening to me!" Not surprisingly, this "you" message was perceived as a criticism. "It's your fault!" is the underlying message. Peter then tried a humorous approach, as he termed it. "Are you guys wearing earmuffs?" No one laughed.

Impulsive, opinionated thoughts are best "censored through sensitivity." Since Peter wishes to be better understood, *Feeling language that uses the "I" message is easier to listen to.*

"I may not be describing this very well!" indicates that Peter is taking responsibility for his own miscommunication. Or, "Sometimes I get carried away with my ideas and get verbal diarrhea!" shows the listener that Peter is at least conscious of his shortcomings.

4. *Solicit feedback from the listener.* Following your explanation or comment, *ask whether the listener understood.* "Is this making any sense to you at all?" Or, "I'm not sure whether this subject is something you're that interested in!" ensures that listeners realize that you are being sensitive to their reactions. Slowly, Peter is learning that not everyone shares his particular interests.

The unique views and values of the listener need to be addressed. The black-and-white, concrete Thinker who is driven to find pragmatic answers to questions concerning ideas and goals tends to be most interested in getting from idea A to goal B. Peter, however, is now aware that Sally is more interested in hearing about the people-side of the projects he is working on. As his feelings surface, Peter, too, expresses genuine concern and appreciation for the people who work for him. He also understands that they have a life outside his sphere of influence. Before, these people had a job to do!

5. *After listening to the feedback on your thoughts, invite the other to share his/her own views. A two-way exchange of views is peer communication.* Peter is now growing increasingly impatient with people who monopolize conversations. When he catches himself doing so, he now says, "I've had the floor long enough. I'd really like to know how you feel about this whole thing." His fresh curiosity about how different people see the same situation led Peter to criticize his former indifference. "Before, I didn't give a damn what anybody else thought! People were just getting to be a great nuisance." When he had asked his managers for their thoughts, as Peter tells it, "I was just being Mr Nice Guy. I couldn't tell you two minutes after what the hell they said."

Although *discussions* typically involve an exchange of ideas, *arguments* attempt to convince the other that your view is right or even superior. Narcissists, who have to be "right" and have their own way, introduce a strange twist. According to their reasoning, "If you disagree with me, that means *you* think that I am wrong." Peter's paranoia had turned innocent conversations into defensive counterattacks. He would conclude, "If everyone thinks I am wrong, then nobody respects me." Two people could not possibly both be right in the world he had created!

To encourage discussion and preserve harmony, listen carefully to the views of each person involved in your conversations. *Agreeing to disagree* is possible only when people truly respect the rights of individuals to hold their own unique views.

6. *Don't use closure statements.* People with controlling natures often add closure statements at the end of their thoughts. Peter would end his remarks with a concluding phrase such as, "This makes sense to me," or "That's what I think!" Such a habit is like putting a strong "period" at the end of your sentence. It suggests that the speaker's conclusion is sacrosanct, the final word.

Instead, *leave the subject open-ended or solicit the opinions of others.* Peter, realizing he needs time to digest new or conflicting information, has learned to buy time. By using supportive Feeling language, he reveals new sensitivity: "That's an interesting idea, but new to me. I'd like to talk this over with you after I've had time to absorb it."

7. *Avoid being short, blunt, or obtuse.* Clear communication results in shared knowledge. Remember, Thinkers tend to formulate their ideas, and package them *before* they speak. Feelers often *talk through* their thoughts before reaching a conclusion.

Short, blunt, sharp remarks tend to jar the listener if there is no lead-in information. Key facts are often left out when people forget to tell you what the subject is. Who or what is this person talking about? Obtuse thinking confuses rather than informs.

The *intensity* of your communication may convey an emphasis you do not intend. It's like underlining as you speak. Is the weight or the formality of my words appropriate to the subject matter? Am I raising my voice without realizing it? Again, watch your listener for clues. You may be shouting and not realize it.

8. *Express your thoughts within a context.* When you state an idea, *try to lead into it with a preamble or introduction.* Dropping thoughts without a context is like discharging a bomb without targeting it! Listeners cannot share your perspective or see the setting of your experience. Peter understands that his "left field" delivery alienates others. Learning to set the scene, Peter introduces his views on a local political issue: "Yesterday I was watching a panel of experts on the six o'clock news discuss the new legislation about waste disposal sites. My opinion is totally different from those guys'!" Peter may then state his thoughts and offer his solutions to this particular problem.

9. *Convey your enthusiasm or keen interest.* Because thinkers tend to intellectualize, they often fail to reveal how strongly they care about something. Others may be misled by the flat tone of their delivery, which contrasts with the intensity of their voice or strong body language. The listener is left with the question, "which signals should I follow?"

Peter is learning to *add a feeling component* to his delivery. He wants others to understand how emotionally involved he is in his concern for the environment. This subject is an important one for Peter. His listeners may well attend more closely if he emphasizes this commitment. "I'm quite excited about this new program," conveys Peter's true experience.

Enthusiasm and excitement are communicated through Feeling language's use of superlatives or emphasis. Peter would not have used words like *excited* before. In the past, his strong Thinking, rational, logical, pragmatic side dominated his language. "That's an interesting idea" would be as close as Peter would come to revealing the emotion behind his thoughts.

10. *Be honest and keep your integrity.* Focus on honesty by being *totally responsible for the integrity of your own thoughts and behaviour.* A word of caution here. The feelings expressed in the words you choose must be genuinely experienced. Do not say what others want to hear, unless it is your truth. Manipulative behaviour comes easily to people who grew up in dysfunctional families, since as children it wasn't safe to make waves. When Peter was polite and accommodating in the past, he had an ulterior motive. When he wanted something, he knew exactly what to say. He knew how to please, and how to convince. Much of the time, though, Peter was not even aware of his own manipulation. He acted as he always had in the past.

The dishonest used-car salesman who knows exactly how to disarm a reluctant buyer is a familiar prototype. Hopefully, such manipulations signal "buyer beware." However, more naive clients may be caught falling for such a convincing sales pitch.

B. Openness

Feeling behaviour and language foster *sensitivity, empathy, thoughtfulness, grace, diplomacy, and harmony.* Together, they encourage discussion rather than argument. An open sharing of ideas and experience brings people closer together, and encourages good listening *and* communication skills.

Openness leads one to *be other-directed and considerate* of the welfare of others. Controlling leads to manipulation and the loss of respect for the rights of others. To counteract his controlling nature, Peter had to let go, and develop his newfound sensitivity and respect for others.

1. BE AWARE OF YOUR PROJECTIONS   Openness will be achieved only when controlling stops and power struggles end. People like Peter control using clues gained by interpreting others' messages. They project by second-guessing what others want them to *say, think, do, or feel.* Only when Peter stopped externalizing and learned to internalize was he able to curb his second-guessing tactics.

Internalizing taught Peter to listen to his own reactions, and formulate both his own thoughts and feelings about the situation. Then he conveyed these ideas, using an "I" message. He also learned to communicate his views only when he was fully in control of his emotions. If he was not, he delayed problem-solving by rescheduling, or he left the scene to regain personal control. His tendency to *write scripts,* to rehearse a dialogue between himself and another person before the conversation even began, gradually stopped. He thus learned to *honour his own and others' ego boundaries.*

Not only is scriptwriting disrespectful and patronizing, it is a waste of energy and time. Remember that more than half the time you will be wrong in your perceptions.

2. STOP CONTROLLING   *Risk being more open, flexible, and spontaneous.* Concentrate on staying on your our own "side of the fence." *Your own reaction is your responsibility,* so verbalize what you think and feel with great care. Communication should be free of judgment. Put simply, you are trying to convey a description of *your* experience of the situation. This is your reality, but others' perceptions may be quite different. Their rights and dignity must be left intact.

It is not your responsibility to make assumptions about how the other person will respond to your words or actions. A good *rule of thumb* to guide you is: *Ask instead of tell!* Interpreting what others are likely to say or do is controlling behaviour. Peter used to take great pleasure in telling others what *he* thought they thought, even though he got incensed if others did that to him. Peter now tries to phrase questions that leave the initiative with the other person. For example, Peter asked Sally one day, "I'm having trouble understanding why you said that to Penny! I'd appreciate it if you would help me out." Sally, in turn, truly valued his curiosity. She sensed that Peter no longer felt he knew her better than she knew herself, as in the old days.

Make an effort to understand the reactions of others. *Reach out* by asking questions, such as "Could you tell me why ... ?"; "Were you upset by ... ?"; "What did you think when ... ?"; "How do you feel about what was said... ?"; "That sounds pretty disturbing. Was it?"; "I'd have some trouble handling that. Did you?"

3. OPEN BODY LANGUAGE If you are *genuinely concerned about another person*, this *positive attitude will show in your body stance*. Ask yourself what message your body is conveying. Are you making eye contact as you speak? Are you showing resistance or defending yourself by crossing your arms over your chest, crossing your legs, or holding your thighs tightly together? Are you fidgeting, unable to focus, and impatient to have the floor once again?

Occasionally, my clients rehearse for me what they wish to say in a job interview. When I point out their defensive postures or uptight body language, they are often surprised. Typically, when bodies are tense, breathing is constricted as well. No wonder it is hard for them to think clearly during an interview.

4. MOOD PROJECTIONS One cannot remain open and sensitive to others when caught in the clutches of a fully developed mood. Put simply, if you are caught in a mood, do not project your negative feelings onto others. *Recognize the earliest signs of a mood beginning* and intervene. For techniques to help you control your moods, see "The Road to

Recovery" chapter in my book *Workaholics: The Respectable Addicts.*

Hard as it is, try to *respect other people's moods,* but don't take responsibility for them. It is their mood, not yours. The initial tendency is to project onto that person your version of why he or she is caught up in a bad mood. This often happens because the ego-centred part of us tends to assume that the reason for the other person's mood lies with us.

The safe thing to do is to *offer empathy only.* Refrain from suggesting going somewhere or doing something to pull them out of it. When Sally withdrew and cut herself off from Peter, he would suggest that they go to a show or out for dinner. Sitting in stony silence in a restaurant, or becoming more agitated by the loaded emotions presented in a movie, is no solution for someone caught in a mood. Over-stimulation only increases feelings of helplessness or anxiety.

Give support by showing concern and asking if there is anything you might do. "You seem a little down today. Would you like me to make you some tea?" is Feeling language. Each of us is responsible for getting out of our own mood. So relax and be patient.

Above all, *do not try to problem-solve. Avoid criticism or judgments* at such time. Someone caught in a mood is unable to Think or Feel, let alone seek solutions to problems. Projecting your version of the problem onto someone else only compounds the problem. Resentment results when unsolicited advice is given. It is likely that the moody person will lash back and an endless discussion will ensue that goes nowhere. Sound familiar?

Give space and allow time for the other person to work through unhappy feelings. Go and do your own thing. No one in a mood needs to be burdened further by your upset reactions.

If you wish to follow it up later, you might ask, "I would really like to know what was bothering you the other day." Chances are the other person will then be in a better position to answer that question. However, some people resent this invasion of privacy. They have let go, so why bring up old stuff? As Peter, who hates redundancy, says, "Why beat it to death?"

C. *Generosity and Appreciation*

Genuine caring and appreciation, especially in Extraverts, *need to be shared* to be fully conveyed. Introverts, however, because they keep feelings locked safely inside, often neglect to verbalize appreciation. Introverts conserve energy, whereas Extraverts expend energy and, coincidentally, beget more by doing so!

For Thinkers, it often isn't logical and rational to care so deeply. So appreciation from them is often scarce. Ideas and goals are safer targets for their energy. People who demand and expect certain behaviours from Thinkers may be experienced as troublesome or tiresome.

1. GRATITUDE   I believe that one of the secrets of happiness is to be truly grateful. It is relatively easy to appreciate the good things that life sends our way. The more difficult task is to be open when negative situations knock on our door. It takes courage to open that door and be receptive to whatever *life lesson* is sent our way. It helps to lighten things up with humour: "I hope I grow an inch with this one!"

2. SHOW ENTHUSIASM   Appreciation is conveyed by *expressing enthusiasm for other people's ideas, thoughts, and deeds.* Praise, encouragement, and supportive words come from the Feeling side. Whereas Peter would say, "Good work!" if a job was well done, he had difficulty saying to his wife, "That was a wonderful thing you did for your sister." Superlative words like "wonderful," "terrific," or "great" seem unnatural and may sound phony to a Thinker. Yet, under-

neath, Peter envied Sally's enthusiasm and the ease with which she performed thoughtful acts. Thinkers, because they are naturally competitive, tend to place things on a hierarchical basis and rate themselves in relation to others on that ladder. Therefore, they are reluctant to elevate others above their level of competence.

Thinkers need to counterbalance their naturally critical and skeptical reserve. "My ball team would laugh themselves silly if I used the language you're teaching me!" challenged another determined Thinker. I laughed and encouraged him to try out some new language that evening at the office game. "What a great hit!" was the most Jake could imagine himself saying, as he left the office muttering. Jake, like Peter, soon discovered that when he showed enthusiasm or said supportive things, people beamed back. It didn't stop him feeling silly for a while though.

Another Thinker, working on developing her Feeling, burst into my office one afternoon. "I've just made friends with my arch-enemy!" Patricia enthused. This man got the promotion she had aspired to. "You know, this guy isn't half bad. When I told him about this journey I'm going through in here, he started to tell me about the problems he is having at home." Patricia empathized: "No wonder he was such a pain in the butt." By articulating her feelings at the office, Patricia found that others, who secretly had been afraid of her, now responded with smiles and, as she quipped, "relief." No one could accuse Patricia of being humourless now.

When another client, Joseph, was thanked by his wife, Clare, for the dinner the two had just shared in a new restaurant, he replied curtly, "Don't thank me. It's your money, too!" When Clare protested about her husband's lack of manners, together we discussed how this situation could have been handled with more grace. When Joseph was asked for suggestions, his blank stare revealed his puzzlement. Often, the person must learn a *new set of adjectives and verbs* that sound like a foreign language. He may not understand yet what is wrong with what he used to say.

3. BE SUPPORTIVE Generosity can be shown by *supporting others' independent actions*. A very controlling mother once told me, "I want the kids to get their act together before I let them go on and do their own thing!" After a discussion about how she could show her support using Feeling language, Geraldine offered, "I know they're going to be okay, and I wish them well on their journey." Her sincere expression of faith in her children was in stark contrast to her endless advice and fretting.

4. COMPLIMENTARY COMMENTS Don't hesitate to compliment someone about how well she looks or what a good conversationalist he is. Many times, people do notice such things, but nothing gets said or done to acknowledge the person's particular talent. "You look really *great* today!" is Feeling language. "Smart suit!" conveys the compliment, but it lacks the personal touch. *It takes energy to reach out*, and thus many people refuse to grow because of psychological laziness. They restrict their responses to what comes naturally and miss out on the smiles and joy that compliments elicit from others.

5. BE GENUINE *If what you have to say is not honestly felt, don't say it*. People feel manipulated, patronized, or put down when others deliver insincere messages. When a message is negative, take special care to be diplomatic, gracious, and thoughtful in how you phrase your thoughts.

D. Warmth and Sensitivity

Warmth and sensitivity describe two specially appreciated attributes of the feeling side.

1. WARMTH   Warmth is often conveyed through *body language, smiles, and gestures that enhance the gift of words or tokens of appreciation.* Reaching out to touch or even leaning forward towards someone as you speak can add a deeper meaning to your message. Gently touching someone's arm or shoulder is easier and more natural for extraverts and for feelers. Others may feel awkward at first performing such gestures. However, next time you wish to show appreciation in a social situation, try introducing warmth and see what happens.

2. SENSITIVITY   It helps to be sensitive to the "why" behind people's behaviour. The focus needs to be on *understanding, not on judging the possible motivation of an act or communication.* Feelers, whose values centre around people and relationships, often have an easier time being gracious in awkward situations.

Sensitivity is especially necessary when gifts are offered and received. Accepting gifts of any kind is difficult for someone who needs to be in control. Whether it be a compliment or an actual gift, the receiver may neglect to affirm the gift-giver. Thinkers, because they tend to be skeptical, often question the giver's motivation. This discomfort may produce a defensive acceptance, such as an ungracious "You shouldn't have done that!"

However, if this same person is open to sharing, he may learn to *comment on the feeling* behind *the gift.* Whether a person likes the gift or not should not affect appreciation. For example, Peter learned to respond, "What a nice idea!" or "That's very thoughtful of you. Thanks so much."

Peter confided that he was often unhappy about the gifts he received. As he explained, "I have very definite tastes!" Many Thinkers do not even realize it, but they often say nothing at all at the time the gift is given. Or they look very uncomfortable. The rationalization offered is that they don't want to "hurt" others' feelings by saying anything.

Feelers' gifts are often simply an expression of their warmth or sensitivity. There need be no ulterior motivation, other than the wish to show appreciation. Successful gift-giving is complex and not an easy art.

E. Diplomacy and Criticism

The other side of the coin to gift-giving is *offering construct-ive criticism*. Here, generosity of spirit needs to be the focus, not power-plays.

1. FAIRNESS A balanced presentation in which the speaker *offers support along with the criticism* is best. No one "*always* does something" or "*never* does something."

When criticism is appropriate, soften your delivery by con-firming a positive aspect first. Peter, with his tendency to blurt out negative statements, might say something like, "That was a rotten thing you said to so-and-so!" Instead, a more gracious tone is achieved when he says, "You're usually polite. In this particular situation, your words came as quite a surprise!"

2. OBJECTIVE EMPATHY If someone else is telling you about a goof she made, or a time when he showed poor judg-ment, further critical judgments are rarely helpful. In fact, the person's shame is compounded. The individual now has a "*double whammy*" to contend with. Because Sally was so naive, she did not realize the impact on her daughter when she became overly involved in any painful situations Penny experienced. Years before, Penny had come home from school one Valentine's Day. She was devastated because she hadn't received one card. The look on her mother's face, unfortu-nately, doubled her grief. In Penny's eyes, she had failed her mother, too.

Sally's objective thinking was not working in this situa-tion. Her ego boundaries blurred across into Penny's territory and she took on her daughter's pain. If she had been able to be more objective, her reply might have been, "Gee, honey, I can't imagine how that happened. Are you okay?" Penny could then have vented the hurt she was experiencing.

When someone tells a painful story, it is important not to jump in and side with someone else in the story. Parents' criticisms, especially at such times, can have a powerful impact on children. Soon, that child will "neglect to tell the whole truth." Why tell somebody something if you will be further devastated by doing so.

3. SHARING SHADOWS   At times, however, it may be supportive to share your own foibles or weaknesses with others. However, *be careful not to pre-empt the storyteller.* One day, Peter wanted to know what was wrong with telling one of the kids what he would have done, or how he would have handled a similar situation when he was young. I answered by describing a theatrical stage, with a father and son standing in the spotlight, centre stage. The son is telling his dad a sad tale about something that happened the day before. The father responds by going off on a tangent. He makes an "end run," so to speak. It's as though he has walked away from his son across the stage while telling him how he would have handled that situation.

I asked Peter to imagine that he was the lighting manager for that theatre. "Where would you direct the spotlight during this scene?" Peter's response followed as insight crossed his face. "On the father, of course. He's the guy whose going on and on!" The son, standing in the middle of the stage, alone, would likely feel unheard and misunderstood. The focus of the conversation had shifted to his father's ideas and past experience.

Keep the spotlight on the speaker is good advice. Remember to listen fully to what the other person has to say. By asking questions that elicit more information, you not only show your interest and concern but you will likely learn more about the speaker's emotional reactions. Brevity on your part is important if you do decide to share. For example, after his son has talked through his problem, Peter might show empathy by saying, "Something like that happened to me when I was a kid, too!" If the son wants to ask questions about what *did* happen to his father, then his dad has been invited over their respective ego boundaries into the son's territory. This is a far cry from unsolicited advice.

F. Harmony

If people always have to be right and have their own way, apologizing will not be part of their repertoire. For instance, narcissists, with their strong sense of entitlement, think that what they are doing is just fine. After all, they are special and unique. What applies to others does not necessarily pertain to them.

1. APOLOGIZING   It's the old story. People would rather be right than happy. Value systems enter into this dilemma. If ideas and goals mean more to you than nurturing a relationship, then it makes sense that backing down from a position, or defusing a contentious issue, is not an option for you. Ludicrously illogical examples occur. After one husband threatened to leave his wife during a heated argument, he later told me, "I can't possibly apologize. Once I've said I'll do something, I do it!"

An apology does not necessarily suggest that you are "wrong." *Two people may both be right for different reasons,* but not in the narcissist's world. He interprets other people's contrary views as an indication that they think that it is *he* who is wrong! Swallowing pride and demonstrating humility do not come easily to people who have become arrogant. As a consequence, other people with a strong need for harmony who seek conflict resolution in their dealings with them will be left frustrated. There can be no resolution when narcissists remain convinced they are right.

2. DIGNITY   Acknowledging and affirming another person's reality, while at the same time holding on to your own beliefs, is possible. While pride can be a foolish emotion, personal dignity must be honoured. *Acknowledge the other person's point of view*, even if you do not agree with it. To ensure that you actually do understand their views, you may need to rephrase and check out your accuracy.

Peter learned to say, "Let me make sure I understand exactly what you are saying." He would then paraphrase, as best he could, and then ask if his interpretation fit.

3. LIGHTEN UP!   Because Thinkers have such highly focused awareness, they often come across as very intense. Sometimes, *a reason to apologize stems simply from the heated delivery of an argument*. Intensity drives home a thought, and this strong focus may convey more than you intend. Sometimes it is derogatory or tough language, such as swearing, exaggerating to make a point, or even attacking someone personally, that heighten the impact of your statements on others.

Peter began to realize how he overpowered people. He wanted to learn to state his opinions without overwhelming his listeners. Probably the best way for him to do this, if he catches himself forcing an issue, is to *comment on his own delivery*. A statement such as, "You'll have to excuse me. I really do get carried away with my ideas sometimes!" may soften his message. *Laughing at your own foibles* often serves to break the ice. It isn't helpful if others get defensive and shut off, especially if you are trying to be understanding, rather than judgmental.

4. BRIGHTEN UP   Peter, without realizing it, had developed a permanent frown, two lines deeply furrowed in his brow. His rigidity and stubborn nature had left a permanent reminder. When my clients are getting in touch with their feelings, I often notice a change in the shape of their faces. As the *rigidity* of the psyche lessens, their *features soften.* Their cheeks take on a more rounded shape, and muscles around the mouth relax.

Peter, aware of his facial tension, began to do exercises to relax these muscles. He opened up his jaw and purposefully yawned whenever he became tense over some issue. He even practiced smiling in front of the mirror in the morning, to start his day.

His newfound inner harmony and openness towards other's differing ideas showed in Peter's more relaxed state. He no longer kept his arms and legs tightly crossed as he had in the past. It had been his unconscious defensive response against an increasingly chaotic and negative world.

5. SMILE, AND OTHERS SMILE BACK   By frowning, you may be delivering negative vibes to those you encounter each day. A smile, in contrast, can relay positive energy as a precious gift to others. Your choice!

G. Humility

Individuals who have achieved inner psychic balance show humility because they know the struggle they had in order to achieve this hard-won self-knowledge. Life lessons taught them that "a little knowledge is a dangerous thing!" Therefore, in order to remain open and receptive to new ideas, they now refrain from forcing a decision and are ever conscious of the big picture. "What I don't know today, I can learn tomorrow" might well be their motto.

Mature people are well aware of their own weaknesses, not just their strengths. Bravely facing the whole complexity of humanity, they consider both the positive and negative aspects of the people involved in any situation. Naivety, or remaining credulous and unworldly, is not an option. There is an acceptance that life is difficult.

These wise people have learned not to problem-solve for others, but *simply to listen.* By doing so, they keep their relationships on a peer level. They willingly share power through compromise, taking turns, or mediating through dialogue to reach a mutually agreeable solution. They recognize that since we are all special in the eyes of God, each of us deserves to be treated as an equal. Through acknowledging their own humanity on the journey towards self-acceptance, they've developed a comfortable humility. There is no longer a need to prove themselves to others.

The healthy balance between their Thinking and Feeling functions facilitates a more holistic point of view. Thus wisdom guides their decisions, care and consideration is shown for others, and the search for truth remains an ever-present goal.

CREATIVE PROBLEM-SOLVING

In chapter 11, the end of this journey we have traveled together, a method of problem-solving will be offered that has been adapted from ideas presented in Matthew Fox's book *Creation Spirituality: Liberating Gifts for the Peoples of the Earth.* The title of a popular song by Tina Turner, "What's Love Got to Do with It?" will serve to introduce the themes of maturity, spirituality, creativity, and joy. A journey that takes us towards any or all of these destinations will serve us well.

11

Problem-Solving Through Creativity

The Logical Circle

You're only young once, but you can be immature forever.

"How will I know when I'm better?" is a question often asked by impatient clients who want recovery to happen *now*! My standard answer, after many years in practice, is: "When the power of love and compassion in you is stronger than the power of greed." This will signal that feelings really work, and that values have shifted accordingly. As one client put it, "My wife and my kids are on the front burner now, and I intend to keep it that way!"

In reality, however, all of us experience continual internal struggles between Thinking's goal-oriented focus and Feeling's concern for people and relationships. On a ski trip to St Anton in Austria, an older member of the group followed a different trail and became separated from the group. It was about 10:30 in the morning. We waited for some time, to no avail, then continued skiing. At the top run the group gathered, and I listened as someone suggested going to Stuben, a nearby village, for lunch. Several people chimed in with their support, thinking this was a great idea.

"What about Kevin?" was the cry from the Feelers in the group. They assumed that our lost skier would likely wait for us at the inn in St Christoph where we had planned to have lunch. "We've got to stick to our plan."

A chorus of protest rose: "Let's go to Stuben! None of us has been there." This time, the Feelers grew visibly upset and put down their collective feet! "No way! We're not going to abandon Kevin!" After much disgruntled banter, the decision was made: "On to St Christoph!"

My comment to the man beside me was, "Well, the Feelers won this time!" He replied, "I was sort of on the fence on that one!" Later in the week, a sigh passed through the group as we passed Stuben en route to Zurich airport. "Well, maybe next year!" was heard from the back of the bus. The Thinking side of us hates to lose.

No one was wrong here. Both groups valued different things. However, my experience observing such life situations shows that Feeling types often have to shout to get their thoughts acknowledged. The truth is that all of us sit on the fence at times and go against our natural disposition. The difference is that Feelers, who make decisions based on feeling values that include honesty, sympathy, empathy, compassion, fairness, self-control and duty, are more likely to suffer guilt and remorse when they lie or act in a way that goes against the grain. Thinkers, because they are more focused and goal-oriented, became absorbed in getting from A to B. Their pragmatic nature permits them to rationalize and justify any of their decisions that go against society's rules and regulations. "I'm rushing, Officer, because I've just got a call that my wife is ill!" The real reason is that he is late for an important meeting. Safety factors in general – and even truth – pale beside the excitement generated by reaching some hard-won goal.

In the balanced personality, the person *takes choice seriously*. A conscious decision may be made to use our Thinking function when ideas and goals are the focus and other people's welfare is not directly affected. When people and relationships do matter, it is appropriate to let our Feeling function dominate and influence our decisions. Take care, though, lest the naturally more aggressive Thinking side runs roughshod over the Feeling side!

As a model for mature problem-solving that uses both Feeling and Thinking functions, let me offer what I call the *Logical Circle*, a technique that was inspired by the holistic nature of Matthew Fox's views presented in his book *Creation Spirituality*. Fox speaks of four paths along the spiritual journey that tell us "what matters" (18–26). *Path one*, the Via Positiva, represents awe, wonder, delight, mystery. *Path two*, the Via Negativa, represents suffering, darkness, nothingness, emptying, letting go, letting be. *Path three*, the Via Creativa, embodies creativity, imagination, giving birth to new ideas. And *Path four*, the Via Transformativa, stands for justice, celebration, compromise.

These paths, as envisioned by Fox, represent a sacred hoop in the form of a cross, describing the journey towards spirituality and wisdom.

THE LOGICAL CIRCLE

The title for my model for problem-solving popped into my head one day, a gift from the Intuitive side! *Logical* represents the Thinking side, the hierarchical ladder – straight, linear processing. One goes through logical and progressive steps to get from A to B, in search of the truth. Rational, pragmatic, practical, analytical reasoning best fits this "straight-line" Thinking.

Feeling is represented by the *circle image*. A circle is in harmony with the round earth and universe. It has no jarring or sharp edges. Harmony dictates a mediatory process by which both sides in the issue are considered and the welfare of both participants is paramount. Discussion rather than argument, reaching agreement by consensus, and protecting the dignity and integrity of all are its guidelines.

Concentric circles, I believe, best describe our growth patterns. In the centre of the circle, the ego is present at the child's birth and first days of life. New persons and life experiences offer opportunities to break through to ever-increasing circles of growth. Throughout our life, we go through cycles in which we suffer growing pains and conflict, regress temporarily to gather strength, and then experience fresh insights. Whether it be a positive or negative experience, we have an opportunity to advance. Failure can be a wonderful teacher, *if* we learn our lessons with humility.

As we pass through these circles of discovery and grow psychologically, the Self is slowly defined. *Individuation* is the process by which you evolve to establish yourself as a person – unique and separate from others. Maturity brings involvement in the wider world around us. Transformational growth offers the privilege and responsibility of touching and influencing others' lives. We hear ourselves called to give our gifts away to others still on the inner circles of burgeoning life. Creativity and joy sustain us, helping us through struggle, and even formidable chaos.

The Logical Circle model for problem-solving has *five steps*. It is a journey inwards to discover the Self and to transform what needs changing. Self-affirmation and gratitude for what we do possess can fuel our enthusiasm and renew the energy we need to face the outside world. The following diagram illustrates the first four steps that lie within the circle. Step five lies outside the sphere, where our newly discovered strengths can be channelled into the generosity that inspires us to help others.

Step 1. Wake-Up Call

Reality-testing can be painful. Life experiences often knock us over the head, and thereafter we are no longer the same.

THE LOGICAL CIRCLE

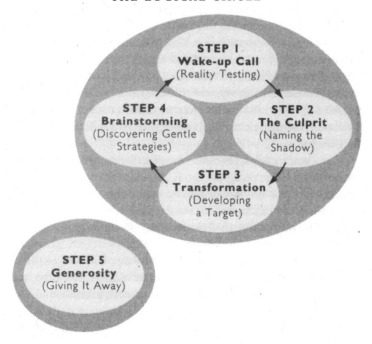

We fail an exam and our career plans or choices are limited. Someone stops seeing us and doesn't call. We don't understand why. A wife decides to separate from her husband, who is shocked. "I thought we got along pretty well!" he protests. Your boss calls you into the office first thing in the morning and gives you the bad news. By noon, your personal belongings are packed up and you are out of there. No warning! No awareness? Life is so difficult, you protest.

Sometimes we receive critical feedback from our *Significant Other*. "Do you know how incredibly controlling you are?" yells a henpecked husband to his bossy wife. A distraught wife, torn between divided loyalties to both husband and child, warns, "That was a really mean thing you said to Johnny! How could you even *think* that way!"

Authority figures often daunt us. "Your performance this term is just not acceptable. The staff are afraid of you. Morale in this office is at an all-time low," announces a supervisor. Your career takes an unexpected dive.

A black cloud seems to be following you around. People who, a year before, seemed to enjoy your company, are now avoiding you. At work your secretary sometimes looks stunned and fights back tears. "What did I say wrong?" you ask yourself. At home your wife is cool and aloof. Well, there's a long story behind that!

It has become crystal clear by now that your own judgment about what is appropriate behaviour can't be trusted. While you instinctively recognize the need to change, you haven't the faintest idea just where to begin. You decide finally that it might be worth it to try out the Logical Circle exercise, and begin by doing some reality-testing.

The *"Wake-up Call"* asks you to write down, number, and describe five recent examples of your own behaviour that proved troublesome to another person, and to state the circumstances leading up to the situation. Choose *different* people and situations for each example. Remember to challenge your honesty by "telling it like it *really* happened," no sugar-coating allowed.

Try to generate your own feedback by analyzing how and why each incident occurred. Ask yourself the following self-confrontational questions.

REALITY-TESTING QUESTIONS

a) What was I actually saying or doing at the time?
b) When did it happen? What time of day or night?
c) Was I aware at the time that I was upset or in a bad mood?
d) Was the other person tired or tense when it happened?
e) Had either of us been drinking prior to the situation?

f) Who else was present who might give me some feedback?

g) Was this unusual behaviour or do I do this often?

h) Who do I tend to behave this way with, or say such things to?

i) Is this a new insight or old news? ·

This list is meant to be only a sampling of the questions you might need to ask. Remember, *growth stems from honesty*, not denial.

Step 2. The Culprit

Now that you have zeroed in on five examples of times when your actions offended others, it is time to *"Name the Shadow."* What is the *essence* of what is wrong with your behaviour or your words in each particular situation? Give a name to the *negative Shadow* you wish to work on. For example, were you being impatient, rude, insensitive, or arrogant at the time? If you chose *insensitive*, free-associate to that word and list one association under the other. Start with at least five related words that come to mind. You can add to this list as you become more self-aware:

> thoughtless
> judgmental
> unfeeling
> indifferent
> inattentive

It is now time to *list alternative words* that could become goals to help you shape future behaviour in similar situations.

Step 3. Transformation Goal

It takes a strong motivation to willingly change some aspect of your behaviour or your personality. Make a true commitment, for the next few weeks, to *concentrate on changing this one flaw in your character*. Set realistic and concrete goals so that you will be able to measure progress along the way. Name the goal words that best express the opposite meaning to the words on your Step 2 list. For example, the opposite of insensitive is sensitive.

insensitive	sensitive
thoughtless	thoughtful
judgmental	understanding
unfeeling	sympathetic
indifferent	concerned
inattentive	fully present

Draw a *square* around each list. The list on the right serves as a guidepost to signify the attributes that you wish to develop in yourself.

Step 4. Brainstorming

Brainstorming, a term coined in *Applied Imagination* by advertising executive A.F. Osborn, describes a problem-solving technique. A group attempts to find a solution to a specific problem through the spontaneous generation and amassing of ideas, with a moratorium placed on all criticism of ideas presented by its members. Individuals can also brainstorm independently.

Brainstorming taps into our Intuition, as well as the Thinking and Feeling functions. As applied in Step 4, creativity and imagination are used to help shift the focus of attention away from the identified negative "Culprit" trait (i.e., insensitive) that caused the problem in the first place, to discover and generate fresh and clever ideas about how its *opposite* trait (i.e., sensitivity) could have been used in the present situation and in similar situations in the future. Innovative solutions often cause great discomfort because people are challenged to use facets of their personality that seem foreign or awkward compared to their natural way of being and of doing things. Patience, persistence, and compassion are essential to sustain the haltingly slow *transformational* process. Enthusiasm and support are great, but not everybody naturally possesses these attributes. For many, becoming more enthusiastic is in itself a goal.

In our therapy sessions, the client and I spin ideas off each other in order to become more effective at brainstorming. My part in this usually consists of asking questions or making comments that relate to what the client is saying. You may wish to ask a close friend, someone who is also interested in personal growth, to think of all the different ways you might transform the behaviour you have chosen to target. Hopefully, one suggestion will generate another as intuitive answers pop up unexpectedly, as if by magic.

SALLY   Let's retrace the first three steps Sally took leading up to the brainstorming process.

Sally's *Wake-up Call* came from her own internal confrontation. She had been noticing the following behavioural patterns in her recent interactions:

a) "People take advantage of me. It happened last week when Belinda expected me to look after her daughter when she went to the dentist."

b) "I can't say no. I was furious, but I didn't say anything. No one else was there to give me feedback on how I handled myself."

c) "I block when I get so upset. Something in me just shuts down."

d) "I lie. I tell people what they want to hear. I didn't say a word to Belinda, but I was steaming inside."

The *Culprit*, the Shadow Sally decided to work on, was her reluctance to offer her own truth, which she blamed on her *naivety.* "That's what causes me to lie. I can't stand the part of me that tells others what they want to hear. I'm such a coward. Worse still, I do this with almost everyone. Even my husband and my mother! I've been vaguely aware of this for a while, but our session last week really brought it home. Boy, is this sick or what!" She laughs.

Her free associations with the word *naivety* are listed here, along with her *opposite* goals (Step 3).

naivety	truth
denial	honesty
dizzy blonde	smart
irresponsible	responsible
childish	adult
unworldly	well-informed

Sally's *Transformation Goal,* the target that she chose as opposite to her naivety, was to "always seek the truth." Any time Sally felt "stupid" about something, she resolved to ask herself, "What might be a more intelligent, rational, or logical way to handle this situation?" Her thinking cap would go on, ready to brainstorm.

Brainstorming, for Sally, was a natural process. Now that her Feelings were working well once again, her Intuition clicked in easily. Ideas popped up, one after another, and she needed little assistance. These are the notes I made as Sally worked through how she was going to be less naive in the future:

– "I've got to open up more. Extravert. Say what I really think!"
– "Use the "I" message to describe my half – what I think, what I feel, and what my gut tells me is right."
– "Risk the other person not hearing or being hostile. I've got to be more brave if this is ever going to happen."
– "I need to be more independent. When my husband talks for me, I need to ask him to let me figure this out."

- "Then I need to go away and figure out how I feel. I need to *thoroughly feel*."
- "I've got to ask myself what is rational and logical here? Be skeptical!"
- "Am I looking at the facts, or only seeing what I want to see?"
- "Look at the big picture. Stand back. Gain some objectivity."
- "It's lonely being naive. Not part of the world. I need to read and expose myself to new ideas."
- "Ask myself if I'm being consistent with my value system? Is this keeping my integrity?"

Sally continued to work on this list at home. Any time she heard herself tell people what they wanted to hear instead of her truth, she would correct herself as graciously as she could. Other times, when a new idea popped up, she would *add that solution to her list*. When she found herself going blank, she would run through some of her brainstorming ideas to see if one of them would work for this particular occasion.

Rereading her list after some frustrating situation, Sally often discovered that associations pulled up more gifts of wisdom. Sally grew very fond of her "Clever List," as she called it.

PETER   Peter's *Logical Circle*, as described here, shows how he battled with one of his most troublesome Shadows, his *impatience*.

The *Wake-up Call* for Peter arose from his awareness that the Gerbil Wheel existence he was living left him rushing through all aspects of his life. People and their needs were a nuisance that he barely tolerated. Nowadays, Peter honestly did want to spend time being fully present, especially for Sally and the children.

Reflecting on his own behaviour the week before, Peter observed:

a) "I'm still trigger-happy. The other night I jumped at Sally out of the blue. She was just minding her own business, doing her own thing. There's still part of me that wants all her attention."

b) "I didn't get an immediate response from one of the kids, and I started yelling. I'm a bit better, but my expectations still run me."

c) "At work, someone was hesitating in the middle of trying to explain something that was painful for him. I wanted him to hurry up and stop wasting my time. There's that selfishness again. I guess that's behind a lot of my impatience."

The Culprit, in all three examples, Peter decided, was his strong *impatience.* "It's behind so much of what goes wrong for me. I steamroll over people because of it, and I can't delegate properly because people have to fit into my agenda and my timetable."

Peter realized that he had been like that even as a teenager. It was worse when he was moody. "But I have to admit, I never saw half of this before." He laughed. "I was like that road-runner cartoon. You couldn't see me for the dust I kicked up chasing after those hare-brained schemes I cooked up. I didn't want too much time to think!"

Peter's free associations with the word *impatient* are listed below, along with his *opposite* goals (Step 3).

impatient		patient	
intolerant		tolerant	
March Hare		tortoise	
insensitive		sensitive	

bulldozer
poor listener

gentle
good listener

Peter's *Transformation Goal*, (i.e., patience), required a radical departure from the way he had lived his life until recently. "How do you use a bulldozer gently?" was his $64 question. "It will be a red-letter day for me when I'm content to be a tortoise." His laughter had a wistful quality, I thought. Hard edges were falling off Peter at an alarming rate.

"Brainstorming is something I do at the öffice," Peter kidded. His humour had peppered our conversations of late, and the sarcasm and black humour of the early sessions was scarce. The notes below follow Peter's brainstorming (my comments are in parentheses). Peter needed more support because his Intuition, like his Feelings, was slow to return to its former level of functioning.

- "I've got to relax more. Believe it or not, I keep trying those six calming techniques you taught me. Got to watch my breathing though – I can feel the tension choke up in my throat."
- "I'm so intense, it isn't funny. Instead of being so damned goal-oriented, I've got to trust the process more. It reminds me of the day you told me about knitting that yellow sweater!" (My analogy had been that if I'm knitting a sweater, I may worry throughout about whether it will fit Johnny. In my anxiety, I won't hear the clicking of the needles, the feel of the wool, the subtle smell of lanolin, nor will I notice the sunflower yellow of the garment. The joy of knitting will be totally lost in anxious fits of measuring and stretching, or worrying that the arms will be too short, or the bodice too wide.)
- "If people are going to mean more to me than getting from A to B, I need to be more curious about what makes people tick." (It may mean asking people enough questions

to know their stories. Also, it might be helpful to educate yourself about developmental capacities related to the ages of your children. Do you think you expect too much?)

- "Since I was overly responsible and never had a real childhood, I'm probably unrealistic in what I expect."

- "Even at work, I'm unrealistic. I fail to understand other people's strengths." (Do you think you need to challenge your judgment here? Did you ask yourself whether this person has the skills to do what you expect of him?)

- "The part of me that has to have my own way, wants to be right – the words single-minded, rigidity, and distancing come to mind. Take a couple of steps back. Ask myself: Is it really vital that I be right?" (Do you think the need to be right has anything to do with this inability to get vicarious pleasure from others' situations that we spoke about last week?)

- "If I can't get vicarious pleasure or pain out of someone else's happiness or discomfort, then I'm cut off, removed. That's when I get judgmental and critical. I guess I'm frightened."

- "Instead of putting words in others' mouths and "fixing," I need to wait until they're finished. I could show them I'm interested." (I wonder if sympathy would show on your face? Try this. Think of yourself as gentle for a moment. How does this make you feel?)

- "It's reassuring. Trying to comfort. Being patient, concerned." (What do you think about using the gentle shepherd as a role model? I introduce the idea of God as a *serving* God, being there to serve us, as well as our serving Him.)

- "If I take on the servant role, I'm going to have to be there for others without expectations – be patient!" (Try to free-associate to both the Hare and Tortoise images.)

HARE	TORTOISE
rushing	unhurried, slow

out-of-breath	not sweating
on a Gerbil Wheel	lumbering
in a frazzle	time to see things
frantic	methodical, steady
exhausted	relaxed

(That's quite a choice you have there! Which one will get the upper hand, do you think?)

Peter and I could go on indefinitely as we exchange ideas, as *"anything goes."* I suggest to him that the images of the Hare and the Tortoise might appear to him at the most surprising times!

Step 5. Generosity

This step represents the point in life's journey when the mature individual, with a strong sense of Self and confidence intact, turns outwards to *ever-expanding concentric circles* and devotes time and energy towards benefiting others. Knowledge, wisdom, creativity, and joy, acquired from the inwards journey, provide the strength and energy needed for the tasks at hand. *Give it away!* There is more where that came from, if you use your resources wisely and well.

TOWARDS BALANCE, WISDOM, AND MATURITY

Where does your power come from? The title of Tina Turner's song "What's Love Got to Do with It!" springs to mind. Without the power of love and compassion for oneself and others, the transformation of the Shadow aspects of the Self is not possible. Instead, in individuals whose insight and feeling are missing, shame often invites destructive impulses. When their security or power is threatened, for example, these handicapped people become vindictive and are often driven towards revenge. Ultimately, they also punish themselves as their dark Shadow traits alter their own personality. Dr Jekyll gives way to Mr Hyde. Healing solutions come through understanding and forgiveness. Freeing others by forgiving them for the pain they have caused us is an admirable gesture. Left undone, however, it can be one of the most difficult stumbling blocks to ongoing growth. It helps to remember that through forgiving others, we also free ourselves. Again, there is a choice to be made. Do I remain a bitter, resentful, and angry person, or do I allow my spirituality and the power of love to work its magic in my life?

Next time some upsetting or traumatic situation presents itself and you experience acute discomfort, instead of reacting immediately, try this exercise.

Look up and imagine a large stop light flashing bright neon red. Stop in your tracks! This scene may turn ugly or have dire consequences if you let go and lose control. Or you can choose to learn something new! Try to open up, and allow yourself to remain vulnerable while you get your act together.

STOP........WAIT........WATCH........LISTEN........LAUGH

Your laughter may be fed by pure anxiety, or it may convey surprise and true humility. "What lesson is knocking on my door today?" you might well ask. Or, "How will I transform this lousy state of affairs?" You need time to think and feel. It takes time for information to register. Listen to what your Sensation (that is, your sight, touch, taste, smell, and hearing) tells you. What is your gut reaction, your Intuition, shouting out?

Resolve to allow all this information to perk and bubble up over time. See what wisdom surfaces from this crazy mixture. You may not be able to understand why all this is happening in the "big picture" of your life experience. Trauma tends to make us short-sighted and trigger-happy. Taking *time-out* before we act is often the wisest decision.

Develop a sense of wonder at such times. *Stay free from judgments*. Whatever has happened just is! Why it happened may take weeks to figure out, or even months. Sometimes, there is no answer to some questions.

In my practice, I frequently work with families whose members suffer from depression, anxiety, and physical and psychological signs of stress due to workaholism, alcoholism, or eating disorders. Many of these families are caught in power struggles, in which the husband, wife, or children compete with one another. *Greed* typically plays a part in all of these traumas. Excesses of anything are rarely healthy, and greed is typically a recipe for disaster. Just read your newspaper each day for the latest "casualty" – some well-known public figure, business tycoon, or pillar of the community who has fallen from grace. Such scenes are played out at every level of society. None of us is free from the possibility of disaster. God, in His wisdom, left us with the freedom of choice.

Will you shape your destiny and determine your fate through the power of love and transformation, or the power of greed and vindication? *Your choice!*

THE BALANCED PERSONALITY

Maturity, wisdom, spirituality, creativity, and joy – all are fostered by a balanced life and a well-developed personality.

The doing-performing-Thinking side of the personality is capable of changing attitudes, values, and directions. It does so through *will and self-determination*. We make choices and solve problems that ultimately determine where our energies go. We can choose to invest in a variety of interests and goals. Or we can remain single-minded and restrict our focus to a limited vision or goal. Unfortunately, the latter choice is often attained at the expense of our family's best interests and our own health.

Our being-Feeling side should play a strong role in determining what choices we make. It is other-directed, open, and vulnerable. Its warmth, enthusiasm, wisdom, and joy influence how we treat ourselves and look out for others.

Purposefully working on your less-developed opposite functions is a useful exercise towards achieving a balanced and mature personality. If you are an Intuitive type, for instance, your balance will come from working on your Sensation side. You might try a process I call "Watching Water." Find a comfortable spot looking out over water. Forget whatever else you might be doing. Concentrate on the surface of the water. Every time the wind changes, look for new patterns. Be alert to shifts in sunlight and notice the ever-changing hues. Do the clouds form stories in the sky? Do you hear bird sounds? Do you feel the wind on the hairs on your arm? Do the sun's rays make the water shimmer and send arrows across the surface that sparkle and shine luminously?

Because this takes extra effort and patience, you will have to *stop what you're doing to make this happen*. However, its rewards are great as you begin to notice small and precious details. It will quiet your restlessness and ground you in the moment. You will be thoroughly present, not wondering what you're going to do next.

Each one of us can benefit from knowing what our personality type is, and where our direction of growth lies. By entering into the opposite territory, we gain new insights, fresh energy, and enthusiasms that have lain dormant. We discover feelings and thoughts we really never knew existed in us. The Introvert who purposely tries to be increasingly friendly and interested in people, who becomes curious enough to ask questions about others' opinions, will be rewarded with smiles and gratitude from those who wondered if he really cared about them or if she even noticed they existed. Your world will be twice as big, and your adventures surprising! As one of my clients exclaimed, "Something really good happened this week. I decided to take that guy I told you bugged me so much out for coffee. It's hard to believe, but that man is a comedian in his spare time. I guess he exaggerates a lot because that's adaptive when you're telling jokes. We really had quite a fun time! This is great!"

If you take the time and energy to take risks, you, too, will see and feel things that are totally new. This is what real living is all about! Why not start growing and expanding your universe today!

You might start by reminding yourself to take action, to work on changing bad habits and behaviours that prevent you from living a balanced life.

Tips for Living the Good Life

Be open to change. Growth is never easy, but its rewards are great!

1. *Take your empathy-compassion temperature every evening*:
    a) How did I interact with each member of my family today?
    b) Was I patient and polite to my colleagues and staff?
    c) Did I remember to take good care of *me*?
2. *Do some serious reality-testing of your honesty*:
    a) Did I say yes when I should have said no?
    b) Did I agree to do something in less time than is realistic?
    c) Did I promise something I can't deliver?
3. *Avoid being critical, judgmental, impatient, rigid*:
    a) Was I open to different ways of doing the same thing?
    b) Was I able to delegate and really let go?
    c) Did I overreact when others made mistakes?
4. *Listen to others:*
    a) Did I look for openings in conversations to turn the conversation back to myself?
    b) Did I rehearse what I was going to say, instead of listening?

    c) Did I try to control by "fixing" others, instead of understanding them?

5. *No excess adrenalin-pumping please:*
    a) Did I over-schedule, and find myself rushing from A to B?
    b) Did I try to do two or three things at once?
    c) Did I push myself to play better, go faster, or win, instead of relaxing at "play"?

6. *Stop overloading yourself:*
    a) Did I deal with each problem, one step at a time?
    b) Did I create artificial, self-imposed deadlines?
    c) Did I try to finish everything before I left work?

7. *Make your car a sanctuary:*
    a) Did I distract myself with business worries or phone calls?
    b) Was I courteous to other drivers?
    c) Did I enjoy the silence or listen to relaxing music?

8. *Avoid business lunches:*
    a) Did I talk business during lunch today?
    b) Did I drink to relax?
    c) Did I invite friends who are in different fields to join me?

9. *Remember, change involves risk:*
    a) Was I prepared to disappoint others and allow them their anger?
    b) Did I leave work on time, without apologizing?
    c) Did I "chat" with myself when I started "slipping back" to old ways?

10. *Make home a refuge:*
    a) Did I leave my briefcase at work?
    b) Have I asked people not to phone me about business at home?
    c) Do I protect my family's privacy, free from e-mails or faxes?

    d) If I work at home, do I keep time free for relaxation and fun?

11. *Lighten Up*:
    a) Did I laugh enough today?
    b) Did I compliment someone, or show my appreciation?
    c) Did I share something interesting or fun with others?

12. *Get a life!*
    a) Am I fun and interesting to be with, both at home and at work?
    b) Do I truly love people and not use them?
    c) Am I grateful and appreciative of all that I have now?

BON VOYAGE

Good luck on your "*Journey from Numbness to Joy.*" Remember to feel compassion and take care of yourself! Be realistic, not idealistic. You're well on your way when you recognize that half of life is positive and half is negative. You'll need your sense of humour and your spirituality because there will be detours, distractions, even roadblocks in your way. Life can be like a bowl of cherries, but cherries do have pits.

Balance and moderation in the external world are crucial for a healthy life-style, and your psyche will remind you of this. It is just a matter of time before people crash when they are spinning out of control on a fast-tracked Gerbil Wheel existence. Esther de Waal, in *Seeking God: The Way of St. Benedict,* speaks of the present-day dilemma in our society of searching for personal fulfilment while admiring expertise, specialization, and professionalism. St Benedict's dictum that body, mind, and spirit must all command equal respect speaks across the centuries.

Monastery life involves time for prayer, study, and work. De Waal sees the Benedictine life as an equilibrium, a holding together of ultimate values in one centre. Maintaining a balance between polarities, "the monk lives constantly at the point of tension between stability and change; between tradition and the future; between the personal and the community; between obedience and initiative; between the desert and the marketplace; between action and contemplation" (95). Such duality is never simple. Balancing the tugs and pulls we all experience on a daily basis is a demanding and difficult task.

One cautionary note: It is wise to keep in mind that *maturity is clearly linked to the ability to produce and appreciate humour.* Mature people laugh at themselves, remain flexible, and accept their limitations. They maintain a realistic perspective on life that views situations and personal weaknesses from a humorous standpoint. Harvey Mindess, in his chapter entitled "The Use and Abuse of Humour in Psychotherapy, " in *Humour and Laughter: Theory, Research and Applications* observes that humour highlights an awareness of our common absurdities. It sees that nothing is exactly as it seems or as we claim it to be, that what we profess is at best only partly true. Humour lets us know that "we are all more unreasonable, corrupt and pretentious than we openly acknowledge" (338). This, says Mindess, should leave no cause for alarm or indignation.

Achieving Inner Balance must be about reality and truth, not idealism and pretension. Mystery, magic, and joy are as much a part of life as pain, suffering, and guilt. When everything starts to go wrong in your life, pay attention – it is time to grow again. No one ever said life was not a challenge. Experience life fully – laugh, cry, mourn, and celebrate, and *remember to feel it all.*

Appendices

Learn to Internalize Your Feelings

A Summary

CHAPTER 7

Step I

Awareness: What emotion are you *feeling* right now? When something happens, immediately tune in to your body.
1. What *physiological* changes (i.e., in your muscles and nerve endings) are occurring that alert you to a shift or change in emotions?
2. What is happening to your *energy* level? Are you pumping excess adrenalin and feeling light, or experiencing a decrease in energy and feeling *heavy*?
3. What do you notice about your *body position*?

Practise: *Stop* a number of times throughout the day, and identify what your body is telling you. Establish which combination of changes typically signals each major emotion. Identify the *earliest* signs of the emotion so that it can be recognized quickly in the future.

Labelling: Use your thinking to *name* the emotion. Sometimes you will know the label immediately (i.e. anger). Other times, you will need to work backwards to figure out what happened in the recent present or past that may have set off this particular emotion.

Achilles' heel: What are your weaknesses or sore points? Watch for situations that typically trigger certain feelings, the ones that cause you to overreact or be impulsive. Act right away to alleviate stress, and make the situation easier to handle.

Step II

Justification: Use your *thinking* to test whether or not this emotion has validity. Is it based on what is actually happening in your immediate environment? Or is a layering of old feelings over present ones unconsciously heightening your present response?

Conscious data:

1) *What* just happened?
2) *Who* said what?
3) What *specifically* are you reacting to in the situation?
4) Is a troublesome *dream* still affecting you?

Unconscious data:

5) Are you *overreacting*, or acting *impulsively*?

Stress level: Pay attention to how stressed you are right now. Are you still comfortable? Or are you becoming overstressed? Watch for outward signs of agitation, irritability, frustration, etc.; or inward signs of lethargy, alienation, hopelessness, etc.

Step III

Experiencing: *Feel the feeling*. Stay with it. Let your emotional reactions be okay, even if they are negative. *Simplify*. Lower your expectations. *Nurture* yourself. Use your senses to feed yourself. Look for humour in the situation!

Exception: *Anger, anxiety, fear, pain*. Problem-solve as soon as you become aware of the earliest signs of these four feelings.

Defenses: If overstressed, *act immediately* to avoid becoming immobilized by your defenses (i.e., projection of blame, obsessive thinking, rationalization, dissociation, compartmentalization, repression, reaction formation, regression, sublimation).

CHAPTER 8

Step IV

Problem-solving intervention: Take some action to make things better for yourself. Be conscious of your own stress level and aware of what is happening to the other person, before proceeding.

Timing: Are you being sensitive to the other person's well-being, both emotionally and physically? Can that person listen right now? Is he in a mood? Is she unwell, too young, elderly, not very bright? Is he distracted by other problems, etc.?

Time of day may be important. Is this individual a morning or evening person?

Complications must be considered. Are alcohol or drugs involved?

Appropriateness: Do you live or work with this person? Is this really your problem? Is this issue important enough to expend your energy on?

In a group or public setting: Is the setting or situation suitable for your intervention? Is it possible to signal that you are distressed, without embarrassing others? Can you follow through later and discuss your feelings then?

Option one: If you have figured out what the problem is, how you feel about it, and are still emotionally in control, proceed to *Step VI – Problem-Solving*.

Option two: If you are still *overly upset*, or *unclear* about exactly what is troubling you, postpone your intervention, and proceed to *Step V – Rescheduling*.

Step V

Rescheduling: *The boiling point*: Let the other person know how you are feeling (i.e., too angry, upset, stressed-out, confused, anxious, etc.), using the "I" message.

Set a time to deal with the situation when *both* parties are free to exchange views, and listen to each other's experience of the same situation.

Leaving a situation: Take time out to get yourself back in control. You want to be able to think clearly and to experience your feelings fully.

Always say why you are leaving.

Remember to say when you are coming back to talk: Nonverbal communication is ambiguous. It leads to misunderstandings and confusion. No one need feel abandoned.

The triangular pattern:

1. Make a conscious decision to leave when overly stressed.
2. Regain your control by performing one or more active or passive calming techniques (e.g., breathing, meditation, visualization, humour, touch, spirituality).
3. Follow through on your promise to return, and proceed to problem-solve.

CHAPTER 9

Step VI

Non-controlling communication: Once you have figured out how you feel, and you're certain that your emotions are under control, it is time to communicate your thoughts and your feelings in a responsible manner.

First assumption: You need to take responsibility for informing others about *what is happening to you*. However, the other person must be *left free to respond* in his or her own way (i.e., *if* he can, *when* he can, and in the *way* he chooses).

People have difficulty hearing when they are being controlled or manipulated.

Second assumption: Neglecting to inform the other person about your reactions is irresponsible passive-aggressive behaviour. Others should not have to "fish," to ask questions about what is going on with you. Describe your reactions, *but stay on your side of the fence*. Ego boundaries need to be respected if there is to be trust. Responsible communicating includes listening.

"I" messages: Responsible communication informs the other person about what you *feel*, what you *think*, and if appropriate, what your *needs* are. It is easier to hear if you talk about feelings first. Be careful not to tell the other person what to *do* about your needs.

Try to *be brief* and to the point. *You do not need to defend* how you feel! No one has to agree with you about *your* feelings about what has happened.

Stay in your own territory: You have power to change yourself and your actions. Be clear and succinct. Be firmly assertive, but not invasive.

A safe atmosphere: There should be no blaming, judging, interfering in others' business, or talk about being "right." The listener has no need to become defensive and launch a counterattack.

Avoid using "you" messages, *which cross over to the other's* side of the boundary.

"You" messages are controlling. Blatant messages tell the other person what to *do*, *say*, *think*, or *feel*, etc. However, covert messages do not necessarily begin with "you." Finger-pointing, non-verbal communication such as sighing or tuning out, as well as expressions such as "Nonsense!" or "You've got to be kidding!" put down or negate the other person's right to have his or her own ideas or feelings.

Name-calling, insulting, interfering, etc. only challenge other people to defend themselves with a counterattack.

The Teeter-Totter power struggle: When someone else has a personal problem, and you offer advice, you are "minding the other person's business." By doing so, you take on responsibility for what happens next. By problem-solving for others, you rob them of their own experiencing. Both parties often end up resenting each other.

Good listening: *Do not give advice*! Instead, *offer empathy and support* only. Good listeners respect other people's right to solve their own personal problems, or even to make mistakes. Listeners need to act as a sounding board so that others can bounce off their own ideas as to possible solutions, ones that suit their unique set of needs, values, and personality preferences!

Second-guessing is unwise: Second-guessing what is going on with others is disrespectful. A good rule of thumb is to *always ask rather than tell*! If others are present and it would be awkward to ask the person to explain, try to refocus your energy on what you are doing. Plan to check out your perceptions of the situation later. Ask for more information so that you can understand the other person's experience. Listen carefully to what is said, and refrain from judging.

Two-way communication fosters a sharing of information, which will ultimately lead to a better understanding of differences. Friendship and intimacy grow when respect, trust, empathy, and truth are present.

Additional Functions from Jung's Theory of Psychological Type

During the 1950s and 1960s, two researchers, Isabel Briggs Myers and her mother, Katherine C. Briggs, used C. G. Jung's conceptual framework to develop a psychometric questionnaire to determine psychological type. Myers and Briggs discovered that people could be classified into sixteen specific types. The resultant Myers-Briggs Type Indicator was intended to foster understanding about the similarities and differences among human beings. Since 1975, the Myers-Briggs has become the most widely used personality measure for non-psychiatric populations.

Starting with Jung's four functions – Thinking, Feeling, Sensation, and Intuition – and the Introverted – Extraverted attitude, Myers and Briggs added a Judgment-Perception preference for relating to the outer world.

In chapter 2, we learned about the Thinking and Feeling functions. Here we will discover the roles that the other functions play in our personalities. Each function is greatly influence by whether individuals, by nature, are Extraverted or Introverted in the way they approach the world. How are people energized, and what conditions restore this energy? We will also learn how different people perceive information, and whether Intuition or Sensation is the dominant function used to perform this processing. Lastly, we will look at how individuals deal with the world around them. Is Judgment or Perception the preferred function when decisions or plans are to be made? Judgment attitude prefers organizing, making decisions, and reaching closure. Perception attitude chooses to remain open, to postpone closure, to live and let live.

EXTRAVERSION AND INTROVERSION

Jung coined *two motivational concepts: Extraversion and Introversion.* These terms indicate our psychological modes of adaptation – where our focus lies, and where we draw our energy and enthusiasm from. *Introverts* derive their motivation from internal or subjective factors. *Extraverts* are influenced by information from the external world. People and situations affect their judgments, perception, feelings, affects, and attitudes.

All of us turn outwards to take action and go inwards to reflect, but we tend to be more comfortable in the one that is the most natural to us. Although the terms are well used, their meaning is often misunderstood.

As Jung points out in *Psychological Types*, the two types tend to speak badly of one another and to come into conflict. "The Introvert sees everything that is in any way valuable for him in the subject; the Extravert sees it in the object. This dependence on the object seems to the Introvert a mark of the greatest inferiority while to the Extravert the preoccupation with the subject seems nothing but infantile autoeroticism" (517).

Problems arise when the Introvert develops inwardly but remains at a standstill outwardly. Conversely, the Extravert may develop external relations but neglect inner growth. In time, if psychological growth is to take place, both types need to develop their opposite functions to reach an adult, mature level of functioning.

Extraversion

Extraverts are action-oriented and do their best work externally, preferably with other people. They adapt quickly to their environment because they are curious and directed outwards towards what is going on immediately around them. Consequently, Extraverts pay a great deal of attention to the real outer world of people and things, and to the interaction that takes place between themselves and others. They are attracted to breadth, and are afterthinkers who understand life after they have lived it.

Extraverts are open, confident, assured, trusting, action-oriented people who like to explore and to seek adventure. They enjoy meeting people and travelling to new places. They are challenged by the new and untried. Sociable, friendly, and accessible, they tend to be the centre of attention, even the life of the party. They are talkative, engage others easily in conversation, and are comfortable in new groups. They tend to have many friends and relationships, although they may be fickle or flighty on occasion.

Extraverts expend energy rather than conserve it. They are expansive and tend to express their emotions as they go along. Early in their development, they take initiative, learn quickly, and play freely with objects because of their risk-taking, optimistic nature. In extreme types, a weakness lies in their tendency towards intellectual superficiality. Also, because they are so other-directed, they tend not to take care of themselves. Their energies are invested in nurturing and caring for others instead. As a result, they are prone to become selfless martyrs who eventually feel taken for granted. They resent the demands others make on them but refuse to see how they contribute to this cycle by not being honest about their own needs and limits. Their ego boundaries may be blurred and enmeshed with those of others.

As Isabel Briggs Myers notes in *Gifts Differing*, Extraverts are "The civilizing genius, the people of action and practical achievement, who go from doing to considering, and back to doing" (56).

Whether one is Extraverted or Introverted only becomes apparent when either attitude is coupled with each of the four functions. For example, Extraverted Thinkers have very different personalities from Introverted Thinkers. The former let you know their opinions and thoughts on a subject, while the latter may be churning inside but neglect to tell you about it.

Introversion

In *Gifts Differing*, Myers defines Introverts as "The cultural genius, the people of ideas and abstract invention, who go from considering to doing and back to considering" (56) Introverts are independent because everything they do rests on their own decisions. They are reflection-oriented and have strong powers of concentration, which they use to focus on their thoughts. Reserved and cautious observers, they pause before new and untried challenges. They tend to stay on the periphery of life's circle, rather than plunge in. Spontaneity is difficult for them.

Because they are slow to take action, Introverts are reluctant to discuss things with others until they have had the opportunity to think them through to a conclusion. Inward-directed, they only trust their inner values, which are based on internal, subjective experience. When reacting to an idea or situation, they turn inwards and formulate their own unique version of it. This interpretation becomes their reality. Consequently, Introverts often remain oblivious to, or uninterested in, the objective environment that lies outside their experience. Internal reactions are more interesting to them. They are attracted to depth and tend to be intense, so may become passionate about an idea or thing. Introverts are forethinkers who cannot live life until they understand it. Introverts tend to be closed, timid, cautious, and prone to pessimism. They are reluctant to risk themselves to explore new people, places, or adventure. Energy is cautiously conserved and limited. They prefer the tried-and-true, home turf, predictable food, and familiar customs.

Taciturn and shy, Introverts tend to bottle up their emotions and carefully guard their reactions from others. Sharing and venting feelings is foreign to them unless pressure builds to intolerable levels. A great deal of energy is suppressed simply because they are terrified of strong responses in themselves and in others. Consequently, they remain well-defended against outside influences. Introverts are therefore prone to extreme sensitivity and often suffer from chronic fatigue.

Introverts are often described as reserved, solitary, and private people. They definitely prefer their own way. Therefore, outside influences are met with mistrust and much resistance. Things and ideas must be understood before they are willing to submit to such alien rules. Introverted children are often fearful and reluctant to confront unknown objects and people. They want names, meanings, and explanations for things because their defensive attitude makes them question and hold back. They must summon the courage and energy to assert themselves over familiar objects and finally master them.

Introverts prefer a few good relationships and relate better on a one-to-one basis or in a small group situation. They are able to extravert socially, but tend to become drained easily by too much interrelating. They may leave a party early and renew their energy by withdrawing into their internal world.

In extreme cases, there is a weakness towards impracticality, being other-worldly and not grounded in reality. Because of their subjective orientation, they are prone to ego-inflation and arrogance, and therefore tend to believe that their way is the best. Introverts are consequently attracted to control and power as a means of getting their own way.

In trying to determine if you are Extraverted or Introverted, think back to childhood. If two young children are playing in a park where there is a new slide, the introverted child will stand back watching the other children for some time. Eventually, he will summon up the courage to approach the ladder and will climb slowly, pause, and then continue until he reaches the top. After moments of hesitation, he will finally swish down, and look somewhat surprised but pleased with himself. Remember, Introverts take comfort in conquering something new, in making the unfamiliar familiar!

The Extraverted child, seeing the slide, will rush to the bottom of the ladder, climb eagerly to the top, and triumphantly slide to the ground with great glee. Only then will she think about the experience and draw her own conclusions. Recall that Extraverts understand life after they have lived it. Life for them is to be experienced and lived fully.

SENSATION AND INTUITION

These are the *information-gathering functions* that allow us to process information about the world around us. Sensation is a conscious process primarily interested in concrete actualities. Intuition is largely unconscious and concerned with possibilities. K. Bradway, in "Jung's Psychological Types," suggests that sensation people outnumber intuitives three to one (129-35), so the interplay between these types is weighted against Intuition.

Sensation

Sensation works on two levels. On one level, Sensation *perceives a physical stimulus*, such as a person or an object, through information gathered from the *five senses* (seeing, hearing, touching, tasting, and smelling). Facts, figures, and other details are processed and observed without judgment. On another level, *internal bodily reactions* to that object or person are conveyed and *registered in consciousness*. Our psyche seeks the practical, concrete reason for what is occurring or being done.

In other words, sense impressions bring a scene to life, and our faculties respond physiologically. We become aware of our thoughts, feelings, and ideas about the concrete image. As Jung explains in *Psychological Types* (462), a flower is always seen along with its stem, leaves, and its habitat. We experience pleasure or displeasure according to its aesthetic appeal. We smell its fragrance and savour the beauty of its special hue. Going further, we even question the motivation of the gift-giver. Is it an innocent and spontaneous gesture, or one steeped in dubious meaning?

Sensation people are sensible, practical, observant, and realistic. Their energy is directed towards actual here-and-now experience. Their trust is placed in the concrete, that which is accessible and observable.

It is important to note that Sensation people distrust words, spoken or written, that come from others. According to Isabel Briggs Myers in *Gifts Differing* (57), words are merely symbolic. They must be translated into reality and experienced before they mean anything. Therefore, Sensation people often have to bang their heads against a closed door three or four times rather than learn from others' experience.

Sensation types are seen as ploddingly slow because they process data so thoroughly. It takes some time to translate sense impressions into thoughts and feelings. They distrust quick answers because they are not closely connected to their imagination. Sensation types value soundness and a practical approach to learning. For all the facts to be registered, things must be said and read slowly, not skimmed over. They cannot be rushed or things become a blur. They seldom read just for pleasure, unless the book contains information they are particularly interested in. They learn new skills step by step and need plenty of practice time to familiarize themselves with all the facts and details.

Sensation types crave enjoyment and seek pleasure in the art of living the good life. They are reluctant to save for a rainy day or to protect future security. The saying "A bird in the hand is worth two in the bush" fits their philosophy. They like to imitate. They want what others have, and want to do what others are doing. Physical surroundings are important to their sense of well-being.

Sensation people, Isabel Myers further states, are consumers and natural pleasure lovers. They contribute to public welfare by supporting every form of culture and recreation. Comfort, luxury, and beauty are their aesthetic pleasures. They can become frivolous, self-serving, and greedy for more and more stimulation to fill up an inner emptiness. Sensation alone can resemble a butterfly let loose in a field of daisies, seemingly flitting from one flower to the next without digesting anything. Without the achievement of some goal, and the imagination and vision of Intuition, life can lack meaning and fulfillment. Growth comes through developing their intuitive skills.

It has been my observation that Sensation types tend to terminate the therapeutic process prematurely simply because they are feeling better and life is more enjoyable. With their focus on the here-and-now, it may be that their imagination does not function well enough for them to see the possibilities for change in the future. "Short-term pain" for "long-term gain" doesn't make sense to them. As we will learn, Intuition introduces goals and guideposts to chart progress, and also provides the drive necessary for growth.

Intuition

Intuition is an instinctive function that gathers information in an unconscious way. Carl Jung in *Psychological Types* explains that Intuition uses a sixth sense to focus its perception on everything – both outer and inner objects and their relationships. The laws of reason, and the process of sifting through all the data, are not involved. Answers pop up unannounced. As Jung further explains, "In intuition a content presents itself whole and complete, without our being able to explain or discover how this content came into existence" (453). This may cause problems, for example, in school when the Intuitive child is certain he knows the answer, yet is unable to justify to his Sensation-type teacher how he got it. This intrinsic knowledge, stated with quiet certainty and conviction, can be quite threatening to others. Therefore, Intuitive people may be accused of guessing or cheating, or of being irrational, opinionated, arrogant, or superficial.

Jung delineates *two levels* of Intuition. Subjective intuition is a perception of unconscious data that has its origin within the observer. Objective perception of data, on the other hand, depends on subliminal perception of the object along with the feelings and thoughts that object evokes in the person. Jung further distinguishes concrete and abstract forms of Intuition, which differ depending on the degree of sensation involved. Concrete intuition is a reactive process that responds directly to given facts, what is actually there. Abstract intuition involves an act of will, an element of direction, or a goal. It mediates connections between existing ideas, or it creates new ones. Intuition looks at the big picture and seeks to grasp the essential patterns. Brainstorming, for example, is a collective intuitive process used to generate new ideas. Group members pool their information and experience, and new insights emerge.

Intuitives are imaginative, creative, and speculative, especially about their current inspiration. They see meanings, relationships, and possibilities beyond the information presented by the senses. Intuitives tend to day-dream and to be idealistic. They are restless, and instead of enjoying the present, their energy is directed towards anticipating the future. They are able to delay gratification in the present for future gain or good. They often fail to appreciate and enjoy what is happening around them. At the theatre, for example, the thoughts of an Intuitive may stray. She is off "scriptwriting," anticipating the good time that will be had by all after the play at the local restaurant.

Intuitives love the abstract, the symbolic, the theoretical. Words, metaphors, books, the theatre are therefore fascinating. According to Isabel Briggs Myers, Intuitives listen to the enticing visions of possibilities that "vary from the merest masculine 'hunch' and 'women's intuition': through the whole range of original ideas, projects, enterprises, and inventions; to the crowning examples of creative art, religious inspiration, and scientific discovery" (*Gifts Differing*, 57).

These people are quick to thought and to action, and therefore often can be impulsive. They rush through things without savouring the experience. I suggest that Intuitives should rely on their gut reaction but wait overnight or a day or two to make a final decision. This allows time for their less-developed Sensation to provide the facts and figures to support or reject the quick answer.

Care should be exercised lest these independent and ingenious people get caught in the "bigger is better" and "it's never enough" syndromes, which lead a person from idealism towards workaholism. What is just around the corner is always worth striving for, and this individual may sacrifice everybody and everything that gets in the way of some sought-after goal. There is a strong irony here because the workaholic eventually loses both his Intuition and his Feelings. Negative

Sensation, the inferior function, becomes ever more powerful. When this happens, concrete dualistic thinking (right-wrong, black-white, dominant-submissive, etc.) dominates, and the person gets picky and argumentative about what he or she thinks is right. The big picture gets lost as obsessive details command all their attention.

Intuitives, Myers further states, are relatively indifferent to what other people have and do. They are independent of their physical surroundings and often pay scant attention to the details and facts before them. However, show an Intuitive an empty room and she or he will use imagination to decorate it, set a mood, or even devise a story with a whole cast of characters, in no time at all!

Unless Intuition is tempered by realism, there is danger that idealism and perfectionism will distort reality. Also, Intuitives can be fickle and lack persistence unless a balance is sought through the development of a judging process (i.e., judgment or perception).

JUDGMENT AND PERCEPTION – THE ADDED VARIABLE

Well-balanced individuals must develop perception to support their judgment, and judgment to support their perception.

According to Myers, Judgment types believe that life should be willed and decided. Closure, achieved through making decisions, reaching conclusions, and settling things, is important for their stability. On the other hand, Perception types regard life as something to be experienced and understood. Their preference is to keep plans and opinions open-ended and subject to review. They make a series of decisions and, even after deciding, they are still reluctant to finalize things in case new information or valuable experiences change their present point of view.

Judgment

Judgment, based on Thinking and/or Feeling, provides a con-
tinuity of purpose and a standard against which one can criticize or challenge one's actions.

People use their Judgment attitude to gather information,
form opinions about whether to agree or disagree with the
facts, or come up with their own conclusions. For some, being
decisive is easy, while others seek closure simply because they
dislike having things remain undecided. Their own point of
view and being "right" are important.

Judgment people are outcome-oriented. They enjoy settling
and finishing things. Upon reaching a conclusion, they take
appropriate action to wrap things up. A sense of progress and
completion bring them a sense of well-being.

Strong Judgment individuals often make decisions about
what others should or should not do simply because they
value closure. In order to get things settled, they are prone
to freely offer advice and suggestions based on their own
experience and information. More timid types think such
thoughts and develop expectations for others, but do not
speak out publicly.

Judgment people often force a decision because they make
the assumption that all the evidence is in. Anything more is
considered extraneous and therefore irrelevant and immater-
ial. In fact, pushing for closure often means that people miss
new information or later developments because their perception process is shut off prematurely. This impulsiveness can
backfire and result in rigidity and error. There is no given-
and-take, no co-operation or consensus. In an extreme case,
someone who is caught in the compulsive drive to get from
point A to point B will ignore all feedback, sacrificing it to
speed. There is no reality testing along the way. "I'm in an
awful rush! Don't confuse me with the facts" might well be
his or her response.

Judgment types like to schedule ahead and organize their lives and their activities well in advance. Sunday night you may find them anticipating their extracurricular activities for the entire week, and planning in some detail how to spend Saturday morning, afternoon, and evening. Often they make decisions impulsively, before it is necessary or even wise to do so. Disappointment over "rained-out" plans is a common complaint among these folks.

Their expertise lies in sorting, ordering, arranging, separating, and listing things. There is a "best" way of doing things, meaning an exact, purposeful, rational way. Judgment people don't handle surprises well and therefore are uncomfortable with unexpected happenings. "Be Prepared" is their motto. Self-discipline and will-power help sustain all their efforts.

Extreme Judgment types with inadequately developed perception (i.e., sensation or intuition) lack the openness, understanding, and experience of life necessary to keep up-to-date and informed. They become narrowly rigid and thus incapable of adapting or of seeing any point of view except their own. These people fall back on old ways of doing things. Fearful of losing control of their own and others' behaviour, they have problems relating to external control and authority.

Perception

Perception, based on data and impressions gathered by Sensation and/or Intuition, informs our understanding. It opens up our minds to immediate and present knowledge, and provides the details and realities of life as it unfolds. Perception people are process-oriented and prefer to keep their options open. They like to hear about what others are doing, and are more likely to ask *why* questions than to tell others what to do.

Perception types make *series* of decisions based on their personal reactions to ongoing situations and events. Rarely do they make a final decision until forced to do so by a deadline, crisis, emergency, or someone else's ultimatum. Even then, they keep wondering if they have made the right decision. Ideally, problem-solving is achieved simply through understanding and exploring different perspectives. Action is not necessary, and closure is resisted.

Perception people are spontaneous and possess the ability to stay thoroughly in the present moment. They are "here-and-now" people, interested in actualities. Often their intentions to do something in the future are forgotten, and things are left undone. Their well-being depends on being open, curious, flexible, and able to adapt as you go. "Let's wait. Let's see what happens. There's no rush. Something will show up." These are their refrains. This tolerant, live-and-let-live, relaxed attitude fosters an adaptability to handle accidental, unexpected, or unpleasant happenings. However, this focus on the present means that they are often late and unaware of time. Other people's need to schedule and be on time is lost on them. Perception individuals shun fixed plans and dislike scheduling of any kind. Consequently, they are often unclear about what they want to do next. This makes decision-making difficult. When asked the question "What are you doing on the twenty-fifth, two weeks from now?" their reply takes the form of a protest. "Give me a break! I can't even begin to think that far in advance!"

Starting is easy; finishing is not. Starting something new and fresh is exciting for these people – that is, until the novelty wears off. Finishing is difficult because the discipline to make decisions, organize a plan, and see it through to a conclusion, no matter what, is not their natural expertise.

Extreme Perception types need well-developed judgment processes (i.e., Thinking or Feeling) to give their life direction and structure. Otherwise, they get so caught up experiencing life that they fail to criticize and govern their own actions. What they perceive as necessary freedom can be seen as irresponsible or lacking in purpose by others. They may be all sail and no rudder.

Myers cautions that it is what we *naturally* tend to do that determines our type. Our natural inclinations, however, may be profoundly affected by others. She states, "A person's idea of what is right may be an acquired ideal, borrowed from another type" (*Gifts Differing*, 74). A person's actual behaviour may reflect habits or efforts developed to please a parent of the opposite attitude.

Perception types appear lazy and aimless to Judgment types. Conversely, they see Judgment types as driven, set in their ways, and lacking a zest for life. Needless to say, Judgment and Perception types often drive each other crazy! The following story was told to me by Coleen Clark, who introduced me to the Myers-Briggs Type Indicator. Imagine a scenario in which a Perception person, Rose, says to a Judgment person, Sydney, "I think I'd like to go out for a corned beef sandwich tonight."

Sydney gets busy organizing his thoughts about which restaurant has the best corned beef. He goes down his mental list and makes a decision about which is best. He is about to suggest Ben's, across town, when Rose pipes up, "On the other hand, I wouldn't mind going for a pizza!"

Sydney, in disbelief and annoyance, asks, "Whatever happened to my corned beef sandwich? My mouth was watering!"

Rose quickly recovers and anxiously begins to offer further suggestions. "Chinese food, Caesar salad, steak" – she goes on and on. Rose really doesn't know what she wants. Making a series of decisions is easy for her. Sydney needs to step in and diplomatically suggest that they try Ben's this time. Rose can make the decision about where they go next time.

A CAUTIONARY NOTE

In this simplified explanation of the different functions, the meaning and effects of coupling the Extraverted-Introverted functions with Thinking, Feeling, Sensation, and Intuition, as well as adding the Judgment-Perception variable, cannot be covered here. The sixteen different personality types are quite distinct, and even one function change profoundly transforms the personality type.

It is important to have a well-trained and qualified practitioner administer and analyze the Myers-Briggs Type Indicator Test to ascertain your true type. In my practice, people often score the opposite on one function from what they really are, the function they were born with. There are a number of reasons this occurs. The individual may have had to adapt in order to survive in a dysfunctional family or in an unhealthy work situation. An example would be working for a workaholic boss or an organization that does not value and nurture its employees but cares only about the bottom line and productivity concerns. In such a setting, it is essential that the individual protect himself and develop and maintain a strong objective, analytic view of his role and personal values. Many people sell their souls to serve the organization and lose the essence of the Self.

Social pressure in our patriarchal society also makes it difficult for male Feelers and female Thinkers not to follow the traditional, stereotyped roles society tends to impose. To overcompensate, males often strive to be sensitive and nurturing and females become obsessed with succeeding in the business world, trying to be better than the men.

Family influences can often push a child away from his or her best function. I was an Extraverted Intuitive child in a household of Introverts. My parents would occasionally let me "get lost" because they worried about my "Curious George" nature. I well remember standing in the entrance to a store in Niagara Falls and suddenly realizing there was no one in sight whom I recognized. Fears of abandonment are innate, so the young child in this situation not only experiences fear but is made to feel "bad" for her natural curiosity.

An Intuitive child, similarly, may distrust his best function when his seemingly fantastical ideas cause concern for other more fact-oriented, concrete family members. These effects can be oppressive and discouraging when one person in the family is outnumbered by other personality types and labelled "different," or worse, "weird." Children want to fit in but also be unconditionally accepted for who they are.

BRAVE NEW WORLDS

By purposely developing our opposite functions, we enter a somewhat strange new world where our energies can flow into exciting and fresh adventures. An Inferior function does not develop by itself, we must be determined and purposeful in our actions. Introverts who challenge themselves by introducing themselves to strangers and make new friends will be energized and fulfilled by their efforts. It will become easier each time they make a friendly gesture. Intuitive types who learn to truly appreciate small, delicate detail will enrich the way they view their world. Beautiful and precious details will be seen in paintings that once were glanced at only briefly.

People have to learn to appreciate and value their opposite functions, however, before they will give themselves permission to risk such adventures. An admirable goal is to strive to achieve balance in our personality by developing *all* of our functions – the ones we were fortunate enough to be born with, and the ones we ourselves make special efforts to develop.

APPENDIX 3

Which Is Your Inferior Function?

SHADOW SIDE	HEALTHY SIDE
NEGATIVE THINKING	POSITIVE THINKING
Idealistic, perfectionistic	Realistic, principled
Irrational	Rational
Illogical, distort	Logical, analytical
Dependent on outside affirmation	Independent evaluation
Aloof	Involved
Subjective point of view	Objective viewpoint
Tangential, cryptic, confusing	Focused, precise, clear
Judgmental, high expect ations	Fair assessment, reasonable
Skeptical	Open-minded
Arrogantly opinionated	Reasoned personal opinion
Erratic, unpredictable	Reliable, predictable
Overly-competitive, aggressive	Competitive, assertive
Envious, jealous	Supportive, loyal
"Help" or "fix" others	Problem-solving skills
Controlling	In control
Overly responsible	Responsible
Obsessive, narrowly-focused	Organize facts, ideas
Overly sensitive	Tough-minded
Uncomfortable dealing with feelings	Task-oriented, impersonal
Hurtful without knowing it	Business-like, short
Reprimand, scold, lecture, preach	Explain own reasoning

NEGATIVE FEELING	POSITIVE FEELING
Moody, repress feelings	Handle full range of feelings
Withdrawn, reserved, secretive	Sociable, friendly, open
Overly-generous pleaser	Caring, concerned, respectful
Distant, discourteous	Warm, polite, courteous
Neglect to tell the truth	Honest
Personally irresponsible	Responsible, dependable
Takes everything personally	Sensitive
Inconsiderate	Considerate
Careless, indiscreet	Thoughtful, tactful
Self-doubting, insecure bravado	Self-assured, humble
Naive	Insightful
Overly-focused on others, selfless	Self and Other-directed
Conditional expectations	Unconditional regard
Complaining	Supportive attitude
Intolerant	Accepting, tolerant
Self-sacrificing, martyr-victim	Firmly assertive
Quarrelsome, grouchy, unruly	Conciliatory, value harmony
Give in, defer	Consult, negotiate
Impatient	Patient
Easily discouraged	Committed, follow-through
Mean-spirited, selfish	Generous, unselfish
Avoid unpleasant confrontation	Diplomatic and gracious
Neglect to compliment others	Praise and give affirmation

NEGATIVE INTUITION	POSITIVE INTUITION
Make errors of facts, not precise	Visionary, "big picture" focus
Faulty sixth sense	Unconscious gathering of data
Slow to figure things out	Answers "pop up" unexpectedly
Uncertain, puzzled, confused	Wise, "knows" what's right
Impulsive about reaching conclusions	Quick to conclusions
Distrust gut reaction	Trust gut reaction
Cleverness dulled	Ingenious, imaginative, clever
Head-in-the-clouds, fantasize	Curious, original
Limited ideas	Brainstorm, generate new ideas
Creativity dulled	See endless possibilities
Fearful about future	Future-oriented
Resist change, new ideas	Enjoy solving new problems
Bored with repetition, routine	Enjoy complicated situations
Follow misguided inspirations	Creatively inspired
Mistakes in judgment	Good judge of people
Lose objectivity	Remain objective, stand back
Lose perspective	Keep things in perspective
Unclear about priorities	Know what is most important
Pessimistic	Optimistic
Threatened by too much detail	Like theory, abstract, symbolic
Impulsive, want it now	Delay gratification/future gain
Restless, impatient	Love life is as it could be
Neglects language, reading	Fascinated by language/books

NEGATIVE SENSATION	POSITIVE SENSATION
Unrealistic	Realistic, see what is there
Short-sighted views	Observant
Dualistic thinking, limited options	Thorough gathering of data
Overly-detailed, picky	Present detailed picture
Overly concrete	Concrete in perception
Flighty	Down-to-earth, grounded
Impractical, silly	Practical, sensible
Dwell on past regrets	Present and past-oriented focus
Discontent, dissatisfied	Fun-loving, content, satisfied
Get mired in details	Step-by-step learning
Dualistic black/white thinking	Consider all options
"Show me," "prove it"	Illustrate through examples
Selective scanning	Seek out all facts, figures
Selective listening	Use all five senses
Overwork a project, overcorrect	Thorough, efficient but slow
Distrust the process	Process-oriented
Rigidly follow rules, regulations	Respect rules, tradition
Distrust others' words/writings	Trust own experience
Resist learning new skills	Rely on tried-and-true skills
Wary of experimenting, new ways	Like established, proven ways
Rigid about routines, precision	Enjoy routine, being precise
Want what others have	Delight in possessions, beauty
Seek extra stimulation, highs	Value security, stability
Overspend, frivolous, greedy	Appreciative of simple things

Quiz

What Is Your Level
of Narcissism?

ARROGANCE

1. Do you believe you are "special," "superior," or "different" from others?
2. Have you ever been told that you are arrogant?
3. Do you tend to exaggerate your own potential?
4. Are your plans overly expansive or diversified?
5. Do you have difficulty accepting your own limitations?
6. Do you think that certain rules and regulations don't apply to you?
7. Does your personal well-being frequently override concern for others?
8. Are you entitled to special treatment and privileges?
9. Do you think others have no right to criticize you?
10. Do you fail to appreciate what others do for you?
11. Do you resist asking for help because you are so talented?
12. Do you think that people should go out of their way to promote your career?

CONTROL AND MANIPULATION

1. Do you always like to be "right"?
2. Do you manage to arrange things so that you get your own way?

3. Do you set up situations so that you are the centre of attention?
4. Do you find yourself saying things to elicit sympathy from others?
5. Do you expect your spouse to think the same way you do?
6. Are you quite different in public than you are in private?
7. Is being "in charge" very important to you?
8. Can you be cold, calculating, even ruthless, to retain control?
9. Does your family's schedule revolve around your timing, your plans?
10. Is delegating responsibility, without checking up, difficult?
11. Do you find it intolerable if others fail to respect your authority?
12. Do you dismiss people who challenge you from your life?

DISHONESTY, DENIAL, SECRECY

1. Do you keep your mistakes or failures to yourself?
2. Is privacy extremely important to you?
3. Do you promise to do things, and then not follow through?
4. Do you tell other people what they want to hear?
5. Do you often neglect to tell the truth?
6. Do you refuse to ask for help lest others find out you have a problem?
7. Do you "forget" your temper tantrums or rages after they occur?
8. Do you sometimes "pretend" you have no money, when this is not true?

FEAR OF AGING

1. Do you pride yourself on your youthful appearance?

2. Do you avoid thinking about your old age or retirement?
3. Do you hang on to business interests far too long after retirement?
4. Do you try to influence how new management runs things after you leave?
5. Are you able to mourn when someone else dies?
6. Is supporting your spouse difficult when a family member dies?

INSECURITY, LOW SELF-ESTEEM

1. Do you sometimes feel "phony"?
2. Do you distrust words, and emphasize action instead?
3. Do you watch others to see how you should act in social settings?
4. When things get too emotional, do you laugh instead of crying?
5. Are you fatalistic?
6. Do you ever secretly worry that you are going crazy?
7. Do you find yourself questioning your own judgment more and more?
8. Would you describe yourself as a loner?
9. Do you sometimes feel empty and emotionally bankrupt?
10. Do you worry that people seem to be avoiding you?
11. Is it difficult to get vicarious pleasure out of others' success?
12. Do you take things too personally when others fail to show respect?

PERSONAL PERSONA OR IMAGE

1. Is your persona, how the world sees you, overly important?
2. Is failure one of your deepest fears?
3. Has work become a form of self-aggrandizement?
4. Do you dress to project a certain image?

5. Is being recognized by the maître d' of a restaurant important?
6. Do you neglect to reveal your failures or losses to others?
7. Do you pride yourself too much on staying independent?
8. Do you believe that you are entitled to get what you want?

POWER

1. Have you always been quite ambitious?
2. Are recognition, status, praise, and admiration necessary for your well-being?
3. When you are successful, do you still crave more recognition?
4. Do you resent interference or a challenge to your ideas or plans?
5. Do you sometimes intimidate others to get your own way?
6. Have you ever become ruthless in your dealings with people or business?
7. Has success in your career become all-important in your life?
8. Do you resent it when other people's needs interfere with your own?

PUNISH SELF/AND OTHERS

1. Do you neglect to exercise, or eat properly?
2. Are you smoking or drinking too much, or using drugs?
3. Have you become obsessed with your work?
4. Do you neglect to go for a medical check-up on a regular basis?
5. Can you be vindictive at times?
6. Do you punish others by refusing to do what they want to do?

7. Have you become selfish and careless of others' feelings or needs?

8. Do you see others, but not experience them or their point of view?

9. Do you blame others when things go wrong?

10. Do you have temper tantrum-like rages when you don't get your way?

11. Do you work to avoid dealing with personal responsibilities?

12. Has your family's welfare become less important to you?

Bibliography

Allemang, John. "Critical Thinking." *The Globe and Mail,* 12 June 2010.

Bandler, R., and J. Grinder. *Frogs into Princes: Neuro Linguistic Programming.* Utah: Real People Press, 1979.

Birnbaum, J. *Cry Anger. A Cure for Depression.* Don Mills: General Publishing, 1973.

Bradway, K. "Jung's Psychological Types." *Journal of Analytical Psychology* 9 (1964).

Campbell, R. *Psychiatric Dictionary.* 5th ed. New York: Oxford University Press, 1981.

CBC *News.* "More than 30% of Canadians say they are workaholics: StatsCan." 15 May 2007. http://www.cbc.ca/canada/story/2007/05/15/workaholics-study.html.

Clark, C. "Myers-Briggs Type Indicators." Pamphlet, 1987.

Coupland, D. *Marshall McLulan.* Toronto: Penguin Canada, 2009.

Davitz, J. R. *The Language of Emotion.* New York: Academic Press, 1969.

"Death by Overwork in Japan. Jobs for Life." *Economist.com,* 14 Jan. 2008.

de Waal, E. *Seeking God. The Way of St. Benedict.* Minnesota: The Liturgical Press, 1984.

Estes, C. P. *Women Who Run with the Wolves*. New York: Ballantine Books, 1992.

Forbes, "Hardest-Working Countries." 28 May 2009.

Fox, M. *Creation Spirituality. Liberating Gifts for the Peoples of the Earth*. New York: Harper Collins, 1991.

Freeman, A. "Japan Gets a Life." *The Globe and Mail*, 13 March 1993.

Friedman, Meyer, and Ray Rosenman. *Type-A Behavior and Your Heart*. New York: Knopf, 1974.

Fulford, R. "Her Elements of Style." *Maclean's*, 4 May 2009, 2.

– "Rediscovering Frank Lloyd Wright." *The Globe and Mail*, 26 January 1994.

Greimel, H. "Government Urges Japanese to Work Less, Have Babies." *The Globe and Mail*, 3 April 2002.

Hart, A. *The Hidden Link Between Adrenalin and Stress*. Dallas: Word Publishing, 1991.

Hedges, C. *Empire of Illusion. The End of Literacy and the Triumph of Spectacle*. Toronto: Alfred A. Knopf, Canada, 2009.

Hellmich, N. "When Working Hard Starts to Work Against You." *USA Today*, 13 August 1992.

Hyder, Q. *The Christian Handbook of Psychiatry*. Old Tappan, NJ: Fleming H. Revell, 1971.

"Jobs for Life: Japanese Employees Are Working Themselves to Death." *The Economist,* 19 December 2007.

Jung, C. G. *Psychological Types*. Bollingen Series 20. *The Collected Works of C. G. Jung*, vol. 6. Princeton, NJ: Princeton University Press, 1971.

– *The Portable Jung*. Edited, with Introduction by Joseph Campbell, translated by R.F.C. Hull. New York: Penguin, 1991.

Kanai, A. "Economic and Employment Conditions, *Karoshi* (work to death) and the Trend of Studies on Workaholism in Japan." In R. J. Burke, editor, *Research Companion to Working Time and Work Addiction*. Cheltenham, UK: Edward Elgar Publishing, 2006.

Kawahito, Hiroshi. "Overwork Kills Many, Japanese Group Says." *Toronto Star*, 17 March 1991.

Kazdin, A. *Glenn Gould at Work: Creative Lying*. New York: E. P. Dutton, 1989.

Kelly, D. "Bridget Fonda: 'Burned Out' at 30." *The Globe and Mail*, 30 October 1994.

Killinger, B. *Integrity: Doing the Right Thing for the Right Reason*. Montreal: McGill-Queen's University Press, 2007.

– *Workaholics. The Respectable Addicts*. Toronto: Key Porter Books, 1991.

– "A Shift to a New Perspective." (Unpublished paper).

– "The Place of Humour in Adult Psychotherapy." Ph.D. Dissertation. York University, 1976.

Kintsch, W. *Learning, Memory, and Conceptual Processes*. New York: John Wiley and Sons, 1970.

Kohut, H., and E. Wolf. "The Disorders of the Self and Their Treatment: An Outline." *International Journal of Psychoanalysis* 59, no. 413 (1978): 413–25.

Kornblum, J. "Study: 25% of Americans Have No One to Confide In." *USA Today*, 22 June 2006.

Krech, D., R. Crutchfield, and N. Livson. *Elements of Psychology*. New York: Alfred A. Knopf, 1974.

Kuerti, A. "All that Glitters Is Not Gould." *The Globe and Mail*, 12 February 1993.

Lasch, C. *The Culture of Narcissism*. New York: Warner Books, 1979.

Lazerson, A., ed. *Psychology Today: An Introduction*. New York: Random House, 1975.

Leonard, L. *The Wounded Woman: Healing the Father–Daughter Relationship*. Boston: Shambhala Publications, 1982.

Lowen, A. *Narcissism: Denial of the True Self*. New York: Collier Books, 1985.

Macdonald, N. "Who Needs a Break? *Maclean's*, 6 July 2009.

Mate, Gabor. "Why Can't Johnny Adapt?" *The Globe and Mail*, 29 November 2008.

Mindess, H. "The Use and Abuse of Humour in Psychotherapy."
In T. Chapman and H. Foot, editors., *Humour and Laughter: Theory, Research and Application.* London: John Wiley & Sons, 1976.

Murray, S. E. "Come and Find the Quiet Centre." In *Voices United: The Hymn and Worship Book of the United Church of Canada.* Toronto: The United Church Publishing House, 1996.

Myers, I. B. *Manual: Myers-Briggs Type Indicator.* Palo Alto, CA: Consulting Psychologists Press, 1975.

Myers, I. B., and P. Myers. *Gifts Differing: Understanding Personality Type.* Palo Alto, CA: Consulting Psychologists Press, 1980.

National Defence Council for Karoshi Victims. *Karoshi: When the Corporate Warrior Dies.* Tokyo, Japan: Mado Sha, 1991.

Nussbaum, Martha. *For Profit: Why Democracy Needs the Humanities.* Princeton: Princeton University Press, 2010.

Oates, W. *Confessions of a Workaholic.* Nashville: Abingdon, 1971.

Osborn, A. F. *Applied Imagination: Principles and Procedures of Creative Problem Solving.* Rev. ed. New York: Scribner, 1957.

Peck, M. S. *The Road Less Traveled: The Unending Journey Toward Spiritual Growth.* New York: Simon and Schuster, 1978.

Pittaway, K. "Overwork: Setting Boundaries in Hard Times." *Pathways,* January/February 1994.

Sanford, J. *Evil: The Shadow Side of Reality.* New York: Crossroads, 1984.

– *The Invisible Partners: How the Male and Female in Each of Us Affects Our Relationships.* New York: Paulist Press, 1980.

Schary, D. *Heyday.* New York: Little, Brown, 1981.

Sharp, D. *The Survival Papers. Anatomy of a Midlife Crisis.* Toronto: Inner City Books, 1988.

– *Personality Types: Jung's Model of Typology.* Toronto: Inner City Books, 1987.

Smith-Lovin, Lynn, Miller McPherson, and Matthew E. Brashears. " Social Isolation in America: Changes in Core Discussion Networks over Two Decades. " *American Sociological Review* 71, no. 3 (2006): 353-75.

Weber, B. "Enfant Terrible of Chess Won a Battle of the Cold War and with It the World." *The Globe and Mail*, 19 Jan. 2008.

Worth, D. "Non-Contact Therapeutic Touch and the Healing of Wounds." *Journal of Subtle Energies* 1, no. 1 (1990).

Index